LIVING SOULS
IN THE
SPIRIT
DIMENSION

"Chris Hardy's latest work follows a series of provocative but well-researched and brilliantly written books on fringe consciousness topics. But this is more than a personal history of her remarkable experiences in what she calls the 'transdimensional reality.' Hardy cites serious research that supports the importance of near-death experiences, out-of-body experiences, after-death communication, and similar topics for a full understanding of the many dimensions of human nature. *Living Souls in the Spirit Dimension* is written in a reader-friendly manner that clarifies the complex phenomena she describes."

STANLEY KRIPPNER, PH.D.,
COAUTHOR OF *PERSONAL MYTHOLOGY*

"Chris Hardy is a natural mystic as well as a fine scholar. In this delightfully readable book she shares her experience on both sides of the veil and gives us an image-rich history of attitudes and beliefs about death from throughout the world."

ALLAN COMBS, PH.D.,
PROFESSOR OF TRANSFORMATIVE STUDIES AT
THE CALIFORNIA INSTITUTE OF INTEGRAL STUDIES

LIVING SOULS
IN THE
SPIRIT
DIMENSION

The Afterlife and
Transdimensional Reality

CHRIS H. HARDY, Ph.D.

Bear & Company
Rochester, Vermont

Bear & Company
One Park Street
Rochester, Vermont 05767
www.BearandCompanyBooks.com

Text stock is SFI certified

Bear & Company is a division of Inner Traditions International

Cataloging-in-Publication Data for this title is available from the Library of Congress

ISBN 978-1-59143-372-9 (print)
ISBN 978-1-59143-373-6 (ebook)

Printed and bound in the United States by Lake Book Manufacturing, Inc. The text stock is SFI certified. The Sustainable Forestry Initiative® program promotes sustainable forest management.

10 9 8 7 6 5 4 3 2 1

Text design and layout by Debbie Glogover
This book was typeset in Garamond Premier Pro with Guardi LT Std, Texta, and Gill Sans LT Std used as display fonts

To send correspondence to the author of this book, mail a first-class letter to the author c/o Inner Traditions • Bear & Company, One Park Street, Rochester, VT 05767, and we will forward the communication, or contact the author directly at **https://chris-h-hardy.com**.

CONTENTS

LIST OF ILLUSTRATIONS

COLOR PLATES

ACKNOWLEDGMENTS

With this book, I want to acknowledge the Great Work that is accomplished by the lovers of Sophia-Wisdom—the questers, philosophers, scientists, and artists of the Deep Reality of the Self and the World Soul—those of the past who have enlightened us and those of the future who are illuminating the other side of our collective face, that of our emerging potentials.

To all these questers who are now dwelling in the hyperdimension of souls, some temporarily so, my deep gratitude for your ceaseless caring and for your inspiring (and sometimes visible) presence, prodding us and making us—the ones living on Earth—more attuned to the soul dimension.

My heartfelt gratitude to my publisher, Ehud Sperling, and to Jon Graham and Christian Schweiger for welcoming this book and for their support in launching it.

I would like to thank Jamaica Burns Griffin for her excellence in editing and her deep understanding and respect of my text that made this work as smooth as an author could ever dream of. Thanks as well to Elizabeth Wilson for the highly competent and smart reviewing and editing.

And finally, I want to express my thanks and deep appreciation to the whole team at Inner Traditions • Bear & Company for their professional talent and great synergy, especially Patricia Rydle, Jeanie Levitan, Maria Loftus, Kelly Bowen, Aaron Davis, and the ubiquitous gate-opener Manzanita Carpenter-Sanz.

By the mere light of reason it seems difficult to prove the immortality of the soul. Some new species of logic is required for that purpose and some new faculties of the mind that they may enable us to comprehend that logic.

DR. RAYMOND MOODY QUOTING
EIGHTEENTH-CENTURY SCOTTISH PHILOSOPHER
DAVID HUME,
PARIS, JANUARY 17, 2017

A Leap into the Spirit Dimension

A whole array of psi capacities just bloomed in my life when I started meditating at eighteen years old and soon experienced transcendent states of consciousness. In brief, it was for me a tremendous leap to a higher spiritual state and, as it happened, this leap opened the gates of several types of psi. Among these was the ability to see and communicate with the deceased souls as well as with nature spirits. I could also perceive the energy of consciousness, which I now call syg-energy—meaningful energy, as opposed to matter energy. I could see it not only around people (as auras), but also as rays darting from sacred monuments, syg-energy fields (or syg-fields) bathing sacred places, or imprinted on sacred objects. In contrast with this sudden new perception, some precognitive abilities did appear but developed slowly, emerging in flashes or in dreams; and I had a still-crude telepathic hearing.

From what I observed in many countries I visited at length, telepathy is the most widely distributed of all psi phenomena, being practically innate in some cultures and countries. In India, for example, it stems from the people's natural ability to enter into high meditative states—fruit of millennia of tradition; just as it is innate for the people of Sub-Sahel Africa to see and talk to the spirits of their deceased parents and relatives and to recount it to their kin. Telepathy is also

1

widespread and developed to a sophisticated level in the United States, but it would be more fair to say that it's on the rise all over the planet. We are, collectively, in the process of making a leap in consciousness, and sensitive people everywhere are developing all kinds of talents in the range of spirituality, psi, mind-body integration, and self-development.

Call it a leap for us—undergoing that change in our lifetimes—but still, as far as humanity is concerned, it takes a few generations. As it is, the first wave of this leap struck in the late 1960s and early 1970s, and it raised the consciousness of all sensitive individuals, irrespective of their age, culture, education, social conditions, and milieu. The awakening process, the trigger, may take as little time as a strong experience, or a few weeks. And it suffices for a person to set for oneself the aim to discover more of their own inner Self and psi capacities, for them to launch their inner path of knowledge. What generates the leap is in fact our own higher Self or soul, and what facilitates and sustains our inner path is to become more and more connected and in sync with our Self and its innate purpose of self-betterment and permanent learning.

In our times of global awakening, and more so with each new generation, it's often enough to sense that such and such deed or mind feat is possible, for it to emerge spontaneously in our lives. As I came to understand it, you don't need to believe in anything—you just need to be curious and give it a try, and then you'll know for yourself. Keep the intent like a polar star in your mind and, when things start happening, test yourself in all kinds of ways you may imagine. Keep the tests and yourself safe, knowing that you could meet success, failure, or else incomprehensible results. Note all the details in a journal, and then try another test. The more fun the test, the more enthusiastic and carefree your mindset (while still remaining focused), and the more chances you'll have to succeed.

What's strange in my case is that I had practically no gift, and just a few anomalous experiences, before I started to read ancient spiritual texts and to practice meditation by myself. I would meditate, invent or try some practice on the spur of the moment, only when I felt it to be the perfect thing to do at that moment. (As far as meditation or self-development techniques are concerned, I'm allergic to practicing at precise times and with a preset program.) Not that everything worked out right, but even in the failed tests, or the hardships in my life, there was enormous matter for learning.

The primary focus of this book will be on communicating with the souls of the deceased, and I'll recount my own experiences as they happened to me, not by chronological order, but by their type. This will allow us to bring in the pertinent research done in this domain, often by notorious psychologists, through field studies and surveys of real-life experiences in the general population, some dating back to the end of the nineteenth century. We'll discover astonishing data; for example that a 1971 survey found that nearly half of the widows interviewed in several U.S. towns had seen or heard an apparition of their deceased spouse.

Now, there is a new understanding about the Beyond, or soul dimension, that emerges out of the real-life experiences in seeing and communicating with the deceased (we are talking about tens of thousands of cases, most of them well documented and checked by careful investigators). And this is what I'm most interested in discussing and presenting in this book, starting with my own intrusion into that realm of the spirit. In fact, these real-life experiences are literally lifting the veil on the mysterious reality of the dimension of souls—whether that of the deceased living in the Beyond, or that of our own Self able to travel out of our body, or ascend in meditation, and penetrate the hyper-dimension (see fig. I.1, page 4).

We can trust those who had such experiences, because these are often at odds with their own beliefs. Practically all researchers stressed that fact. For example, W. F. Barrett, a physicist at the Royal College of Science in Dublin, in his 1926 book *Deathbed Visions,* had cases of terminally ill children who were astonished to see angels without wings. We can certainly trust the children to express truly what they are perceiving (see for example Dyer and Garnes's 2015 book, *Memories of Heaven*). As the renowned psychologist Frederic Myers noted as well,

Fig. I.1. Unveiling the mystery of the dimension of souls,
Elmwood Cemetery, Memphis, Tennessee
Photo by Adarryll Jackson Sr. (www.instagram.com/adarrylljacksonsr)

some percipients saw the apparition of a person they didn't know had died, and believed they were there for real while talking to them, before they just evaporated inexplicably; then they would get the sad news afterward. In other cases, several people present other than the terminally ill patients themselves, such as nurses or parents, had perceived the apparitions of the deceased. Also, we have cases by the thousands of apparitions of living persons, sometimes doing an ad hoc experiment of appearing in their etheric body to a friend far away without having told them beforehand about it; this was the stuff of the monumental collection published as *Phantasms of the Living.*

The most telling information we get from real experiences is that we live in two dimensions at once; we do have, as humans living on Earth, a part of our being that is immaterial and appears mostly in a human form—called etheric body, astral body, energy body, or dreamtime body—and that is able to exit from our biological body and travel or just move instantly through space. And it is also as an immaterial body that the deceased appear most of the time to their living friends or relatives. However, it has been my experience that they appear to us in several ways, and that they choose to do so. We'll see in my conversation with physicist and Nobel laureate Wolfgang Pauli that he appeared to me as a blob of energy in an apple tree during an hour-long discussion. But then, on introducing his long-term friend Carl Jung, he took suddenly the appearance of a full but small body still within the energy bubble, which became an elongated oval. At the very moment he mentioned Jung and pointed with his hand behind him, Jung appeared at a distance, also as a full but tiny human silhouette within an oval bubble. My father and several visiting scientists appear as a head only, hovering near the ceiling, or near my desk. Whereas some others enter walking by (or through) the door, in a fully dressed dream body, and even sit down on a chair and behave like friendly guests. From this, we can deduce that the etheric body is only an appearance they take so that we may recognize them—and in fact, surveys show that they often don the very clothing they had on the day of their death, or that they used to wear at home. Their real form, in fact, is a field of energy, a syg-field, and they can choose to appear in whichever form they want.

As the most knowledgeable and dedicated researcher in this domain, Frederic Myers, concluded, and as we'll see throughout this book, the amount of evidence and its astonishing variety point to the deceased being complete personalities, extremely mindful, displaying all the signs of intelligence, reasoning, precise memory, intention, and more often than not, humor. They are full of attention for their loved ones still living, showing love, caring, and often easing things for them (like the example of a deceased mother prodding and helping her daughter to acquire a new medical degree). Their mental capacities encompass the domain we would call supraconscious, because they display a knowledge of the far past and of the future, and a keen understanding of spiritual growth. Yet, as underlined by Myers, their apparitions far outstrip being explained by the psi of the percipients (such as a hallucination just for the sake of becoming conscious of a future event).

However, understanding that yes, after death we keep on living in our very individuality and mindfulness, yet in an immaterial body or form, is far from enough for me.

The nature of this soul dimension that obviously is somehow shared by our etheric body and by the deceased as well, is what I always wanted to understand. And along my very serpentine path of research, I finally came to fathom this soul dimension as a hyperdimension in the universe—the famous 5th dimension featured in the movie *Interstellar*. The still-rare physicists who have modeled this 5th dimension see it mostly (or solely) as a 4th dimension of space—as a tesseract or hypercube. My own research in cognitive sciences, psi, and transcendental states led me to envision it as a full-fledged cosmic *consciousness,* on top of being a hyperspace and a hypertime. The conception and the writing of the core of the theory came as an intense visionary and creative state and was completed in eighteen days and filled about a hundred and twenty pages (practically unchanged in the published version). However, two years later, I spent nine months of arduous intellectual work in order to connect my cosmological theory to other physics theories, until its publishing in 2015 as *Cosmic DNA at the Origin.* And it is during these nine months—and that's indeed extremely meaningful— that I had very frequent visits from scientists while working at my desk, and we would converse for ten to twenty minutes. They were clearly interested in such a work and theory that could bridge the two dimensions—that of the living (in our 4D matter world) and that of the souls (in their hyperdimension of consciousness).

It was a breakthrough for me when I fully understood that we, the people living on Earth, have a part of our being that is constantly connected to this hyperdimension. And there is more: our Self—the higher consciousness we gain access to in deep meditative and altered states— is bathing and dwelling in it; we also access this soul dimension during the sleep state, and that's how we get dreams that give us guidance, strength, and an inkling of the future.

The knowledge displayed by the deceased—of world events, of the advancement of their own domain of research, of future events, and about a science and facts still unknown to us—has led me to get, with time passing, a clearer idea about what occupies them in the soul dimension. That, and my curious questions to some of them.

For one, all souls in the hyperdimension are intent on learning and rising to higher domains of frequency/quality of their souls.

The persons who have recently died are mostly busy reviewing their life, sorting out their good and bad deeds, learning from their mistakes, and caring for their loved ones on Earth. Some, more elevated and/or more knowledgeable, are definitely helping the newcomers to go through that preliminary phase of reckoning, more or less prolonged depending on their past life and their willingness to do so. It seems that there are sub-realms in terms of their elevation, or soul-frequency, or depth of understanding and knowledge.

The souls are also interconnected within vast networks according to the domain and path of their quest; just like, through the internet, we form networks of minds connected to specific themes and topics. This would correspond to the alchemist concept of *egregore*—a collective consciousness field of like-minded persons, with common values and practices. This has been recognized as far as religious creeds, or brotherhoods, or communities or systems of knowledge are concerned (such as the egregore of the Templars). But I believe it's the way the hyperdimension is organized: around meaning, domains of interest, of research, or of activity.

This was made clear to me on several occasions, especially when, at the end of our conversation, I asked Pauli if he was still in contact with Jung—that's when he introduced Jung by pointing to him. While gesturing so, Pauli explained, "Of course! We're always connected. In fact we're working together!" By this and other discussions, I learned that, at a certainly high level of consciousness, the souls or Selfs are forming vast communities involved in a given frequency-domain* of knowledge and action or dedication.

I came to understand, through my communications with ascended scientists, that the quest for an integration of science with an inner path of spiritual knowledge—what would be in effect a new scientific paradigm generating a new golden-age civilization—was such a vast network in which deceased scholars were in synergy with living researchers and experiencers.

The work of ascended souls is twofold: one, to keep on learning and accessing higher syg-frequencies (and in doing so, interact with alien civilizations having shared values); and two, to steer and support the consciousness leap now happening on Earth. Interestingly, the whole of nature (and not only humanity) is undergoing some type of leap to a higher sentience or consciousness. The leap is reverberating in all the living, not only in animals, but also in all natural systems on Earth, including rocks and crystals.

Thus, according to their specific domain, for example psychology or physics, the ascended souls would befriend the Selfs of the researchers who are the most promising in their own judgment and give them support, guidance, and help. And the same would go for the souls dedicated to saving the environment, for musicians and artists, and so forth.

This picture of a hyperdimension—in which the souls of the deceased are not only individualized but supraconscious, intent on pursuing their own research and spiritual path—is what some skeptics as well as some conservative religious authorities would too readily dismiss as an afterlife rosy tale. But it's not the case. Not only does this outlook on the spiritual dimension stem from numerous real-life experiences, but it is further supported by several domains of scientific investigation

---

*We owe this interesting and fecund concept to brain scientist Karl Pribram (1991); however I'm using it in an unorthodox way.

that we'll also explore—beyond the apparitions of the deceased, the out-of-body experiences (OBE), the near-death experiences (NDE), and memories from dead-brain episodes; finally, it is also corroborated by psi capacities (totally anomalous as to the 4D matter laws), by the visions of mystics, and by heightened states of consciousness.

Let's just remember that Christian priests, along the centuries of the Middle Ages and well into the sixteenth century, were mostly intent—in their religious teachings—on raising the fear of hell and on stressing in minute details the torments endured by the "sinners" (a category that included all non-Christians); and theirs was also a belief in the saints enjoying paradise for eternity in such a way that I wouldn't consider it anything but horrendously boring even for an afternoon.

My approach is not bound to a specific belief system but rather to real experiences that I and other authentic questers have lived. In fact, my path of knowledge, since I was an adolescent, has been, through extensive immersive travels, to tread many cultural and spiritual paths and learn as much as I can from these different world-visions and practices. My approach is as much a yogic one as a phenomenological one: learn from real experiences, strive to attain glimpses into the soul dimension by meditating and self-development techniques; then analyze and compare various occurrences, sort out their common traits, and only then look for the more global picture.

As I said, it's often enough to know that something is possible, and how someone else has achieved it (ongoing mistakes and failures included), to open for you a path of exploration and to make it a new potential in your life. This is why I want to share with you some of my real-life experiences, and how we can weave them into a coherent framework. I confess that I also love to ponder these anomalous happenings that befell me and I delight in recounting these stories, because often, when I do that, another facet of these experiences is illuminated, especially when comparing them. Expect from me no lies, no embellishment, and no masking of failures, that's all I can promise. I can't promise to tell you all, even in this specific domain, for a whole range of reasons. But I hope to make inroads progressively. As for what I can't tell clearly at the moment, the most productive way to ponder these weird domains at the fringe of our collective knowledge is certainly through science fiction, in a casual and imaginative way.

Have fun and don't restrain yourself from a bit of experimentation.

1
MY FATHER'S PASSING

My father, Victor, was in his late eighties when I first experienced a telepathic conversation with him; he who had been a brilliant mind, self-taught, and steeped in literature, philosophy, and the arts, was now in the grips of senility. His loss of memory had become dangerous for him in a large city such as Paris, and my mother had opted for them to move to Provence, where they dwelt in a picturesque village surrounded by vineyards.

As for me, I was living in an apartment building built atop an antique water mill with its huge wooden wheel, and set on a tiny island on the Essonne River, south of Paris.

I was sitting on an armchair in the living room, my eyes lingering beyond the balcony on the trees bordering the downstream edge of the island, where the two water streams connected again, with ducks gliding over the water around a small beach and jetty on the opposite side a few yards away.

Suddenly, I heard distinctly my father's voice. He confided to me, with a sober tone:

"Look, now I've become a real burden for you all. I think I should just die and lift the weight off your backs."

I was startled by the equal, coldly reflecting, style, and began a quick-thinking assessment.

At this point in time, he was just unable to think straight about anything, and furthermore, he was not aware of his deteriorated mental and memory condition. Many a time, he would argue about an event in the past shared with his longtime wife and maintain he was right, getting upset with my mother—where it was his own memory that failed him. Even at his best, he could do no more than follow my mother's lead as to what to do when, and back her stand on any issue.

The last time I had called my parents while I was traveling in India, just to say hello, my mother had to repeat to him a few times, before letting him on the phone: "It's *Christine,* your *daughter,*" to jog his memory on one and the other. Then, when I had him on the phone, I reminded him that I was in India at the moment.

"India? India?" said he uncomprehendingly.

And I explained, "You know, India, the country in Asia." When, after a few minutes, he caught on to the fact that I was in the East, in India, he burst out:

"In India, *oui* . . . But then, you don't give a damn about anything, do you?"

His tone had been matter-of-fact, not a reproaching one, just implying that I was in a carefree state, in my own world. My parents had, in fact, been so used to my frequent impromptu travels that, all along my late teens and my twenties, the first question they always asked me eagerly whenever I would call them was, "So, where are you at the moment, where are you?" And of course both of them, but my father especially, had positively loved the freedom with which I was living my life as a teenager.

"Well," I answered with a laugh, "that's about right!"

So, sitting in my armchair by the glass panel of the balcony, and hearing his voice in my head expressing a complex reasoning, and stating his senile condition as a fact (even if my mother was the one to take all the weight on her), I inferred he must have been at this very moment in deep sleep, and that it was his Self (or soul) talking to me, with crystal-clear thoughts unhampered by his deteriorated brain.

Often during sleep, the personal consciousness is able to exit the brain-body and to ascend to the level of the Self—the higher personal consciousness who indeed is the entity surviving death. The Self has been called *soul* in Christian religions; *atman* in Advaita Vedanta (philosophy of nonduality), Hinduism, and Buddhism; and the *ba* in Egypt.

The Self (thus named by the eminent psychologist Carl Jung) is the core of the individual consciousness who resides mostly in a higher dimension, beyond the brain-body and beyond spacetime. It is in this hyperdimension (HD) of consciousness—the *semantic* or *syg-HD*—that the Self of all individuals resides; and this is precisely why it is the dimension where dwell the souls of the deceased. (The triune hyperdimension is composed of the syg-HD as cosmic consciousness, hyperspace, and hypertime.)

Thus, while my father's body was in deep sleep, his Self had the ability to confer telepathically with me. As I know now, his Self could have conversed with my own Self, impervious of distances, without even my ego, in my ordinary state of consciousness, being aware about the exchange. It's only my long practice of meditation and self-development techniques that finally enabled me not only to "hear" such exchanges, but to respond to them or even drive them. So I answered:

"Well, Dad, if you're talking so clearly to me using a fairly grounded reasoning, then it's because at this very moment your mind is merged with your immaterial Self, who is reaching out to me from the other dimension. And it means you can get any help and advice you need from other souls residing in this dimension, in order to ponder what to do. Then it's up to you to decide; you certainly have a better grasp of the whole issue from your actual standpoint than I can have myself . . . As for me, I'm certainly not going to push you toward the grave; you're welcome to stay, and I don't have any advice to give you."

About six months later my father fell ill and was taken to the hospital in Carpentras. No specific illness was diagnosed, yet he presented with some difficulty in the ability to breathe and was unable to do more than lying in bed. By a stroke of bad luck, my mother was herself in another hospital in Avignon, for a minor operation, and my brother had taken care of my father during our mother's illness.

I was informed of Victor's transfer to the hospital, but to all of us, it seemed a minor and temporary problem. I had no more news because it was difficult to talk to my mother in the hospital and impossible to communicate with my father who wouldn't have recognized my name or voice.

Yet, four or five days later, while I was as usual spending my night writing (on whatever book was on my desk at the time), a bell in my head suddenly sounded an alarm. I knew something was wrong and my father was dying. I had the sudden realization that, if I wanted to see him alive a last time, I had to drive to Provence the very next morning.

It was still early in my writing night, and I made the decision on the spot. Now, I had to call my mother before departing, to let her know I was coming and to arrange for getting the keys to their house—and therefore I had to wait until 8:00 a.m., her usual awakening time (back in 2001, there were no cell phones). Then I would leave right afterward. Getting up at 6:30 a.m. meant that I had to soon suspend my night's work to allow myself five hours of sleep (my usual sleeping time) ahead of my seven hours drive to Provence.

At 8:00 a.m. the next morning, I was reaching out to my mother in her hospital room, and before I could explain myself, she exclaimed:

"Ah! Christine! *I called you* because your father is in a critical state, and if you want to see him a last time while he's still alive, you have to come immediately."

"Well, this is exactly the intuition I had in the middle of the night! And as it is, I'm fully dressed and ready to jump in my car just after we hang up. But what do you mean by 'I called you'? I'm the one to call you, no?"

"No, I left a message on your answering machine yesterday evening, to call me back."

"Ah! I didn't see it! But look, I'll head directly to the hospital in Carpentras—will be there in about seven or eight hours."

"After you'll have visited him, come see me at Avignon's hospital; as we knew, the cyst the surgeon removed was innocuous, but he wants to keep me under observation two or three more days, due to my age. I'll give you the house keys."

On my way I went. Ormoy, where I was living, is a far suburb, about twenty miles south of Paris, and it has a quick access to the Sun Highway, going straight to Provence and Marseille.

I had been driving for three hours when, to my astonishment, I started to hear the very clear thoughts of my father talking to me. Simultaneously, I was perceiving his face in the corner of my eyes, strangely embedded between the left corner of the windshield and my driver's window (left side of the car). His eyes were a bit higher than mine.

I reduced my speed and veered to the slowest right-side lane of the highway, on which there was little traffic anyway.

Victor was very excited, and he started talking without any preamble (just like the previous time in Ormoy), as if he was confident that I could hear him clearly.

"Figure that I've seen everybody! They all came and talked to me. It's hard to believe but that's what happened! I've seen Lulu (one of my uncles, the husband of my mother's sister, Denise), and Maman Angèle (my maternal grandmother) . . ."

At that point, two streams of thought occurred in my mind. The first was the assessment that, since he wasn't dead himself, he must have been unconscious at the moment and accessing (sporadically) the other dimension. This explained why he was talking to me in such a clear way—it had to be either being unconscious or being asleep, as in our previous exchange. But this time, given the circumstances, I inferred that he was drifting in and out of consciousness—meaning accessing the hyperdimension during the unconscious phases.

The second stream of thought had to do with the experience he had, because both Lulu and Angèle were deceased, the first one for a few years, and my grandmother for about two decades. And thus his experience seemed to fall into the category called deathbed visions or apparitions, a neutral term, despite the fact they are more like visitations from the Beyond dimension. I understood that he was now very near to his death—the welcoming committee had come, and he was himself closing in on the soul dimension, spending more and more time there, I suspected.

My father didn't seem to react to my own silent assessment that his time had come. Or else, his excitement over the experience he had just undergone didn't leave room for a gloomy mood.

He went on enumerating all the deceased of the close circle of the family, his parents and parents-in-law and their descendants, about seven or eight people altogether. There seems to have been only one exception to the panel who had come to greet him. He explained:

"The only one I've not seen is Denise [the younger sister of my mother, Yvonne] . . . because Denise is in a very specific situation right now and she must not be disturbed."

I now regret that I didn't ask him details about the so-important task that demanded Denise's whole attention—to the point that she didn't come to greet her best ally and friend in the close family. (Denise had passed away fifteen years earlier.) In contrast, Victor organized a wonderful two-day reception for the centennial birthday of his mother-in-law, Angèle, despite the fact he had had dire and bitter quarrels with her occasionally; and yet, she was there to greet him.

It was quite a shock for me when I realized his impending death—one more sign, after my nightly intuition and my mother's warning—but this one the most ominous of all. And that made me more attentive to what he had to say to me and less prone to interrupt his narration.

Strange as it appears to me now, that was about all that Victor conveyed to me; and yet in my vivid memory of this event, I keep the impression that we talked together about half an hour. Let me point out that this type of discrepancy between, on the one hand, what is felt to last a long psychological time, duly corroborated by the clock, and on the other hand, the small bulk of information being consciously memorized, has been quite frequent during conversations I had with deceased persons.

All the while we talked, my eyes were focused on the road ahead, but my attention was attuned to this spot on the left of the windshield, in the corner of my eyes, where I could sense his head and his presence. (I'm so used to experiencing sudden visions, heightened states, or mental connections while driving that I know I can handle it without risk.)

But the greatest surprise was yet to come.

Hours later, I exited the highway at Orange and went straight to Carpentras hospital, at that time still in the historical building at the center of this small town. Having gotten directions to his room at the reception desk, I went there . . . and was surprised to find my sister, a dermatologist, standing next to his bed and attending to my father.

After a quick hello to her, I turned to my father and saw that he was unconscious. My sister confirmed that he was drifting in and out of consciousness, and that she was watching his breathing closely. That day, she had closed her own dermatology office to rush to the hospital and take care of him.

I bent over the bed, stroking his forehead and talking to him, but he didn't open his eyes at that point.

My sister Colette, with her strong character and in her capacity as a medical specialist, had taken over the reins of the medical treatment given to my father. She told me she had required a scan of all the internal organs, but that it revealed nothing. She was adamant that they hadn't performed a full scan of the abdomen as she had asked, but only of the chest, and that's why they had not found out the problem. She was, as usual, furious and fulminating against my brother who, in her eyes, hadn't taken Victor to the hospital until the morning after he had choked at dinner on eating an apple a few days earlier.

As usual also, I didn't relate to, or interfere with, the vindictive way she was putting out steam.

Then, suddenly, she bent over Victor and started pressing rhythmically on his chest, urging him:

"Breathe, breathe, come on Dad, breathe!"

Then, after she deemed the fit to be over, she turned toward me:

"Sometimes, he just stops breathing, and I have to press on his chest and force him to breathe . . ."

I approached him from the other side and held his hand, speaking softly and comfortingly, caressing his forehead. Now my father opened his eyes, and I was able to exchange a few innocuous words with him; he smiled at me, but his eyes remained a bit vague, as if he didn't recognize me fully. Then he drifted again.

That's when my sister started to tell me the strangest of stories— what she had seen happening in the morning.

So basically, before I even had time to express my own stupendous experience, my sister recounted to me that, in the morning and for a quite long moment, our father had been fully conscious with his eyes wide open.

At this point, I must describe the large rectangular hospital room. On one small side, it had an empty bed; on the other were two beds set along the long sides and facing the large room. One bed under the window was occupied by another patient, a mostly sleeping old man, for whom I never saw any visitor. And opposite the window was Victor's bed, with a space of about thirty inches running between the length of the bed and the wall, to allow passage of the nurses. And in between these two beds was a large space of about two yards with the bed tables at the back, and where my sister had her chair, largely unused as she remained mostly standing.

So she told me that Victor was looking intently at the center of the ceiling, and his eyes widened in astonishment as he suddenly greeted my Uncle Lulu with effusion:

"Oh, Lulu, it's so nice of you to have come! Oh, I'm so happy to see you!"

And all the while he talked thus to Lulu, his eyes were slowly moving down, as if accompanying Lulu's movement, who seemed to have descended from the ceiling slowly to settle finally on my father's left, in the small passage between the wall and the bed. Then Victor's eyes remained fixated on a spot there, as if Lulu had been now standing next to him, while he kept talking to him further, witnessed my sister.

After a short while, Victor's eyes were again focused on the center of the ceiling, and he was now greeting another person with the same enthusiastic emotion and joy.

"Oh, Maman Angèle, I'm so happy to see you; it's so kind of you to have come!"

And again his eyes would slowly accompany the person's descent all the way to the same side of his bed, while talking to them, and then he would keep looking straight at a spot there.

My sister told me the whole operation was repeated a number of times, greeting thus all the deceased parents of the proximate family—who seemed to have lined up one by one along the wall to his left. After she had finished relating this astounding observation, I told her how Victor had appeared to me in my car while I was driving, and how he recounted to me that he had seen all his immediate deceased relatives, just as she had described it.

I could barely tone down my excitement at what my sister had witnessed—the precise unfolding of the encounter with deceased relatives that my father, himself upbeat by the extraordinary experience he just had, had deemed so important that he had to share it with me.

In my view, it gave a solid ground to the exchange I had with Victor in my car—a telepathic-type experience that, lacking any outside witness and behavioral manifestation, would remain rather anecdotal for a psi researcher, and total fantasy for a skeptic. Quite the opposite, the way my father's deathbed visitation happened, with the spirits of the deceased emerging out of the ceiling one by one, and flying down to stand next to his bed in line, is of such precision and duration that it rules out the concept of a mere hallucination that the skeptics love to readily append to these far-from-rare experiences. (And let me add that my late sister had a rational scientific mind, her science, dermatology, being based on observation and analysis, and she didn't doubt the reality of what she had observed.) Moreover, the fact that Victor's behavior—while following the displacement of the visitors, greeting and talking with each one by their names—was repeated seven or eight times makes the hallucination explanation totally improbable. In contrast, it shows the visit and intrusion of disembodied souls into the material and spacetime dimension of their loved ones still on Earth, in order to prepare them for their imminent transference to another level of reality, the soul hyperdimension. It is also based on surveys of such deathbed visions that I interpreted what my father was telling me in the car as a sure sign his life was ending. (We'll review the data at the end of this chapter.)

A MERGING OF MATTER AND SOUL DIMENSIONS

We have to ponder the fact that, at the moment of death, there seems to be an opening between the dimensions, a sort of coming together or convergence, that allows the two-way contact and intrusion of one into the other and vice versa.

A few times in Sub-Sahel Africa, for example in Mali, I've been able to observe a strange behavior in very old people. They keep to themselves, sitting alone on a mat for hours in a corner of the house or in a shaded spot in the family courtyard, and nevertheless their posture remains erect and they are not asleep. They haven't lost their mind either, because if one goes to greet them, they snap to attention and sweetly welcome you. While withdrawn, their facial expression is extremely peaceful and content, yet alert, and behind their closed eyes, they seem to look intensely at something, to be wholly absorbed in some other level of reality. The impression I got was that they were already mostly living in the Beyond reality, their consciousness focused on and bathing in the hyperdimension. Now that's surely a serene way to make the transition to the afterlife: to disentangle oneself from the material world and from the emotional and societal maelstroms, while one gets more and more attuned to a spiritual dimension.

I do remember that my mother, once her life companion had passed away, told me that she would often talk at length with Victor and get his advice and support. Just as with deathbed visions, there are count-less reports of old-age widows feeling the recurrent presence of their late spouse and receiving great comfort from this ongoing communication. My paternal grandmother used to hear her late husband moving around her flat during the night, but, unlike many others, she felt so perturbed by it that, despite being in great health, she decided on selling her Paris flat, distributing her heritage and moving into a cozy senior home—where, unfortunately, she had to spend the next twelve years, until two years before her centenary. A friend of my family lost her dear husband who was about twenty years her senior, and thereafter married another man who had a fondness for drink and a bad temper. She recounted to me that one evening he got violent and was about to strike her, and a wall behind her made it impossible to run away; she called aloud for her first husband to protect her and she saw him appear and protect her so efficiently that her inebriated new husband couldn't approach her.

While skeptics attribute these visitations to hallucinations, or else a dissociative state and mental disorder, caring physicians, nurses, and psychiatrists have repeatedly stressed their mostly beneficent and calm-ing influence on widows.

The cultural wisdom of the Hindus certainly reflects the natural tendency of aging people to hear and see the spiritual realm. Hindus state that we go through specific ages: childhood, parenthood and pro-fessional life, and then the age of spiritual attainment. In the last age, all men and women, according to the tradition, should detach from worldly affairs and only strive to attain peace and enlightenment.

In this perspective, I assume that individuals approaching the end of their lives—the time of their *transference* to the soul dimension—beyond engaging in meditation and self-development, would also take advantage of their deep sleep and dream periods, when their conscious-ness is able to disengage from the body, to tune in to the soul dimen-sion. In both the waking and the sleep states, they would communicate with resonant souls, be it their spiritual guides or the spirits of loved ones and kindred minds. Then, when their health deteriorates to the point of their shifting in and out of consciousness, they would similarly use their periods of unconsciousness to branch into the soul dimension, just as my father had done.

To get back to Victor's experience, my sister had another surprise for me. She started talking again, now with a somber undertone. The problem was that, from the time I was born when she was two and a half years old, she had entertained a grudge toward the younger sibling—me—attracting all our parents' attention, a jealous bent she had never overcome; and I just recognized *that* undertone of her.

"But one thing I couldn't understand is that Victor saw *you too* arriving in the room—the only one not being deceased . . . So what does . . . ?" She left the sentence hanging.

Judging by her ominous tone, that meant I already had a foot in the grave! I cut her short, sidestepping her train of thought with a crisp laugh:

"Oh! But as you well know, I'm able to crisscross the dimensions, and theirs is one I certainly am familiar with. Nothing to worry about!"

My father at that point made some groans and I tried to talk to him some more, but he didn't open his eyes and soon slumped back into a half-comatose state. I then realized it was due time to go visit my mother, as we had arranged. It must have been 5:30 p.m. already—and as in all hospitals they would soon get their patients ready for dinner . . . better to get on the move. When I left my father's room, my sister was again bent on making my father breathe—a therapeutic relentlessness that her medical profession held sacrosanct at the time; yet, this medical harassment was not favoring the kind of serene transference to the other side that his being welcomed by his deceased loved ones was suggesting. But I kept these thoughts to myself.

We were then in 2001; but when my mother died fourteen years later (aged 101) we had come to the age of "stop the therapeutic relentlessness" motto and to a willingness to ease the final days of the terminally ill. Therapeutic relentlessness, as it turned out, had been appraised in the new light of an aging population putting great logistic and financial stress on the social security given to all. The number of ailing patients was largely exceeding the hospitals' and senior homes' capacity, and any excessive hospital care of terminally ill patients had been relinquished, while the medical profession now favored at-home treatments and a peaceful end-of-life among one's family. But to be fair, we also had had a generation of spiritually aware young volunteers (not abiding by any specific faith) who had devoted their time visiting the terminally ill and helping them with psychic healing, suggestions, and wise paroles. They had followed in the footsteps of Dr. Elisabeth Kübler-Ross and her 1969 revolutionary book *On Death and Dying,* which offered the first glimpses into NDEs and prodded both patients and doctors to stop fearing death and see it as a transference to another dimension.

A half hour later, I was at the main Avignon hospital, and gave my mother some news of Victor, while omitting the anomalous experiences of both my father and me. I knew she absolutely wanted to visit Victor the next day, as she worried it could be her last exchange with him alive. We agreed I would come and take her in the early afternoon, and then drive her back to her own hospital room.

Once in the family house, I prepared myself some dinner with whatever food was available in the freezer and on shelves, and then I crashed on a bed upstairs, where it was freezing cold.

The sad story of my family—which I have to clarify in order for the following accounts to be understandable—is that it had always been plagued by internal feuds. My childhood was filled with the enmity between my sister and my mother—with conflict flaming up on a weekly basis. And with the bullying behavior of my older sister vis-à-vis me, starting from my toddler years. As a result, from as early as I can remember, I felt a total stranger to this family; even before I reached the driving license age of eighteen, I had already squatted my parents' country house in Igny, a south suburb of Paris, and was regularly hitch-hiking from Paris to reside there any time I could, on the pretext I had work to do and exams to prepare for in peace. Work was sacrosanct in my family, and since I was a brilliant student, my parents were letting me free to do what I wanted. Furthermore, I was helping at, or taking care of, their catering shop every Sunday morning and whenever they were overwhelmed with clients' orders—such as all night long on each and every Christmas and Easter eve—and that, in my father's fair perspective, was setting me as a responsible individual, therefore self-driven. As soon as I was in the country house, of course, forgetting all about my dreadful school and suffocating sister, I would dive and revel in my own world, meditating, reading, and writing poetry in the garden and in the nearby woods.

Just after my parents had bought a piece of real estate with my sister in Séguret, a vineyards village, and both households had started to build their own house—just eighty yards apart—a new feud erupted between my brother, who was overseeing the construction of our parents' house, and my sister. So bitter was it that, when my parents moved over to their now finished house, the conflict was inflamed again and the Provence family was split between on the one hand my parents siding with my brother, and on the other hand my sister and her household cutting all relationship with them. I was the only one, residing in Paris, keeping in touch with both sides—needless to say, a position hotly criticized by all!

As had been my understanding and strategy since experiencing a dire family crisis when I was five years old, the farther from them I was, the better I felt, and so I kept to myself and my husband in Paris, relieved that the conflict was set in Provence. That day, when I was five years old, I had been badly harassed and hurt by my older sister; I realized that, her being bigger by two and a half years, I couldn't defend myself physically.

"Since she is stronger, I'll be more intelligent!" I swore to myself, intending to circumvent her efficiently by cleverness alone. And from then on, my tactic was one of smart avoidance and, a few years later, the adamant setting of my own territory in the Paris flat as off-limits to her—all the while for the most part remaining polite and sound.

And so it was that, at the time of my father's last days, she had been informed of my father's admission in the hospital by her colleague doctors, and had neither been in contact nor set foot in the house of my parents for a year and a half—and wouldn't for the next twelve years, until I reconciled her with my mother when I settled in Provence and took care of her.

Early afternoon the day after I visited the hospital, I went to fetch my mother and we drove to Carpentras to see my father. Fortunately, he had a long moment of clear consciousness, no doubt brought about by his wife's presence, whom he was extremely happy to see, as well as me. Colette wasn't there, she had resumed her usual schedule at her dermatologist's office. Then I drove Yvonne back to her hospital and came back to Séguret. A quick hello to Colette's husband Guy and their kids (Colette was still at work), and then, after having a bite, I got myself a book in the large library of my father. I'm used to going to sleep well after dawn, after a night of writing, and so I indulged in reading until about four in the morning.

It must have been about 5:30 a.m. when my sister burst into the house from the terrace door that I had left unlocked, and woke me up the harsh way with loud shouts. I came downstairs, and here she was standing, already clad in a warm winter coat, telling me Victor had passed away during the night and the hospital had just called her to let her know. She was awfully stressed and direly authoritative, enjoining me to get dressed on the spot and go with her to the hospital mortuary where our father's body had been transferred.

As for me, I was shocked by the abrupt awakening in the first three hours of sleep—generally a deep sleeping stage. We had all expected Victor to die any day; to do anything possible to see him alive a last time was one thing, but why was she now in such a rush to pay a visit to his dead body? But I kept mostly silent, just acknowledging the sad news.

Again she tried to enforce her stress on me, by commandeering me to get dressed and jump in her car. I was nearly drawn to follow her lead, when, at that point, I heard a clear and strong voice in my head: *"You get in her car, you die."*

An instant clarity of mind sparked in me; I fended off her deep-seated tendency to control me. Taking some psychological distance, I said:

"Wait! I don't see any reason to hurry up to the mortuary, where he will remain for two or three days anyway until the laying out of the body ceremony. What's the rush for? It's still dark and freezing cold out there. I'm not even awakened yet. Listen, go by yourself if you wish. As for me, I'll have a coffee and take a shower, and will drive to the mortuary in my own car in an hour or so."

Seeing that she wasn't going to have it her way, she got upset and stormed out of the house.

Left alone, I made myself some strong coffee, and had some cheese and tomato toasts—the kind of breakfast that helps the body withstand the cold.

I had had so many interactions with the spirits of the deceased, from a very early age, that these had changed thoroughly my attitude vis-à-vis death. I knew from experience that the consciousness, the soul, of a person remains alive and is able to communicate with living individuals inasmuch as the latter are sensitive and/or loving. Death, for me, meant only the discarding of the body. The trauma, for the ones living, was all about the loss they had to endure themselves. But as for the ones who had passed away, they were mostly happy, liberated from suffering. They were even able to observe their loved ones still living in the matter universe, as if from an all-seeing observatory. And when it came to persons with a debilitating illness, such as my father, then death meant the freedom of their souls, and the possibility of a clear telepathic communication, such as was not possible while they were alive.

The tragedy of death is the psychological pain and suffering of the ones living—the bottomless anguish for the lost companion. At the time of my father's passing, I was still mourning over the absence of my

ex-husband, who had left me for another woman about two years earlier, and it took me some additional years to overcome this terrible loss.
(While it was not caused by death, the grief was as profound.) This, I
could definitely understand and was deeply empathetic toward those
mourning.

Yet, for the minds able to reach to the Beyond dimension and hear
the voices of immaterial souls, the sense of loss for a departed companion
or parent is somehow diminished. Of course our funerary rituals and
customs have all been defined by our diverse religious authorities on the
basis of their pervasive belief in the survival of the souls. Yet, as strange
as it may sound, these customs are at times in discrepancy with the reality of souls being alive beyond. The mourning and mostly dark clothing signifying despair and loss are clearly espousing the emotions and
mindset of the family and friends having lost a loved one, but are at odds
with the supposed new freedom and liberation from pain that most great
religions deem the deceased to enjoy. However, there are some people
who celebrate a burial in joy. Let's mention the tradition of jazz funer-
als in New Orleans: these are all along accompanied by live music, first
expressing grief on the way to the cemetery, then on leaving it, displaying
upbeat music and dancing (see fig. 1.1 on the following page).

Surprisingly, we did hold such a joyful parting ceremony in France,
but only after four days of mourning, when twelve people, eight of them
cartoonists or columnists and their colleagues and security from Charlie
Hebdo, were brutally murdered at the office of the magazine in Paris on
January 7, 2015. After the attacks, silent marches and vigils were held,
especially at Place de la République in Paris, many holding placards *Je
suis Charlie* (French for "I am Charlie"), which was adopted as a rallying cry for freedom of speech and resistance to armed threats, as well as
"Not afraid," and holding pens in the air. On January 11, a day of silent
marching was organized not only in all large towns in France, but also
at the level of each remote village in Provence, and altogether pulled in
the streets an unprecedented crowd, above 4 million people. It felt as
if the whole population was in what I call a telepathic-harmonic field

a

b

Fig. 1.1. (a) "Jazz funeral" style procession in New Orleans to mourn the closing of Public Health Service of the New Orleans Marine Hospital, 1981; (b) Jazz funeral in Memphis for the "King of Blues" B. B. King, on May 14, 2015, with Barbara Blue singing on the left. Ruby Wilson, the "Queen of Beale Street," performed at the memorial, ahead of his burial in Mississippi.

Photo (b) by Adarryll Jackson Sr. (www.instagram.com/adarrylljacksonsr)

(or Telhar field), all of us like one collective soul, feeling the strength of this intense empathy while coming together. We then expressed in a huge silent shout, our willingness to stand for our freedom of speech, freedom of critical thinking, freedom of the press, and resistance to threats. In the last years, it's mostly with such a silent togetherness and supporting each other in resistance that we have responded, in many places, to terror and hate attacks and threats, whatever the motives, religious or political or otherwise, of the perpetrators.

In Paris, because we were giving our fearless cartoonists and humorists a last homage, our biggest TV channel, TF1, organized a stand-up comedy and satirical evening show, in which comics offered sketch after sketch about Charlie Hebdo, keeping us doubled over with laughter for the whole evening. (TF1 had set a no-interdiction rule, in that all were free to use any slang they wanted.)

Back in the Provence house . . . An hour later, when I got into my car, the sun had risen on a crisp whitish and frosty Provence landscape. I drove carefully on the dust path between the vineyards, up to the asphalt road leading to the next village, Sablet. And there, seeing the asphalt had a dark color, I got out of my car to check whether the road was still coated with ice, or if it had fully melted already. I was reassured, it had this damp color and look, but the road was clear of ice—the sun and the rising temperature had melted the frost. So I engaged myself on the mostly deserted road at a normal speed, enjoying the Provence landscape at a season I never had the opportunity to discover before.

A mile after Sablet, the road made a ninety degree turn on the right, while it ascended a hill. Just after the turn, I unexpectedly saw the road covered with whitish frost and realized my car was sliding. The brakes didn't respond anymore. At that point, my mind got into hyperspeed. In a split instant, I took the whole situation in: on the left, the steep hillside that had been cut to make the road, like a wall. On the right, an abrupt, nearly seventy-degree slope down to the level of the vineyard fields—punctuated by a few young trees quite spaced apart—the height of the fall getting bigger with each new yard my car traveled up the road. The scene was surrealistic. My car kept sliding up and taking a slight bent toward the right—all this appearing to me to unfold at an extremely low speed. The brake pedal, the wheel, the tires, none were responding. I instantly got concentrated and calm, hyperlucid, watching the event unfold as if time had been slowed down tenfold. I saw the car move ever so slightly to the right, unstoppable, and then I observed, with an unnatural slowness, the growing height down to the fields at the foot of the hill, through a long opening without any tree. Then my eyes got fixated on three tiny silvery birch trees, way ahead of the front right of the car, about twelve yards ahead, and then I thought: "But I'm heading toward these trees! Am I really going to smash into them?"

As usual for me in extremely dangerous situations, I was totally devoid of fear; instead, hyperlucid and with a decupled speed of thought.

Then the trees moved progressively toward me, with an incredibly slow motion, forward and forward; and that was my last image, just before my right front wheel, that of the passenger seat, overran the side of the road and my car fell over, into a precipitous toppling.

Next perception, I was at a weird angle in my driver seat, looking at the steep slope of the talus running on my left beyond my intact windshield. I was still calm and coldly concentrated—without any psychological shock or panic—and I quickly assessed my situation.

The car had embedded itself within the three birch trunks, right on the passenger door, awfully bent inward. Apart from that door, the front of the car, inside, was untouched; I was perfectly clear of mind, without the slightest pain or hurt. But my driver door, on my left, was above me—the downward slope of the hill must have been less than thirty degrees. The car was wholly overturned on that slope, the road invisible as the trees were planted about three yards downward. My next thought was to assess if the car could still move and fall farther down when I would shift my weight to get out of it. It wasn't oscillating and it seemed securely stabilized by the three slim trunks that had made a deep indent into the front right door. But that was not a sure bet. And thus, I moved very carefully, like an equilibrist on a rope, while I slowly unbuckled, grabbed my handbag, and extricated myself from a crooked position, in order to be able to reach to the driver door above me. Then I couldn't believe how hard I had to push on that door for it to open upward, and then to keep it ajar. I had to climb up through that door, and then scale up the slope in order to reach the level of the road, where I stood, still bewildered, looking at how far below was the ground.

I estimated the height where my car stood compared to the fields below to be about seven yards; without the birch trees, my car would have rolled on itself sideways until it crashed below, something that could well have been lethal for me.

Five minutes later, a car passed by, coming from the north and I gestured for help. The driver, slowing down, took the whole scene in and stopped carefully farther on the hill side of the road. Only the top of my car—that is, its left flank—was visible from farther down the road. The driver, shocked and concerned, made a U-turn and gave me a lift all the way back to my parents' house.

Back in the house, I prepared myself a second coffee and decided to take it easy. There was no way I could reach my sister; cell phones were still nonexistent and I wasn't going to call the mortuary. It was still too early for anything. It was fortunate that my car wasn't obstructing the small road, as it allowed me to get away without involving the police and a towing service. Later, I was going to call my elder brother, whose hobby was car racing, and he would get one of his buddies to come and tow the car. I had remarked that the only part of my Mazda that had been damaged was the passenger door, easy to find secondhand, as well as its metal frame on the roof, just needing to be hammered in place, since my car was so old. So old indeed that, as my brother would explain to me later, it didn't even have an antiskid mechanism. That was real luck: the repair expenses were going to be minimal.

Thus I was making myself some coffee in the kitchen—using my mother's antiquated and slow homemade filter because she couldn't stand coffee machines—all the while reflecting on the series of events.

I wasn't at all astonished by my incredible luck at the presence of the three tightly planted birch trees, so young indeed that their trunks were hardly three or four inches wide, all three forming a pack of about twenty inches wide. My brother later pointed out to me that if there had been only one trunk, even much wider, my car, due to its speed, would have turned around its axis at the impact point and would have fallen down the hill. In my life, I had always had such uncanny events preventing the worst from happening and, furthermore, I knew my life was still ahead, buzzing from the future with achievements I still had to perform. I had had a precise glimpse of some of these events by precognition.

So, ironically, the one troubling detail wasn't in the accident sequence—but earlier when, my sister pressing me to get in her car, I heard the voice in my head stopping me with great force from doing so: "You get in her car, you die!"

I knew this voice, its ominous tone, and its compelling force. I had always abided by it; and it had always been proven right. Frighteningly so.

I was yet to be informed (again by my brother) that in Provence or in any hilly landscape, you have, in winter, to watch for the northern slopes of hills and expect the road there to be coated with ice even though the rest of it is dry and clean.

As I reflected back on the two scenes—the precognitive one and the accident one—even if my sister knew these roads well in any season and was a smart driver, albeit loving to speed along, one had to put in the balance the fact that, with the disturbing news, she was highly stressed and had been awoken badly by the hospital. I couldn't refrain from thinking that, had I been in the passenger seat, even with the trees stopping the car I would've been killed by the impact, given that the metal door and its frame had been deeply bent inward into the cabin.

Of course, reflecting on the precognition that made me take an alternative course, it was strange that I still had the accident. It seemed the probability of accident was too high for it to be averted. Could there have been two possible suites of events? One being deadly for me in the passenger seat, and one being inconsequential if I was by myself, driving my own car, and at the wheel—meaning having full control of the events?

And I'm not excluding a supernatural monitoring, by my own higher Self, of the skidding of the car precisely right into the lifesaving bunch of trees. I've already seen this in action in my life, with indubitable clearness. Its main revealing symptom was the lack of any sensory and bodily perception between the instant I realized I was heading ever so slowly toward the side of the road, and the moment I found myself askew in my seat and assessing the situation within a car that was already impaled on the trees and totally still. A second symptom, absolutely crucial for the Self to take the reins of a situation, is the total absence of fear or of any emotion—just cool observation and realization of probabilities—*before* the Self takes over. (These two topics—the monitoring by the Self and precognition versus probabilities—would each deserve a full study and are beyond the scope of this book.)

With my pot of coffee and a glass, I now sat at the kitchen table to drink it.

That's when the face and shoulders of my father appeared in the right-hand upper corner of the kitchen, just under the ceiling and facing me. And he started talking immediately, without any preamble:

"Oh my! It's hard to believe! These doctors can't let us die peacefully! They have to keep trying this and that! It's like we have to trick them in order to do so . . . It's really something!"

I chuckled, remembering the relentless and rather inopportune actions of my sister, and her mentioning the scanning and tests. And after a brief pause, with a different tone, that of a peaceful realization, he confided to me:

"I'll tell you . . . if only I had known, I would have died earlier!"

That last sentence implied: If I had known it would be like this— that we remain conscious and alive, surrounded by our parents and friends—I wouldn't have suffered and made the others suffer for so long! (See fig. 1.2, page 34.)

I gave him my empathetic assent. Yet, there was nothing one could

Fig. 1.2. *Death's Door*, drawing by William Blake and etching by Luigi Schiavonetti for Robert Blair's poem *The Grave*

do, really, to convey to an atheist such as my father—even with his natural spirituality and high humanist values—that life goes on in another dimension of reality and that regular occurrences of communication render, for some people like me, this fact of survival as self-evident and certain as a phone conversation across thousands of miles.

In fact, after I came back from my two long travels of eighteen months each (in India and Africa), understanding the impossibility of expressing such views in a face-to-face exchange, I had written a long letter to my father, explaining to him what to expect at death, the process, the afterlife, and so on. I had told him that, when the time would come, he should contact me, that I knew how to facilitate his access to the other side and would do it. My letter just elicited, at the time, an immense pain to my father, and stirred in him the feeling of being betrayed. (I must confess that I thought he was going to die soon—this was what had triggered my writing the letter—and had voiced it as a preamble, and this definitely didn't help, especially when it was disproved by later events.)

However, it seems his Self knew better, since it was Victor's Self who had first called on me in Ormoy, and to whom I was now talking! The Self, being the subject of the unconscious, and what all religions call the soul (ba, atman, nagual . . .), is the personal immaterial and cognizant spirit of each of us, who pre-exists our conception and birth, and survives our bodily death. Thus, as soon as Victor began to prepare himself and started to get attuned to the soul dimension during his deep sleep and later his lapses into unconsciousness, he knew that my own Self could easily penetrate and crisscross this dimension, the aborigines' dreamtime. As my sister witnessed it—when his deceased parents and family at large came to welcome him into the other dimension, thus pacifying his intellect before the great leap, and opening it to the dimension of his Self—I was there, as my own Self, facilitating the process, while my ordinary ego, driving my car some 200 miles away, was conversing with him. This is soul-guiding at the moment of death, a psychopomp role that I've always assumed in my life, even before I had awakened to my own Self through my meditating practice.

A PSYCHOPOMP ROLE

In Egypt, various Books of the Dead were depicted on walls or on papyrus in the tombs of pharaohs and notables. At death, whereas the *ka,* or life-force, remains in the body (that is going to be embalmed as a mummy), the soul, or *ba,* exits the body and begins a dangerous journey in an intermediary realm toward the immortal realm or *Duat,* kingdom of Osiris. If it succeeds in warding off dangers, the ba will, at the gate of the Duat, attend the judgment over its own life. The god Thoth, with an ibis head and as the divine scribe, oversees and records the weighing of the heart of the deceased to evaluate their worthiness (performed by the jackal-headed Anubis, against the feather of Maat, the goddess of justice). Then Horus will take the worthy ones to Osiris. (The punishment for bad deeds was thus to be barred from entering immortality and one's heart being devoured.) In the Duat, the worthy ba (somehow integrated to its heart and ka) will be transformed into an *akh* "the effectiveness of the dead," what we may understand as a consciously acting and ascended spirit (see plate 1).

The term *psychopomp* means a conductor of souls to the afterworld. As we know, Thoth has been called Hermes by the Greeks, whose most brilliant scholars went to learn the sciences and sacred knowledge in Egypt. Hermes is, like Thoth, knowledgeable in all sciences and philosophy; the paragon of the architect, "Measurer of the cord," and of the philosopher; the instructor in secret knowledge and divine wisdom; and a psychopomp as well. Hermes supervised the burials and led the souls of the dead up to the river Styx, the frontier to the underworld, governed by Hades (the Latin Pluto) (see fig. 1.3). However, this was only the first leg of the journey, with Charon, the ferryman, taking the soul across it to Hades. Then souls were to be judged, and according to their merits, be sent to the paradisiacal Elysian Fields (to live among the heroes), or to the Fields of Punishment or the Asphodel Fields (two types of purgatory), or else to the Tartarus (sort of inferno). Note how the Greek Hermes, in his psychopomp role, is full of empathy and truly friendly toward the dead soul, especially as he takes Myrrhine gently by the hand to lead her to Hades. I find this Greek cultural depiction of Hermes Psychopomp the nearest and truest to the information we'll gather through direct communications with the deceased and through

a

b

Fig. 1.3. Hermes as psychopomp: (a) supervising the burial of Sarpedon, while his body is carried by Hypnos and Thanatos (Sleep and Death), side A of the "Euphronios krater," an Attic red-figured calyx-krater signed by Euxitheos (potter) and Euphronios (painter), ca. 515 BCE; (b) conducting the deceased Myrrhine to Hades, carved funerary stone lekythos (vase), ca. 430–420 BCE, National Archaeological Museum of Athens. *Photo (b) by Marsyas, CC BY-SA 3.0*

the accounts of survivors of near-death experiences. As we will see soon, the deceased are really welcomed to the realm of the souls by their friendly and caring parents.

The Eleusinian Mysteries in ancient Greece were an initiatic cult revealing the dimension of the afterlife and the cycle of life, death, and rebirth, and fertility; it precedes the Olympian religion, and, in my opinion, was issued from Egypt (and probably either morphed into the Priory of Sion's initiation, or else shares with it the same root-cult in Egypt). This Mystery school is centered around Persephone and her mother Demeter—the goddess of agriculture, growth, and nourishment. Persephone was abducted by Hades (Pluto for the Romans) and became the powerful queen of the underworld. But her mother, Demeter, grieving and desperate, kept relentlessly searching for her. The earth became barren, nothing would grow anymore and life faced extinction. Hermes, then, crossed to the underworld and took her back to her mother. However, she had to spend in the underworld the season when the vegetation stops growing and rose back to earthly life with springtime (see plate 2).

In Hinduism, it is Shiva, the god of the meditative path of learning and wisdom, represented as an ascetic, who, after death, guides the true Self of the quester toward its liberation, *moksha* (or *mukti*). This state of liberation is what all yogis aim at achieving in the course of one life; it is deemed the highest state achievable in a human consciousness. In moksha, the ego (*jiva*) merges with the heightened consciousness of one's own Self (atman), and that spontaneously sets a state of oneness with cosmic consciousness (*purusha,* or *brahman**). Then this state is called *jivanmukti* (liberation in this life), and the liberated one is a *jivanmukta*. But in case the questers have not realized moksha before their death, but are striving for it, they can attain liberation after death (*videhamukti*). The understanding is that once the state of moksha is

---

*The word *brahman,* gender neutral in Sanskrit, means "the cosmic consciousness," as distinct from the god Brahma, masculine in Sanskrit.

achieved, the quester is also liberated from the cycles of life and rebirth on Earth (the wheel of life). This is similar to the Tibetan concept of Great Liberation, called *Thödol* in Tibetan (more in chapter 8).

For me, the encounter with the mystery of death had all begun at a very early age. I was eleven years old when my paternal grandfather, Henri, died. My father had driven us from Paris, my mother and the three kids, in his big car to my grandparents' house in Châteauroux. A mortuary room had been installed downstairs, where parents and relations had paid their last homage to the deceased. The embalmed body of my grandfather was resting on the impeccably set wood-frame bed, dressed in a rich black suit and starched white shirt, his face like a yellowish waxed mask looking a bit younger, without creases. I've the fuzzy recollection his hands were joined over his chest holding his rosary. The bed was surrounded by two heavy bronze candelabra, on foot, supporting large baptismal wax candles reaching taller than my height, their flame pale and cold in the late afternoon daylight, made even more somber by black drapes hanging at both sides of the window. At the foot of the bed was a large incense holder and a bucket of holy water with its aspergillum, the silver instrument for everyone to sprinkle the deceased while drawing a cross with it at the ending of the funereal ceremony. A row of chairs was set along the bed on the window side, for the funereal vigil, where we sat with our mourning parents for a long moment of prayer (see fig. 1.4, page 40).

The burial was to be the next morning and we were to stay over for the night. The adults were now conferring and busy with themselves, not paying any attention to us, the kids. After an austere and melancholy dinner, my grandfather having been much loved by everybody, my mother told my kin where they were going to sleep, assigning beds. Then she turned to me and took me back to the mortuary room; she showed me how they had installed a small bed along the wall opposite the window, and told me matter-of-factly but in a hushed tone:

"Look, you're to sleep here because we don't have enough room for

Fig. 1.4. *Praying Hands,* by Albrecht Dürer (ca. 1508). Pen-and-ink drawing; sketch of the hands of an apostle to figure in the Heller Altarpiece, Frankfurt.

everybody." And she handed me my nightgown and diminutive toilet bag with a towel and just left with a quick good-night. I was a bit concerned, but not afraid, when I found myself alone in front of the body of my grandpa on the queen-size bed, a sheet now covering him save his face, and the curtains drawn for the night. The giant candles, the sole light with a toned-down orange lamp, were now letting out a golden aura over the antique wooden furniture, while effluvia of incense from the funereal ceremony still filled the room. The whole atmosphere was evoking a church, a sacred place and ritual—and I was to sleep in this sacred funeral chamber? Next to the dead body?

Now they were all on the first floor it seemed, and I was alone on the ground floor. As earlier in the day, when we had paid homage to the dead and prayed for him, I was tiptoeing in the room and subduing my breathing—as if I was in a church. I felt as if they had put on me an enormous responsibility—that of being *à la hauteur,* of being able to meet the challenge of such a dignified situation.

I undressed and donned my nightgown in the oppressed and airtight atmosphere. Then I approached the bed from the other side and decided to say goodbye to the grandfather I had loved, who would remain, in my memory, as always pulling out cookies from the oven for me, the kid, when I was staying at their home. But now that I was alone with him, I had no care for punctilious prayers. As I inclined my head toward his, to see him better, I could feel his presence as an aura and a softness above the top of his head. And at the same time, his face was looking like yellowish wax and its features were angular and dire fixated, as if carved in stone. So I talked to him directly to say good-night, yet joining my hands to do so, because the space was so sacred.

Then I went to lie on my bed and got under the sheet and blanket. But it still felt so strange with the soft light and this insistent and troubling mystery. I kept looking at the rigid mask there on top of the large bed. Then I got curious and wondering about the waxlike texture of the skin. And now I had to get up again and get near to his face, from the more lighted side. There was this strange nimbus blob of a presence, a soft yellow-gold presence above the top of his head. I looked at his strange face, the closed eyes, the rigid forehead. I wanted to touch the forehead but I touched instead his cheek, with one finger to sense the texture. And then I was looking at his face again, wondering the mystery.

Now that I ponder this quite out of the ordinary set of events, it's as if I had tamed death, made it something natural that allowed some sort of spontaneous communication. And with the accumulated experience I have got since then, I know that a lot more happened during my sleep, when my Self could penetrate the other dimension and keep exchanging with my grandfather.

From the rare ones to whom I recounted this story, I got only an outcry and shocked reaction: How could a mother ever do something like that? But my mother had a natural underlying connection with nature. Her own grandfather had been a renowned healer, specialized in severe burns—which he would treat both with a laying of hands that stopped the pain and effected a cure, and by applying a plaster of crushed oyster shells that healed the skin and avoided infection. He was a specialist patients would come and consult from far away in the Nièvre region, a few miles from the high sacred site of the Celts—Bibracte. And Yvonne had been partly raised by her grandparents because her parents, who had moved to Paris to make a living, were both too poor in the big city, and too overwhelmed with work, to take care of their three kids there. And in the same vein, she had been the one to take care of all sick people in the family, but in a modern way, through doctors and her own knowledge of medical drugs and ingrained psychological wisdom. Yet, she was only a conventional Catholic, despite fearing death. So, could my mother, at the time of Henri's burial, have yielded to superior forces—to the influence of kindred spirits dwelling in the soul dimension, who couldn't ignore that I had a gift that I was going to develop further—and could she have thus opened unknowingly my first gate of contact with this dimension?

Even if I did burst into tears when my grandfather's coffin was lowered down the grave the next day (something more out of empathy for those in sorrow), the impression that lingered in me was that death was puzzling but it wasn't to be feared. It was a mysterious, churchlike presence under a waxlike rigidity.

STYLES OF INTERACTION
WITH DISCARNATE SPIRITS

Back at my parent's house, after the accident with my car, it was around 1:00 p.m. when my sister who, after the morgue, had gone straight to her office, came back for lunch; she dropped by at my mother's house, still upset, to inquire why I hadn't showed up at the morgue. On hearing about my car accident, she exclaimed, pulling off an ad hoc interpretation from her shallow Freudian studies:

"In fact, it was all an unconsciously deliberate act on your part, wasn't it? So that you wouldn't go to the mortuary!"

The thought surprised me, and I had to retrace her mental circumvolutions to gather that, in her opinion, I had in fact unconsciously provoked an accident (just like one makes a Freudian slip) just to avoid the proximity of death at the morgue. She thought I had a phobia of death! (And this notwithstanding the fact I had risked my life!)

Arguing would have led nowhere. So I recounted succinctly my conversation with our father, which she listened to carefully, and I ended by:

"So, look, if I can talk with him—his alive spirit—in his kitchen, what's the point about going to visit him at the morgue, where only his dead body lies?"

I'm not sure she saw my point. In any case, she remained persuaded I had a phobia.

Meanwhile, I had called earlier first my mother and then my brother to tell them of Victor's passing, and of course recounted my accident. In the evening, my brother brought my mother home after their visit at the morgue. On the way, he had spotted my car and said he would come with a friend who owned a garage to tow it and then repair it.

As soon as my mother was back, my sister stayed away from her and the house, and from my brother as well. They never crossed paths at the hospital or the morgue. The lunch following the burial in my maternal grandparents' town near Bibracte, was every bit of a sad affair. My mother and brother's clan were sitting all together around a long table, while my sister was alone with an aged cousin at a side table. It was so gloomy that I took on myself to sit with her, just for the sake of balance. A friend of the family who had come from Paris took me back to my flat in Ormoy, and it was only a month later that I went back to Provence to pick up my repaired car.

I had no further two-way conversation with Victor until well after his burial. But one day, at the time of sunset in the Loire valley, I expressed to him all my love and my nostalgia for what he had been, in a long, improvised chant. That was my real homage to the person he had been and my deep mourning.

To this day I remain in contact with the spirit of my father, who is making a point of assisting me about family matters and sometimes encouraging me with regard to my research. However, I'm not inclined to speak, in this book, about ongoing situations and matters that haven't been settled yet. But let's have a look at the way these interactions unfold and what it reveals about the soul dimension.

The way the contact with Victor generally happens is that his voice (with or without his head appearing) is suddenly reaching my mind loud and clear; he starts to talk without preamble, mostly providing me some piece of information or some advice. Then I can discuss it with him, ask him questions, reply to one of his statements, ask him for more detail, and he will hear what I say and respond to it. But the dialogue with him isn't as fluid and rapid as with spirits of much higher spiritual realization, extremely used to crisscross dimensions—such as Carl Jung, Wolfgang Pauli, and many eminent thinkers and sages. My father is still somewhat of a neophyte in the syg-dimension; it's as if he were on a stage holding a microphone and talking aloud, expecting me to hear him on the radio; and when, after his flow of words, I ask a question, he is really astonished. Although the conversation aspect has improved since his transference, he still isn't able to move fluidly in our 4D space; to the contrary, he remains fixed high up in one place, generally in a corner under the ceiling of the room I'm in.* Whereas souls of great spiritual refinement will often enter *through* the closed door with the appearance of an immaterial body, yet finely clothed, say something briefly, and wait for me to hear and see them. If I'm standing (for example preparing some food), they will remain standing a yard or two from me. If I'm sitting, for example reading in an armchair, they will come in through the door, and once I've perceived and greeted them, will sit on a chair in front of me. Or if they visit me while I'm working at my desk, they will appear in front, or on the side, of my desk, their head often practically level with me, and will start talking when I'm aware of their presence.

Only on very rare and dire occasions am I the one to talk and/or

---

*Yet I must add that in two separate visits last year, since this text was submitted, he appeared walking through the wall from a corner behind the chimney in my new living place, then walked in the room toward my desk where I was working, and both times he came accompanied—this supporting my point that the deceased take time to learn how to deal with our 4D spacetime.

ask for help from souls residing in the syg-dimension; yet I do initiate the contact more often with spiritual and cosmic guides. The near totality of my meaningful exchanges with discarnate spirits—whether scientists, sages, or parents—as far as I'm consciously aware, have been initiated by them. Yet, sometimes things are quite fuzzy; for example, I ask a question in my head, to myself that is, and astonishingly one of them answers it (generally one whose specialty it is). A quite extraordinary and baffling occurrence was the start of the conversation with Pauli, which we'll examine in chapter 9.

A last point I want to emphasize: my father, during all his life (until his memory loss), had been in high spirits and displayed a great sense of humor. Even when he was hurt or gravely sick, or confined for weeks in the hospital in one case, he would keep on lighting up the atmosphere. I remember, when I was a kid, that meals shared within the family (mostly dinners and weekend lunches) were spun by my father with a suite of jokes and humoristic remarks, while he would also revel in steering the discussion on his favorite writers and painters. Fortunately, the bitter feud between my sister and my mother and her bullying me didn't encroach on the family table. When sitting together, we were a happy crowd, adults and kids exchanging jokes freely and spontaneously, all this interspersed with deep discussions on serious subjects. As for the kids, we had also our share of funny stories to bring to the dinner table, from school or from the art college for my much older brother. Thus, his funny remarks about his own passing and the doctors' mindset were perfectly in line with his humoristic and philosophical attitude all through his life.

THE DYING WELCOMED BY DECEASED PARENTS

The deathbed visions, or "welcome cases," are the visions of deceased parents and loved ones by the terminally ill, as a delegation from the soul dimension to welcome them to it. Typically, one or two days prior to their passing, patients have visions of deceased parents and friends who tell them that their time has come and they will guide them to the Beyond. Sometimes the patients have visions of religious figures and see paradisiacal scenes and landscapes. In other, rarer, cases, beings of light or deceased parents convey to the patients that their time hasn't come yet, and those will survive their illness.

It has been observed by many doctors and psychologists that these deathbed visions have a soothing, and even elating effect on the terminally ill, and that they don't feel any pain anymore in their last instants, being on the contrary filled with joy and wonder. Melvin Morse thus states in his 1994 book *Parting Visions* that these spiritual and ecstatic visions not only pacify the mind of dying patients, but also eliminate the fear of dying and empower them; moreover, they are soothing to the parents and friends who happen to witness them. See the remarkable drawing by William Blake expressing the joy of reunification with loved ones in the Beyond (fig. 1.5).

Fig. 1.5. *The Meeting of a Family in Heaven,* drawing by William Blake (1806) and etching by Luigi Schiavonetti for Robert Blair's poem *The Grave*

A Welcome Delegation and a Hug with One's Deceased Mother

In this case, found on the website LiveAbout in a collection by Stephen Wagner entitled "Visions at the Hour of Death: 13 People Describe Their Experiences with Deathbed Visions," which has all the attributes of authenticity, a terminally ill mother has several visions of the deceased, then they come to welcome her before she dies. There are two striking features in this case (identified with my added emphasis in the following excerpt); first, an alarm clock without batteries rings; and second, during a later apparition to her daughter, they embrace and hug each other.

One morning in the hospital room, about 2 a.m., when all was quiet, my mother stared out the door of her room and into the hall that led to the nurse's station and the other patient's rooms.

"Momma, what do you see?" I asked.

"Don't you see them?" she said. "They walk the hall day and night. They are dead." She said this with quiet calmness. . . .

The night of her passing, she was restless and anxious. A few minutes before 8 p.m. she said, "I have to go. They're here. They're waiting for me." Her face glowed and the color returned to her pale face as she attempted to raise herself and stand up. Her last words were, "I have to go. It is beautiful!" And she then passed at 8 p.m.

Several months later, *my alarm clock (set at 6 p.m.), which was broken and had no batteries in it, went off at 8 p.m.* I could feel the presence of my mother and her amusement at achieving such a task and bringing it to my attention.

A year and two months to the day of my mother's transformation, she appeared standing in my kitchen as whole, healthy and young. I was surprised, knowing she was dead but so happy to see her. *We embraced in a hug,* and I said, "I love you." And then she was gone. She had come back to say a final goodbye and let me know that she was happy and okay. I know my mother is finally home and at peace.—*Moon Sister*

Frederic Myers, in his book *Human Personality and Its Survival of Bodily Death*, gathered a small group of *apparitions of welcome.** These cases showed, said he,

> evidence for the definite agency of some dying or deceased person [producing] *sounds of welcome.* . . . One of our cases is remarkable in that the auditory hallucination—a sound as of female voices gently singing—was heard by five persons, by four of them, as it seems, independently, and in two places, on different sides of the house. At the same time, one person—the Eton master whose mother had just died, and who was therefore presumably in a frame of mind more prone to hallucination than the physician, matron, friend, or servants who actually did hear the singing—himself heard nothing at all. . . . It was during the laying out of the body that the sounds occurred. (Myers 1903, 245; 2012, 107)

Myers states about these welcome cases, "the approaching severance of spirit from body . . . enable[s] the dying person to see spirits who are already in the next world. It is not very uncommon for dying persons to say, or to indicate when beyond speech, that they see spirit friends apparently near them." Myers adds that the true scientific evidence for these apparitions comes from cases "where the dying person is unaware that the friend whose spirit he sees has actually departed." The strongest evidence for survival is given by cases in which "departed spirits manifest their knowledge that some friend who survived them has now passed on into their world" (Myers 1903, 142; 2012, 102). Of course, Victor's deathbed vision is such a welcome case, but it is also an instance of what Myers calls *reciprocal cases,* such as the Miss W. case, in which a dying aunt has a vision of her little niece who sees an apparition of her at the same time. This category is extremely important, as the vision

---

*All references marked as Myers and a page number, will be taken from this book *Human Personality,* unless specified otherwise. The page number preceded by 1903 refers to the original printing, and the second number to the 2012 reprinting.

seen by the dying is not of a deceased relative but of a living sensitive one, who is able, at a distance, to perceive the (half-liberated) spirit of the dying. The synchronicity of the interaction rules out a simple emergence of psi information and corroborates the reality of the spirit as an entity able to perceive and to be perceived as such.

As for Victor's vision of me, I didn't look at my watch in the car after I had the conversation with him. The reason for this, despite the fact that I have been a researcher and steeped in protocols and search for proofs, is that when I get to communicate with the syg-hyperdimension, I'm either in a right-brain heightened state or instantaneously drawn into one. And in these states, the least important things for me are the kind of details that my rational mind would look for afterward. So, it's reciprocal in the sense that Victor, around the time the deceased are visiting him, sees me arriving in the hospital room and talks to me (said my sister, although I didn't ask if my appearance happened in the same manner and at what moment exactly); and meanwhile, that same morning (and probably just after his relatives' visit), I have a vision of him while driving on the highway and a whole dialogue follows in which he explains the visions he just had.

DEATHBED VISIONS: RESEARCH DATA

Numerous studies have been conducted on deathbed visions, mostly through surveys of terminally ill patients and the nurses and doctors accompanying them.

The first systematic study was that of J. H. Hyslop, who engaged in three series of interviews (in 1907, 1908, and 1919), which he presents in his article "Visions of the Dying" and books *Psychical Research and the Resurrection* and *Contact with the Other World*.

Hyslop discovered that such patients were much more prone to having visions of the deceased rather than visions of living acquaintances. The same majority percentage of visions of the deceased, compared to the living, was found in a study by the Italian Ernesto Bozzano in 1923, detailed in his book *Les phénomènes de hantise au moment de la mort*. Then W. F. Barrett, physicist at the Royal College of Science in Dublin, presented his collection of cases in his 1926 book *Deathbed Visions*. He had remarkable cases in which the visiting deceased were perceived by several people beyond the patient, such as the nurses or doctors. In some cases, the etheric body of the patient himself would be seen exiting his body, while the patients would later say that they had an out-of-body experience (OBE). Barrett made several crucial observations: First, the apparitions didn't conform to the patients' preconceived ideas; second, they would see people they didn't know had died (such as cases in which the family had hushed the bad news); third, the apparitions didn't conform to the cultural/religious stereotypes (for example, kids were astonished to see angels without wings).

It was only forty years later, in 1961, that Karlis Osis, then researcher at the Parapsychological Foundation in New York, conducted large surveys and made a statistical analysis of the results in the book *Deathbed Observations by Physicians and Nurses*. He was keen to show that fever-prone illnesses or painkillers didn't increase the frequency of these visions (they would rather suppress them), and that age, sex, and even beliefs had no impact either. Osis compared visions of the deceased with visions of the living from two different groups: on the one hand the terminally ill, and on the other hand the normal population. The statistics showed that the terminally ill had three times more visions of the deceased than the normal population. Let's remember that such apparitions of living persons in an immaterial body are far from rare, and that they happen also to healthy people, for example in OBEs. (More on OBEs in chapter 2.)

Karlis Osis and Erlendur Haraldson, willing to test the influence of culture on these apparitions, had the brilliant idea to conduct two studies in widely different cultures: the first in five states in the United States (1961–64) and the second in northern India (1972–73). They gave doctors and nurses a questionnaire, asking if they had observed their terminally ill patients having (1) visions of human beings, (2) visions of landscapes, (3) a sudden heightening of consciousness—whether these patients had finally died or not. Their findings were detailed in their book *At the Hour of Death*.

About the same number of interviews were conducted, with 442 in the United States and 435 in India. Of the total 877 cases, 163 patients did survive. It was reported that 591 patients had visions of human beings (with 471 of them later passing away), and 112 had visions of paradisiacal landscapes; in 174 cases, patients had no visions but they experienced a heightened state of consciousness and reaching peace and serenity.

As for the traits of these apparitions, most of them lasted a few minutes, but 17 percent exceeded one hour's duration.

- Concerning visions of human beings, 80 percent were linked to the Beyond (either deceased persons or religious figures). In comparison, Sidgwick's *Report on the Census of Hallucinations* (1894) reports, in the general population, only 33 percent of visions being of the deceased, and 67 percent of living people.
- As for the cultural bias, most Americans (66 percent) saw deceased persons, compared to 12 percent seeing religious figures; whereas most Indians saw religious figures (48 percent), compared to 28 percent seeing deceased persons.
- About 61 percent of all patients hadn't been given hallucination-causing drugs. Half the patients had remained conscious, and 29 percent were somewhat perturbed but maintained some degree of communication with the nurses.
- No personal or social factor could be found to trigger the visions. Neither stress nor optimism were causal factors: more patients in a normal state of consciousness (54 percent) had a vision, compared with patients with a positive attitude or with a negative one.
- The certitude of one's own death was not a factor either: many who thought they would survive had visions of people coming to take them, sometimes rejecting them. Only one American was not ready to leave this world, whereas 34 percent of Indians

refused vehemently to do so (regardless of their religion—Hindu, Catholic, or other).

- Finally, not believing in the afterlife didn't preclude having visions: 12 patients were in that position. And that shows clearly that these apparitions are not created by the person's beliefs. Yet, the characteristics of the religious beings will be highly influenced by the patient's religion, and that's where the culture intervenes.

- Among the 471 patients who had visions of human beings and later passed away, in 196 cases the purpose of the apparitions was to accompany them into the other world, despite (in 54 cases) the patients' refusal of such eventuality.

Osis concludes in favor of the reality of the survival of the soul, and the strongest elements in favor of this hypothesis, he states, are the 54 cases in which the patients were reluctant to leave this world (that's 11 percent of them) and yet were peacefully greeted by deceased loving friends and family. Thus, the apparitions seem to show a will of their own, instead of just expressing the desires and the internal dynamic of patients (as would be expected if they were mere psychic projections).

This Osis and Haraldson study strikes a very positive note as to the soul dimension, one that's definitely showing some disparity with the religious Judeo-Christian dogma, with the biblical belief in "the very few" or "the Chosen Few" who would meet the criteria for Redemption. Indeed, among the patients who beheld visions of human or divine beings, among 273 Americans, only one saw a demon; and among 285 Indians, only two saw demons. This is a far cry from the inferno threatened on any nonbeliever of the creed, whatever its type.

I'm fully agreeing with Karlis Osis, Melvin Morse, and Raymond Moody (of whom we will hear more in the next chapter), that surveys amply prove that the experience of deathbed visions is a peaceful and highly positive one, preparing the terminally ill for their transcendence by raising their consciousness and making them tune in to the dimension of souls.

2

VISION AT A BURIAL
AND EVIDENCE OF THE
SOUL DIMENSION

I had always sensed and known that the person who just died is attending his/her own burial ceremonies, but the way I saw it happen at my brother-in-law, Guy's funeral mass was as striking as it was informative.

Let me give you some background details first.

Near the end of her medical studies, my sister Colette joined the team of the famed Doctor Dépinay in Diré, a big town in upper Mali, set on the Niger River. On her return, this year was counted as a (mandatory) internship stage for her medical doctor exam. Then, while she went through her three-year specialty studies in dermatology, she did a number of summer replacements in Ivory Coast and thus kept in touch with her African friends and colleagues who generally move around West Africa within extended families and social circles, the way people move around states in the United States.

Guy's mother, born French, had four kids with her African husband in France before they went to live in Mali, and she had divorced long ago. She was the owner and manager of a quite original café—which was also a restaurant and a nightclub—in the town of Korhogo, in northern Ivory Coast. Guy and his brother Bernard were outstanding musicians who had launched the nightclub and were the main band playing there and running it.

On my second year-and-a-half travel, when I was twenty-three years old, I started from Montségur—the Templar Knights' stronghold in the Pyrenees mountains, in the south of France, and crossed Africa hitchhiking from Tangier, the northern tip of Morocco, all the way to Mombasa, Kenya, where I took a boat to return to India. On this occasion, while crossing Mali, I visited my sister whom I had not seen for more than two years, in fact since I had left for my first long travel to India. I knew she was at Diré's hospital with Dépinay, and, welcomed by Dépinay and his wife to stay at their place with my sister, I remained about six weeks in the region and then my sister accompanied me to visit the Dogon country. We had a wonderful time together, the time of our life, indeed, as if our contentious past had been magically erased and we could enthusiastically join in each other's singular experience.

A few years later, I was twenty-seven, I traveled to West Africa with my boyfriend of the time, Pat, who happened to be the best friend of Guy when both were adolescents and roaming in between Abidjan in Ivory Coast, Mali, and Dakar in Senegal. Pat and I were embarked on touring West Africa in our old car, from Dakar (where a liner from France had taken us with our car) to Abidjan, where we hoped to settle for a while, and where his mother was living. That route crossed Mali and its capital, Bamako, and entered Ivory Coast by the northern town of Korhogo, where we would stay awhile with Guy's mother and brother Bernard. After a long stay in Dakar, we started the trip across Mali. A few weeks later, the night had caught us while we were still driving on one of the worst unpaved and bumpy tracks in West Africa, where the hardened sand is as wavy as on sand dunes, sometimes with literal steps a few inches high, left by the bulldozers used to try to flatten it. We were now hoping to reach Korhogo in an hour or so, and Pat was stepping on the gas, despite this extremely uneven surface making us and the whole car shake and vibrate like crazy and regardless of my repeated calls to ease up (I had warning bells ringing in my head for a while). The heat was still stifling, and I had my arm out of the open window, holding on to the roof. That's when, in a large turn with such a high step, the car made a somersault and rolled over on my side. Next, I found myself lying on my side on the ground with my right arm pinned down under the roof by the hard metal frame, just below the elbow, and the upturned car's weight impeding me not only from pulling away from it, but from making any big move . . . and Pat having a fit—not over my situation mind you—with me telling him to breathe deeply. Then he tried to jack up the car with the wheel crank, but the roof being curved, the car just skidded a bit, pinning my arm down even harder. After some twenty minutes in absolute darkness (some gasoline had leaked from the tank and Pat had cut the engine and the electricity), my ability to move my fingers under the banged roof was dangerously diminishing. And I was trying to figure how much time I had before losing my arm. Fortunately, that's when an African drove by with his wife, and the three of them together were able to lift the car enough for me to pull out my arm. The blood flow painfully returned to my numb arm. The car was beyond repair and we had to leave it there, but the African couple was going to Korhogo; we transferred our trunks to their pick-up and an hour later they dropped us at Guy's mother's downtown.

At that time, Guy and my sister were already living together in Paris and we didn't see them in Africa. But in Korhogo we stayed with Bernard and his mother about a week. Then, on arriving in Abidjan, we couldn't stay in the too-small flat of Pat's mother, and instead dwelt in Guy's elder sister's large home for a good three weeks, before I managed to get a job and we could rent a house. Then I split with Pat a few months later and flew back to Paris.

During this six-month trip in West Africa, I had thus gotten acquainted with Guy's brother and two sisters, as well as their mother, but I hadn't encountered the father who had become estranged from his wife and children a long time ago. In acting like this, we were just espousing an age-old custom in West Africa that consists of having one's house and family always open to a large network of relatives and friends, and to visit and stay in each other's homes for long periods. For example, it's common practice for an adolescent to stay at an uncle's or aunt's house in the capital for the duration of their studies at a good college.

It had been more than two decades since Guy and Colette had moved to Provence and she had opened her medical practice there when Guy died of cancer, and he had lost his younger brother, Bernard, then dwelling in Paris, just a few years earlier. Guy's funeral ceremony took place in a picturesque small village church near their home. It was an intimate service accompanied by the music of the African cora—a small four-string guitar made of a calabash.

The choir, where the priest stood in front of the altar, featured a high lectern for reading and was flanked on both sides by a row of five or six chairs, thus perpendicular to the main rows of chairs filling the church's nave. As it happened, the African side of the family who was attending—Guy's niece and nephew that I had just met for the first time—sat together with Colette and Guy's son and daughter on the right side of the choir. And Colette, her close friends, and part of our own family were seated on the left side of the altar. As for myself, I was sitting on the first row of the nave chairs, on its right side.

The ceremony had started a while ago, and we were still standing, in a deeply concentrated state, when I became aware of a strong presence *above* the row of the Africa-rooted side of the family. I focused my peripheral vision (which I know sees better the etheric and syg-dimension), and now I perceived clearly a group standing there, as if on a second floor of the church, in two rows, the first one being exactly above the chairs in the choir where Guy's children were.

Standing in the first row, nearest to the choir's center, were Guy himself, his brother Bernard, and astonishingly, their father. Then there was a space of about three feet, and in another row behind, the women stood—Guy's mother, and a thin-framed woman in her late teens or early twenties, who was (as I felt it) her daughter.

I was totally dumbfounded to see them there. They were in the same posture as the people attending the mass, standing, serious, rigid, and focused on the priest. They didn't seem to sense that I was seeing them, or at least they didn't react in any way to it. Their features were so clear that I could have drawn a portrait of the father, whom I had never seen even in a photo. I was cognizant of the fact that Guy's mother had died too, and I recognized her by her imposing size, but I couldn't figure who was the young woman.

Guy, as a musician, was a sensitive—he had some psi capacities, namely a rare level of empathy. Many a time we had played music with our Paris group, in the mid-1970s, even before I started living with Pat. And I knew from my travels that most Africans are able, routinely, to see and to interact with their deceased parents and kin. So that, after the ceremony in the cemetery, when only the close family circle remained gathered around my sister near the grave, I went to see Guy's niece and nephew whom I had just met for the first time ever, and who were, as it happened, talking by themselves near the gate. I described to them what I had witnessed, and then voiced my astonishment at the young woman's presence. I asked in earnest:

"Did Guy have a third sister that I didn't know of, and who has already died?"

The niece, dumbfounded, responded:

"Yes indeed; she died when a baby, a few months old, and that's why nobody speaks about her."

Of course, this doesn't explain why she looked like an adolescent, given that it doesn't seem to reflect the time elapsed since she was born, nor her toddler age at the time of death. This point is still somewhat of a mystery to me. But the soul of a baby is ageless, and I imagine that this soul could take on the appearance of a young person in the syg-dimension.

The only other information I have on this subject comes from a sensitive branch of the family, rooted in Burgundy. A young couple lost their baby girl when she was only a few months old. They both were

greatly affected since it was their first child, and the mother was incon-
solable, even after she bore another girl, to whom they gave the first
name of their lost baby, and two sons. They recounted to me that every
year, on the birthday of the girl, they were able to see her among them—
namely crossing the dining room while they had lunch. And they told
me that, each time, she looked like the age she would have been, if only
she had lived! Obviously, this was not the case with Guy's sister, but it's
good to keep in mind these two possibilities.

Let's now have a look at the early researchers at the end of the nineteenth century, who not only launched, as it happened, the new fields
of psychology and psychiatry, but who simultaneously discovered the
unconscious and made inroads in the research on psi and survival.

PSI AND THE UNCONSCIOUS
VIEWED BY THE PIONEERS OF PSYCHOLOGY

The fact that each individual has an *unconscious* (formerly called the
subconscious) that is endowed with capacities vastly different from our
conscious mind, was an assumption already reached by the founders
of the various psychology and psychiatry schools. The pioneers in this
research appear on the scientific scene in the late nineteenth century
in America, England, and France, and all of them are investigating
conjointly psi capacities (a domain called at that time *psychical research*
in England and *clairvoyance* in France) and altered states of consciousness such as hypnosis and dreams. Furthermore, they all know each
other and more often than not, travel back and forth in order to work
together.

Jean-Martin Charcot, professor and doctor of medicine at Paris'
La Salpêtrière hospital, the father of psychiatry and modern neurology,
launches the study of mental illnesses such as hysteria by putting his
patients under hypnosis (see fig. 2.1).

Sigmund Freud attended his world-renowned courses in 1885 and
then started using hypnosis to treat patients before elaborating his own

Fig. 2.1. Charcot giving a clinical course on hypnosis at Salpêtrière. Painting by André Brouillet (1887).

method, psychoanalysis, in 1896. Let's also note in passing that Freud was so fascinated by telepathy that he discussed it at length with Sandor Ferenczi in their correspondence and did several ad hoc experiments with his daughter Anna. On August 18, 1921, Freud announces to his circle the completion of an article, *Psychoanalysis and Telepathy,* that he will however never publish (this interest was dutifully hushed by his biographers) (see Moreau 1976; Devereux 1953).

Charcot's seminal book on hypnosis in 1882 creates a huge scientific interest in phenomena produced during the hypnotic trance, notably clairvoyance capacities. At the very beginning, these clairvoyance or psychical studies are part of the domain of psychology, and the methods used are hypnosis (especially in France), and the mediumistic trance (especially in England and America). A generation later at Paris' *Collège de France,* the field of physiology and immunology is launched by Charles Richet, a Nobel Prize winner in 1913 for his pioneering work on allergy. (He is also the researcher who introduced Charcot to hypnosis.) Richet, who became president in 1905 of the London-based Society for Psychical Research, also instigated the psi research in France in Paris' *Institut Métapsychique International*. His view of psi is particularly interesting for the hyperdimension hypothesis: "It has been shown that as regards subjective metapsychics the simplest and most rational explanation is to suppose the existence of a faculty of supernormal cognition . . . setting in motion the human intelligence by certain vibrations that do not move the normal senses" (Richet 1923).

In the 1890s, Pierre Janet, a former student of Charcot, while conducting a notorious study of hypnosis with Doctor Gibert at Le Havre hospital, discovers the existence of multiple personalities and a "hidden self" in his hysteria patients.* He also investigates their clairvoyant capacities under hypnosis, notably with a very gifted psi subject, Léonie. Janet is one of the fathers of psychology with William James and the one to coin the terms *subconscious* and *dissociation*.

It's also in the late nineteenth century that the father of American psychology, William James, and the pioneer in England Frederic Myers, delved in collaboration into the study of both the subconscious mind and psi capacities. James and Myers took an active part in launching and managing the British Society for Psychical Research (SPR) in 1882 as well as its American counterpart, the ASPR, two years later. Some studies of mediumship were conducted at both sites simultaneously, each one with its network of mediums, as we will see with the cross-correspondences work.

How interesting that all the research on psi in the late nineteenth and early twentieth century was done by the most eminent scholars and pioneers in the fields of psychology, psychiatry, and medicine! It is also remarkable that the early study of psi was done almost exclusively on subjects in deep trance—either mediumistic or hypnotic trance that both generally left the subject with total amnesia as to what had

---

*Read William James's essay on Janet's discoveries online in the Wikisource article "The Hidden Self."

taken place during the session. And thus it was quite obvious that these clairvoyance feats were springing from the subconscious or the unconscious. It's only with the early work of J. B. Rhine at Duke University in Durham (North Carolina) in the 1930s that the psi of subjects would be investigated in a normal conscious state.

The psi information provided by subjects under hypnosis was sometimes stupendous. One day when Janet and Gibert hypnotized Léonie in Le Havre (in the northwest of France) and asked her to visit Charles Richet's laboratory in Paris, Léonie shouted, "It's burning, it's burning!" Truly, that day, a fire had erupted in Richet's lab, as was corroborated later (news traveled slowly in that pre-telephone time).

Interestingly, a similar feat involving clairvoyantly seeing a fire at a distance was performed by the great Swedish scientist, philosopher, and mystic Emanuel Swedenborg, and what's more impressive, in a conscious state during a mundane event (see fig. 2.2).

On July 19, 1759, (a Thursday) Swedenborg was dining with friends in Gothenburg, 250 miles from Stockholm, when, at 6:00 p.m., he suddenly announced to the other guests that a huge fire had broken out

Fig. 2.2. Swedenborg at the age of seventy-five, holding the soon-to-be-published manuscript of *Apocalypsis Revelata*. Painting attributed to Per Krafft the Elder, ca. 1766.
Nationalmuseum, Stockholm

in Stockholm; he went on to give more details as time passed, such as that the fire was now dangerously approaching his home, having already reached a neighboring house. Then, a couple of hours later, he declared with relief that the fire had been controlled and had not consumed his home. The word spread quickly in Gothenburg and the region's governor had Swedenborg come to his place that very evening for a detailed report. (The first courier with the news arrived only late on Monday.) This historic and dramatic fire consumed 300 houses in the Swedish capital.

Another scholar, in fact the most eminent mathematician and physicist of the generation before Einstein, Henri Poincaré, made a careful study of the workings of his own subconscious mind, stressing that it was at the root of his own major discoveries in mathematics (see fig. 2.3). His most famous "illumination" as he called sudden insights, happened after days of being unable to solve by rational means an arduous math problem. In the precise moment he climbed on the step of a bus, while on a trip with other scholars, the solution surged in his mind, perfect and simple. Then he worked it out and discovered a new class of math functions. In his book, *Science and Method,* he devoted a chapter to his theory about this lengthy "unconscious incubation" that led to

Fig. 2.3. Poincaré and Marie Curie at the first famed Solvay conference in Brussels in 1911

sudden insights. What is particularly striking in the case of Poincaré is that he endows the unconscious with the ability to compute complex math problems, and to send to the conscious mind its results.

When it came to Carl Jung, a psychoanalyst and psychiatrist in Zurich—himself extremely gifted with an array of psi talents and a strong and permanent access to the syg-hyperdimension—the reality of this layer of our collective and cosmic consciousness became an integral part of the *depth psychology* that he elaborated. The beginning of his original exploration of the collective unconscious and of the writing of his major works was triggered by or rather corresponded with a dramatic intrusion of a group of deceased persons into his house, after which he wrote his *Seven Sermons to the Dead* (we'll see this in detail in chapter 8).

Jung had also attended spiritualist séances in his youth and had written a study about them for his doctoral thesis. During a stormy discussion with his then mentor Sigmund Freud, when he visited him in Vienna in 1909, as he recounts in his memoirs,* Jung demonstrated with striking evidence that spirits, or the Self, are able to make themselves heard. It was only a few years later that Freud, on the basis of his repeated experiments with his daughter Anna, vouched that telepathy was real; he sent his disciples a memo stating that they now had to take it for granted and also wrote two monographs on the subject. But he wouldn't have anything to do with other psi phenomena, especially mediumship. That's what they were hotly arguing about in Freud's library when a loud knock was heard from the bookshelf; and when Freud got totally upset, calling it utter foolishness and denying this was a proof, Jung replied that to prove he was right, there would be another knock—and indeed at that very moment, there was. That fatal quarrel is what initiated the famous split between the two scholars. As for me, I believe, just as he himself did, that Jung was able to exteriorize his

---

Memories, Dreams, Reflections, chapter 5; the memoir also includes *The Seven Sermons to the Dead.*

own syg-energy in a way powerful enough to create the knocks, what he called a "catalytic exteriorization." Why? Because he explained that he felt an intense burning sensation in his chest at the instant the knocks occurred: "I had a curious sensation. It was as if my diaphragm were made of iron and were becoming red-hot—a glowing vault." Yet, I've no doubt that familiar spirits (such as deceased scholars or guides) would have heard this eminently crucial discussion about their reality and could easily have manifested themselves loudly.

Carl Jung recounts also in his memoirs that, just after this split with his symbolic father, he made a plunge into the collective unconscious that lasted fourteen years. During this phase, he entertained dialogues with ancient scholars, and got into a stable relationship with some of them. His main interlocutor was Philemon, who was, said he, his own Self. These conversations, the reflections about them, and the symbolic drawings and mandalas he makes along the years are the stuff of his most mysterious work—*The Red Book*. This dive into one's inner being, as Jung emphasizes it (based on his comprehensive experience), is *the* path toward realizing the harmony between all inner dualities, including one's own inner man or inner woman—the animus or the anima, the complementary aspect of our psyche to the one we live and express daily. This way of harmonizing our inner duality and reaching a state of wholeness has been codified in all inner and mystic paths, including alchemy, as its aphorism VITRIOL reveals, standing for *visita interiora terrae, rectificando invenies occultum lapidem,* that is, "Visit the interior of the earth and, while rectifying, you will find the occult [hidden] stone [the philosophers' stone or *lapis*]." See fig. 2.4. Note on the right,

Fig. 2.4. The alchemical Grand-oeuvre, with its revealing formula: V.I.T.R.I.O.L.

the Green Lion, symbol of the stage of the universal healing, and on the left the double-headed Eagle, symbol of the harmonization of the masculine and feminine; and, on top, the mystic *athanor* (the alchemical oven) or Grail cup, realizing the perfect Oneness beyond duality—with the fusion of Sun and Moon; see also on plate 3, how the philosophers' stone is represented as a hermaphrodite.

ACCESSING THE SOUL DIMENSION: NDE, OBE, AND SUPER-PSI

When we ponder the question of the survival of souls after death, we imply that they dwell in a higher dimension—the soul dimension, or the syg-hyperdimension as I'm postulating it. In this strong sense, we imply the survival of a whole personality with its memory of Earth intact, endowed with intelligence, perception, intention, and will. And the central philosophical question then is: What kind of signs, or proofs, do we have of an individual consciousness being able to exist and function outside of its body?

For materialist scientists, intelligence is only the product of the brain, as emotions are only the product of physiological and hormonal processes. In brief, no thinking, feeling, or consciousness can exist outside of the brain (which is 4D matter). Therefore it excludes *telepathy* between distant minds, *remote viewing* and *clairvoyance* of events distant in space, *precognition* of future events, or the *psychic healing* (bio-PK) of a sick body (as part of *psychokinesis,* or PK, the mind affecting matter).

Yet, all these psi capacities (apart from PK on hard matter) have been proven over decades of experimental research. Of course we have to remember that modern science, at its onset, had a hard time conquering its space of freedom against the power of the church that maintained as a dogma that the Earth was at the center of our solar system and the universe as well. We lost too many great minds because of its radical bigotry, such as Giordano Bruno, a mathematician, cosmologist, philosopher, and poet, who was the first scientist to claim that stars

a

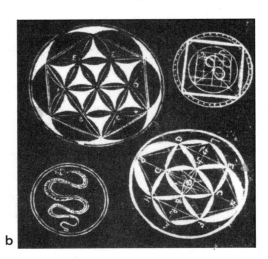

b

Fig. 2.5. Giordano Bruno: (a) portrait from a 1715 woodcut; (b) woodcut from *Articuli centum et sexaginta* ("160 Articles," 1588) showing some of his work on sacred geometry—see on the upper left a version of the "flower of life" pattern

were other suns with their own orbiting planets, and possibly inhabited. Bruno had published two works in 1584 in which he supported and developed Copernicus's heliocentric model (see fig. 2.5).*

---

*For more details, see Bruno, *On the Infinite, the Universe and the Worlds,* and Yates, *Giordano Bruno and the Hermetic Tradition.*

Wisely, Copernicus had published his work just before his death in 1543, with the sun at the center of our solar system (see plate 4), a heliocentric view that only one Greek astronomer, Aristarchus of Samos, in the third century BCE, had expounded.

Worse still, Bruno believed in the transmigration of souls, a kind of universal reincarnation, for all living beings; and finally, his philosophy was that of pantheism—a spark from the divine realm existing in any being and natural system, and moreover he saw this realm as the One, as he endorsed and was greatly elated by Plotinus's ideas. Now, is not that very akin to positing a hyperdimension in all systems and beings? Especially when, as in ISST (or Infinite Spiral Staircase theory, which we will explore in chapter 6), we posit this HD to be (also) the realm of the Self and soul! (We'll discuss panpsychism, a related framework, as well as Plotinus, in chapter 12.) Bruno was burnt at the stake in 1600 for these ideas, because we were supposed to have been created as a unique humanity on a unique planet, sitting at the center of the universe. And the reverberation such intransigence left over the centuries was that many scientists didn't want to even consider anything of the likes of spirits, souls, nor anything infringing on the matter laws of the universe, such as psi.

But physics, in our times, has now proven that ordinary matter (from particles to galaxies) makes up only 5 percent of the total energy of our universe—the rest being unknown dark matter and dark energy. All in all, it sounds like materialist scientists are really running out of matter! And with the physics of hyperdimensions coming in full force as the only possibility to explain a lot of anomalies, the horizon has changed drastically.

Now a funny twist of things happened when data started accumulating: firstly in favor of apparitions of the dead as well as the living in the early twentieth century, and secondly, at the end of that same century, data supporting the reality of psi phenomena, including the most intriguing one, healing or bio-PK. For example, the results of a meta-analysis on bio-PK done by William Braud in 1985, and using the

149 experiments conducted up to that date, showed that 53 percent of them were statistically significant—a very impressive result (when only 5 percent would show something more than chance was involved).*

Some researchers proposed that all apparitions of the dead (such as deathbed visions) and of the living (such as a live person appearing in an etheric or immaterial body) were only hallucinations provoked by the percipient in order to become aware of some real psi information (see the alternative explanations of survival in Braude 2003). Sometimes the psi feats were so complex that one needed to invoke not one but several psi capacities working together in order to explain them—something called the *super-psi hypothesis*. Here is the most extreme one, reaching to the absurd: It has been proposed that the effect of mind over random-ness (namely, an electronic random-number generator, or RNG), instead of being just that, implies having a precognition of the time at which to push the test key in order to get winning results—this, while the num-bers were produced electronically, at a computer speed that exceeded by several hundred milliseconds the muscular time needed just to strike the key. And all this tortuous and convoluted theory could well further only one purpose: to explain away the data and suppress the dreadful idea that mind could have such an effect on physical or biological sys-tems as to allow healing to occur.

Now, if we consider survival from a scientific perspective, it becomes crucial to determine if our consciousness (or a part of it) can or cannot leave our body and wander around. That is, we need to assess if conscious-ness can exist and operate independently from the body. And in fact, we have loads of data to prove just that. They fall in the categories of the near-death experiences (NDEs) and the out-of-body experiences (OBEs).

The most convincing evidence we have from NDEs comes from patients who suffered dead-brain episodes, in which the brain ceases to

---

*For more on psi research, see Mishlove 1997; Radin 1997; Targ and Puthoff 2005; Schwartz 2007; Broughton 1991; Ullman, Krippner, and Vaughan 1973; and Tart, Puthoff, and Targ 1979. On healing and bio-PK, see Benor 2001; Dossey 1989; Schlitz 2015; Yogi Ramacharaka 1965; and Krippner and Welch 1992.

function. However, some patients who survived were able to describe what was happening and what the surgeons were saying in the emergency room, in accurate and later-verified detail. Here is one example.

The person, after an accident, arrived in the hospital already in a coma state. He is seeing everything from above, his body on the surgery table and its terrible appearance after the accident, and yet he has no fear. He mentions that a priest was there too. He describes how one surgeon exclaimed he was going to lose his leg, and later that "it has stopped" when, in the same instant, he saw the green line of his heartbeat go flat on the screen; after which they try to restart his heart. Then he suddenly falls in total darkness and sees a light far away, becoming more and more bright, and now he feels he's floating in the air, surrounded by a beautiful blue color. "It's as if I was in a ray of light and was traveling through it." Then he feels a pressure on his skull, and somebody tells him he has to go back; and he replies, "Why me, Lord?" And he is told that his work is not finished on Earth and that he has to return to it. And now he feels disappointed, because of the incredible peace he has experienced there. (My summary of a case given in Sabom and Kreutziger 1978.)

Some convincing evidence also comes from the experiencers who had been blind from birth and were amazed at being able to see shapes and shades of light (without of course being able to give these colors a name).

Albert Heim, a mountain climber, made a survey of survivors of falls after he had such an experience himself. He describes that he experienced a decupled speed of thought; his mind following several tracks at once; a total absence of fear and pain; the superfast review of his whole life in minute detail; pondering what will happen to his family; and simultaneously, performing incredibly clever actions to protect his body and lessen the impact of the fall. All this at once, during the few seconds of the fall (Heim 1892).

NDEs generally happen during the few minutes or seconds before an accident, when the person sees the danger coming and before they are hit—by a car or at the end of their fall—or else during a coma.

Often, at the beginning of the NDE, they find themselves hovering above their body and perceive everything around it; thus, in the first phase of the NDE, we have sometimes a typical out-of-body experience. Thereafter, at the core of the NDE, the experiencers usually see and move through a tunnel and, at the end of it, meet a being of light, or bathe in a beautiful spiritual light; some describe then meeting with angels, or divine beings, and contemplating paradisiacal landscapes. In his painting *Ascent of the Blessed,* the famous late-fifteenth-century painter from Netherland Hieronymus Bosch seems to have described the light at the end of the tunnel phase of the NDE with astonishing accuracy! (See fig. 2.6 for a detail showing Bosch's stunningly precise depiction of the tunnel that experiencers usually fly through toward the light, and plate 5 for the whole Bosch painting.)

Fig. 2.6. Bosch's 1502 painting *Ascent of the Blessed;* detail of the tunnel toward the light

The NDE experiencers are then told they have to go back and complete their lives (given that the only subjects who can tell their stories are indeed those who survived). In the cases we saw of deathbed visions, it's the opposite, as they are welcomed into the soul dimension.

Francois Brune, a Catholic priest and lifelong researcher on the afterlife and transcommunication with the deceased, who was a colleague member of IANDS (International Association for Near Death Studies), considered NDEs as "temporary death experiences." I do agree that in most cases, the persons undergoing such NDEs access the dimension of the souls, since (1) they are greeted by a being of light and love, and (2) they find themselves in a heightened state of consciousness, filled with love and understanding. They share that, on their return, they were deeply transformed and had awakened to the essential values of Life, consciousness, and love. Their descriptions of the state they experienced are breathtaking, especially the sense of oneness with the Whole and with a divine light—that is expressed in the West only by rare mystics. Here are some excerpts gathered by Brune in *Les morts nous parlent*. One expressed: "I was one with the pure light and love. I was one with God and simultaneously one with all." Another recounted: "I felt filled with bliss and I sensed I was one with everything." Yet another one: "I entered in the arch of pure golden love and light. This radiation of love penetrated me and, immediately, I was part of it and it was part of me" (1:525–30, my translations).

In OBEs, people find themselves hovering above their body, and some may also travel to faraway places and bring back precise information that can be checked afterward. And there were experiments of this sort conducted notably by the famous psychology professor at UC–Davis Charles Tart, who launched the whole research on altered states of consciousness with his notorious book whose title was this same generic term (1969). Let's note that this type of exteriorization from the body and of "travel" in an immaterial body has been widely practiced by yogis and shamans in many ancient cultures.

OBEs make the stuff of most apparitions of the living, as it seems that the etheric body on the one hand can be visible to sensitive persons, and on the other hand, as far as Tibetan and Indian traditions go, it can be made, by meditation and practice, to acquire more of a physical-like appearance. The yogi Yogananda, for example, witnessed the etheric body of his master being so substantial that he could touch his feet in devotion. In *Autobiography of a Yogi,* he reports instances of bilocation as well, when the master was seen as if in a real body by two different groups of disciples in two distant places.

With OBEs and NDEs, we have numerous scientific medical observations and some experimental studies as well, that leave no doubt about the reality of the etheric body as a vehicle for an immaterial part of our consciousness. The fact that our consciousness, in an immaterial body form, is able to perceive, think, remember, and move around as if

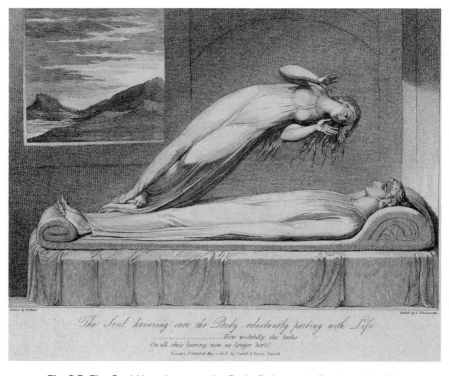

Fig. 2.7. *The Soul Hovering over the Body Reluctantly Parting with Life,* drawing by William Blake (1806) and etching by Luigi Schiavonetti for Robert Blair's poem *The Grave*

space or matter was not a barrier, is one of the most convincing pieces of evidence of the existence of a dimension of consciousness beyond matter and spacetime. In my view, the immaterial OBE body is just the same etheric body that we find ourselves in after we die (see fig. 2.7).

Here is a stunning case of an OBE by a daughter in which she meets, in full consciousness but as an etheric body, the immaterial form of her mother who just died, and sees her being welcomed by deceased parents. This Dr. Jamieson case is recounted by Dr. Raymond Moody, the psychiatrist and philosopher who started the research on NDEs and on the afterlife as well, with his 1975 famed book *Life after Life*. Dr. Jamieson is visiting her mother when the latter has a cardiac arrest; she performs mouth-to-mouth resuscitation but to no avail.

> Suddenly, Dr. Jamieson felt herself lift out of her body. She realized that she was above her own body and the now-deceased body of her mother . . . "I suddenly became aware that my mother was now hovering with me in spirit form . . ." [Her mother] was now smiling and quite happy. . . . Then Dr. Jamieson saw something else that surprised her. "I looked in the corner of the room and became aware of *a breach in the universe that was pouring light like water coming from a broken pipe.* Out of that light came people I had known for years, deceased friends of my mother." . . . As Dr. Jamieson watched, her mother drifted off into the light . . . having a very tender reunion with all of her friends. (*Glimpses of Eternity* 6, my emphasis)

Let's note the stupendous "breach in the universe that was pouring light like water coming from a broken pipe." This, in my opinion, describes the types of curved geometrical structures or vortices that are in actuality physical breaches happening when the hyperdimension intrudes in the spacetime one—such as the energy blobs and oval shapes around the apparitions of Pauli and Jung described in chapter 9, and the funnel instantly connecting two distant places (through the syg-hyperdimension) recounted in *The Sacred Network*, chapter 11.

In an interview titled "Life after Life: Understanding Near-Death Experience" with psychologist Jeffrey Mishlove, Ph.D., on his Intuition Network (linked to the ongoing *Thinking Allowed* TV series), Moody expressed his confidence about the reality of the afterlife, based on his research into NDE:

> I don't mind saying that after talking with over a thousand people who have had these experiences, and having experienced many times some of the really baffling and unusual features of these experiences, it has given me great confidence that there is a life after death. As a matter of fact, I must confess to you in all honesty, I have absolutely no doubt, on the basis of what my patients have told me, that they did get a glimpse of the beyond. (Interview transcript available online at intuition.org/txt/moody.htm)

And in a book still published solely in French, *Donner du sens au non-sens* (Giving sense to nonsense), Moody returns to his primary research as a philosopher of language and logic, to attest with David Hume that, in order to confirm and model the life after death, we need not only new psi capacities, but a new logic as well. I can't agree more and believe that hyperdimensional physics and super-psi can indeed put us on track.

APPARITION NEAR A PERSON WHO JUST DIED

Strangely, it took me a while to find another case of apparition just at or after the moment of death. (In contrast, all deathbed and welcome cases happen generally within two days *before* the person's passing.) But I finally found one: Mrs. Bacchus's case, part of the *Census of Hallucinations* and summarized by Myers (1903, 234; 2012, 103). Mrs. Bacchus (possibly not her real name) is deemed "an excellent witness," meaning a sensitive known to the researchers. In this case, the just-deceased woman, unknown, was in a public place, possibly a hospital or just transferred to a mortuary bed. Mrs. Bacchus sees an apparition of a man next to the bed on which lies the person who just died; both the dead and the apparition are unknown to her, and yet her description is so accurate as to allow a later identification of the apparition as the husband. Myers interprets the case this way: "A lady dies; her husband in the spirit-world is moved by her arrival; and the direction thus given to his thought projects a picture of him, clothed as in the days when he lived with her, into visibility in the house where her body is lying."

I don't agree with Myers that this case "is midway between a case of welcome and a case of haunting," and I don't think that he portrays well what may have happened in the soul dimension. Based on the events at Guy's burial, and my sensing spiritual presences (without definite perception) around the coffin at other burials, I know that the spirit of the person who is dying is attended by their deceased parents, and then the spirit is mostly standing above or near their dead body during all religious ceremonies, thus receiving the influx of spiritual energy and love from the ritual and the people assembled. Spirits are also present each time that a loved one approaches their body or coffin (even at their grave), and the deceased's parents are indeed accompanying them during their final days and then in the sometimes difficult period during which they adapt to their new condition. So in my opinion, the already deceased partners or parents closely watch everything happening before and during the passing and the burial of their loved ones.

APPARITIONS OF THE DEAD: RESEARCH DATA

Let's note first the well-known case of Achilles who did not want his friend Patroclus, who fought with him in the Trojan War and died fighting, to be buried, until the ghost of Patroclus appeared to him and demanded his body be buried so that he could pass into Hades.

As I have already hinted at, a very large body of research was done on the survival issue in the late nineteenth and early twentieth centuries, by the SPR (Society for Psychical Research) in London, the ASPR (the American one), and the Institut Métapsychique International (IMI) in Paris. There are several noteworthy repertories presenting and analyzing tens of thousands of verified cases in the parapsychological scientific literature: most notably, the Gurney, Myers, and Podmore *Phantasms of the Living* (1886), and the Sidgwick et al. *Report on the Census of Hallucinations* (1894). Most later researchers have used these for their analyses and statistics. Concerning Sidgwick's *Census*, 17,000 respondents from the general population answered the questionnaire and sent their personal case (if they had one); then these reports were screened and analyzed, with all possible witnesses interviewed. Out of these 17,000 respondents, 1,684 (or about 10 percent of the general population) had seen an apparition. There was a definite peak in the number of apparitions within twelve hours of the agent's death, and the nearer to the time of death, the more numerous the cases (see fig. 2.8).

Fig. 2.8. Reunion with the loved one after death: the soul of a woman welcomes her just-deceased husband, Elmwood Cemetery, Memphis, Tennessee
Photo by Adarryll Jackson Sr. (www.instagram.com/adarrylljacksonsr)

Other researchers have later gathered new collections of cases—such as Louisa Rhine (1981, 1972), Ian Stevenson on poltergeists and memories of past incarnations, and William Roll on poltergeists.

Return of the Departed Spouse

The Osis and Haraldson survey in the United States and India (conducted from 1961 to 1973, and published in 1977), was followed by two new surveys.

- A. M. Greeley tested the general population in America as to the incidence of an apparition of the dead, asking people if they had ever felt that they were in contact with a discarnate. The statistics he obtained were that 27 percent of the general population had had such contact with a deceased (Greeley 1975).
- In 1971 W. D. Rees did a survey comprised of 343 widows (277 women and 66 men) in various towns in the United States. He found that 47 percent of the widows had seen or heard an apparition of their deceased spouse. None of them had talked about it to their doctor, and only one had shared their experience with a religious pastor or priest (Rees 1971).

Now, we see here that nearly half of the widows had such communication with departed loved ones. And the study proves also that the surveys of doctors and nurses were definitely underestimated, since the strange events are rarely shared with doctors. This is of course a very significant fact; and at the same time, if we take for granted that the souls go on with their lives in a higher dimension, then it's not surprising that they would make whatever effort they can to appear in a clear and recognizable way to their past companions, and as it happens, half of them succeed in being seen and recognized at least once. And, before that, when two people are greatly in love, and one of them passes away, it's fairly sure that they keep in constant contact. As Edgar Allan Poe implies in his poem "Lenore"—the heroine

Fig. 2.9. Henry Sandham's illustration for Poe's poem "Lenore"
(for the 1886 edition of Edgar Allan Poe's original 1845 poem)

being "the queenliest dead that ever died so young"—the lovers will be one day reunited and meet in paradise. Therefore, the poem argues, instead of mourning, it's more appropriate to celebrate their ascension to a new world (see fig. 2.9).

3
PREDICTIONS AND CARETAKING FROM THE BEYOND

As I saw it happen in my life, our deceased relatives can give us hints and precise predictions about our future. In my expert view—both as a researcher on consciousness and psi, and as an experiencer—this reception of information through hearing and/or seeing deceased relations implies a real communication with souls residing in the hyperdimension, even when the exchange happens in dreams. It is not, as some have argued, the triggering of our own psi capacity in order to sense the simultaneous or future death of a friend. Indeed, in a typical precognitive dream—that features an event that will happen in the future—we just see this event unfolding and we don't need any spirit or discarnate intermediary to do so. And so, when we see discarnate or immaterial entities, it's another story altogether: we really have a glimpse of the hyperdimension. Here is an example of a simple precognitive dream.

One afternoon that I had planned to leave Ormoy and go for a long weekend to my writing house, my car just wouldn't start. It's late afternoon already, and whatever I try to do, even asking a neighbor to jump-start it with the cables I carried, won't work. I'm really upset because I don't have the money to call for an emergency mechanic to come from faraway—their prices being prohibitive; and also because I had only three nights to spend there writing, with an appointment pending in Paris after that. So it's with enormous frustration that I take my bag out of the car and return to my flat. I wake up the next day having had a clear dream: My car was still stuck in the building's parking area; a mechanic arrives with his emergency pick-up and gestures with emphasis like an actor showing some tricks. The hood is open, and he has his hands on my engine, two or three moves, and suddenly my engine runs with a roaring sound; the man smiles broadly and, opening his arms wide, makes a victory gesture meaning "T'was really nothing! I told you!"

I ponder it while I'm having breakfast. The dream, I know, tells me it's not a grave problem; my car can be started with some expert help. But how? Jumpstarting it with my cables didn't work. I already have bothered my nice neighbor. Calling a mechanic is too expensive. I know there *is* a quick solution, and I just have to find it. Then my mind drifts, as the previous day, to the fact that if I was at least twenty miles from home, my car insurance would send a mechanic with a pick-up to wherever I was stuck, for free. Unfortunately, I'm at home . . . But wait a minute! It's not long since I've moved in, and I've not changed my address with them yet! This is it: tell them I'm stuck at a friend's place. Next, I call, they send a mechanic right away, and in less than ten minutes he has jumpstarted my car—but this time, using his powerful engine! Just like in the dream, he makes a gesture of satisfaction. And I don't have to pay anything.

This example is interesting because it highlights that precognition has also a practical and survival advantage; it shows how, with a clear precognitive dream, one starts looking at the problem or situation with a different mindset that may be the perfect trigger for finding the solution. And many a time, on meeting great difficulties, I have asked (just before sleeping) to be shown the solution in a dream. And quite often it worked fine.

I've been prone to having such precognitive dreams, or even conscious visions of future events, since my late teens, and these are much more frequent, and quite distinct from dreams in which one interacts with discarnate souls. My take on the matter is that when a luminous being (discarnate or not) talks to me in a numinous, symbolic, and clear dream, this reflects an actual interaction with the syg-dimension and specifically with the Self of that person.

In the case I will recount now, the dream features not only a terminally ill aunt giving me a clear prediction, but the preparation for, and the setting up of, a whole series of events implying her precognitive knowledge of her own passing. This aunt of mine showed, through these events, that she was caring about my life and helping me through various phases. She acted, from the Beyond, as a true ally of mine. (As usual, allow me to set the stage for understanding the dream, by explaining the context and events preceding it.)

While living in Paris, I had decided that I wanted to do a doctoral thesis on the subject of psi or parapsychology, and it's only after a very long search, when I had in fact given up, that I found in Remy Chauvin the professor who, at last, accepted such a doctoral theme and study. Chauvin was a famous ethologist and author, and the prominent academic voice of support in the French media for scientific and experimental parapsychology.

The next summer I took a two-month open-mileage airline ticket and visited the Rhine Laboratories in Durham, North Carolina, then headed by Professor K. R. Rao, Chauvin having established the connection for me. The Rhine lab had been the first psi research lab in the United States, called at the time FNRM (Foundation for Research on the Nature of Man), started by Joseph Banks Rhine and his wife, Louisa Rhine.*

Unknown to most of his colleagues, Chauvin had devised the first experimental study of "animal psi" at Rhine's lab, using mice to test their precognitive capacity, and was successful. He demonstrated that mice had the ability to anticipate which half of a cage would be randomly selected for the trigger of a mild electric shock, thus assessing

---

*More information can be found online at rhineonline.org

positively their precognition and their capacity to avoid harm using it. And he published it under the pseudonym Duval (see Duval and Montredon 1968, and Animal Psi on psi-encyclopedia.spr.ac.uk).

My plan had been to tour all the labs doing research on psi, and the Rhine lab, in the person of Richard Broughton, offered me three days of open phone line and provided me not only with the list of all active labs (and who to consult), but also that of independent researchers. And in one lab, the Psychophysical Research Laboratories (PRL), I was offered by its director, Charles (Chuck) Honorton, the opportunity to come and work in the lab as a research assistant.

With a book on biology to finish with the famed Professor Étienne Guillé,* it was not until the next June that I was able to move to the States.

Myself included, the PRL lab had a team of seven scientists, each one working on the fabulous new desk computer invented by Steve Wozniak and Steve Jobs, the Apple IIe (needless to say, I was on it, literally magnetized, since day one at the lab, and started learning to program in Basic at the beginning of week two). Two months later, I fell madly in love with one of the scientists, Mario Varvoglis, a shared feeling that made us inseparable; and still another few months later, I let go of my flat around Princeton and moved into his. About sixteen months later, I had an astonishing dream. Sometime earlier I had gotten news that my Aunt Denise—my mother's younger sister—was gravely sick and undergoing various medical tests in a Paris hospital.

In the dream, Denise is radiant, luminous, and, smiling broadly, she tells me: "I'm going to make you a gift for your wedding!"

Then the scene changes and now it's my father who is talking to me, saying: "Come with me, I'll show you your new temple."

And soon I behold, farther in a large valley landscape, a temple looking like an Indian one with several aisles and domes, and I'm spellbound by it.

---

*L'Alchimie de la vie [The alchemy of life], Paris: Rocher, 1983

In a second part of the dream, I meet a couple of friends I had at the time in France, colleagues and researchers with whom I was working prior to my departure for the United States. But just before the dreamscape changes, a strange character crosses the landscape in front of the temple, as if swiftly flying through it: the emblematic and symbolic *ageless mystical guide,* the one I recognize as Chidder-the-Green, the mysterious *Al-Khidr* ("the Green One") of the Sufis—the guide and initiator in secret knowledge and wisdom, and the messenger of the gods, thus on par with Hermes/Thoth.

No wonder, then, that in my dreams the rare and mysterious Chidder-the-Green or the messenger Hermes announces the onset of a new cycle, and rebirth. This numinous being abruptly invests the entire dreamspace, generally crossing it from right to left, cutting through it as if he belonged to another dimension, or, in a more recent dream, flying all over me and a group of questers, sprinkling ashes on us all and finally rolling me in these ashes on the ground. He embodies an immortal youth, beardless, thin, agile, flying, and evoking a chasm between dimensions—a transdimensional being—an emanation of Hermes. The fact is, each time this elusive character intrudes in one of my dreams, my whole life is bound to change soon afterward. That time in Princeton was a great example, as drastic changes occurred in my love life, my work, and my country of residence.

Bizarrely, I couldn't fully interpret the dream because I got shocked by the idea of marriage. This type of ceremony, in my eyes, was superfluous; the only thing that counted was the quality of a love relationship, and thus I couldn't fathom thinking about such an eventuality. And, in brief, I just discarded this part of the dream. Yet the new temple definitely appealed to me as a beautiful promise, and furthermore its multiple round domes, each with a spike at the top as so many antennae, evoked a feminine temple and sacredness.

Some two or three months later, while I was busy writing on the parapsychological research and data on survival—believing it was going to be the subject of my doctoral thesis—I became abruptly annoyed and weary with my life in Princeton and at the lab. Social contacts were near to zero on both counts. Princeton was a city that didn't have a single café (apart from a student joint within the university campus) but only ice-cream parlors and restaurants. And there was not enough of a social life among researchers in the field, despite two psi labs in the area. The other lab, the Princeton Engineering Anomalies Research (PEAR) laboratory, was set within the Engineering Department of Princeton University, and headed by physicist Bob Jahn, the department dean, and Brenda Dunne. It was also where the famous *Global Consciousness Project* would be conceived and started by Roger Nelson.*

Astonishingly, these two Princeton labs being in competition for a proper funding and also in terms of research protocols, I was the sole PRL researcher to visit the folks of PEAR, with whom I loved to converse and whose theoretical worldview—based on the physics of fields (EM, or electromagnetic, and QM, or quantum mechanics) and more holistic and spiritual—was immensely more appealing to me than the strict experimental and task-oriented attitude of PRL's team, who adhered to a strict quantum physics framework. I recall only three social gatherings in two years: one at a pricey restaurant in New Hope with the whole PRL team for the one-day visit of a foreign researcher; one at my place with Bob Jahn and Brenda, and Mario of course; and one the next year at another researcher's home, with the whole PRL team. This state of affairs became suddenly insufferable for the Paris-born woman I was. I felt dried up and suffocated by the lack of sufficient lively exchanges during the week, despite the fact that, with Mario, we were spending most weekends in New York, where I had some great friends and where Mario had both friends and family. On top of that, we had launched an exciting research group on psychotronics in New York; about eight members meeting informally every weekend at one or the other's home and sometimes informally in the huge and trendy

---

*See Jahn and Dunne 2009; Nelson et al. 1996; and information on the "Global Consciousness Project" is available at noosphere.princeton.edu

New Age parties of New York. But that was not enough for me. For a few months I was off the lab, working at home on my thesis. But the lab seemed bound to stick to the exact same protocol of *ganzfeld* for studying telepathy; that is, immersing the percipient in a uniform field of perception, or ganzfeld, with white noise and eyes covered with half ping-pong balls. And despite its being very successful, neither Mario nor I could envision spending years focused on it. At that point we decided to move to France where we would start our own independent research lab, and we fixed our move at the time of the summer holidays.

But then I reflected that for Mario to get himself integrated easily in France (in terms of legal and administrative matters, including working) the best way was for us to get married. And so, we got married before leaving; and to make this shift to France an exciting one, we opted for a three-month trip to India—a spiritual and consciousness-raising travel to the East. When we landed in Paris and went to reside in my parents' country house in Igny, it was just for a fortnight before we boarded the flight to India. I went to visit Denise at the hospital; she had been diagnosed with an aggressive brain tumor and was just going to have a last-chance surgery. I saw her again right after this surgery and was shocked: she could hardly speak and was in a wheelchair, having moreover lost the control of an arm and a leg. Her tumor was now at a terminal stage and her fate sealed. Worse still, on getting the news of his wife's brain cancer diagnosis and unavoidable surgery, her already half-paralyzed husband, my Uncle Lulu, had a flare-up of his evolving multiple sclerosis and was now in a nursing home. Sometime after we got back from India, Denise was moved to a more cozy hospital where our family could take care of her for her last few months. As for Igny—my beloved house in the woods in the Bièvres valley, in which I had awakened to my soul and writing vocation, and lived for a good fifteen years—it had been sold. And my father, in charge of my aunt and uncle's affairs, rented us their house south of Paris. Being large but with an unfinished first floor, its rent was at a price I could afford through the selling of my books, whose royalties had steadily gone up.

We had been in this house hardly a couple of months when one day Mario had prepared our lunch and called me to the kitchen table, I was pulling the chair in order to sit when I was suddenly overwhelmed by sensing my mother bursting into tears, and feeling her pain. I froze and said to Mario: "Denise! She just passed away!" and told him what I had just felt. Then I went back in my workroom to wait for my mother's call, which came a short while afterward.

Then, suddenly, all became clear in what I could recognize now as true knowledge of the future handed down to me by the Selfs of my aunt and father during a dream. The marriage had indeed happened, and the marriage gift from my Aunt Denise was the new house we were going to live in for the next fifteen years. I was very grateful to Lulu and took care of him as much as I could, taking him in his wheelchair to the restaurant where we would share with our lunch one of his Sauternes wine bottles that were no less than forty years of age, from a fabulous vintage and exceptional year. Sauternes is one of the select few white wine vintages that can age that much and so well (the red wines don't last half of that age).

After she died, Denise started to appear in my dreams as an ally standing by me, and these dreams would most of the time contain some precognitive information about future events in my life, such as an inkling about how I would fare as an author. For example, we would stroll together through Paris, meeting highly symbolic situations on our way, or she would be in the passenger seat of my car while I was driving. Her appearances in my dreams were never anecdotal; they would instead point to crucial events both in the present and in the future. And this was so for a few years and then she didn't intrude in my dreams anymore. My father's comment about Denise not coming to greet him for his transference to the Beyond—because she had important things to do and couldn't be disturbed—happened a few years after her presence had deserted my dreamtime. And indeed I had had the neat impression that she was already reincarnated, and had a vision of her on one occasion as a kid of about six years old. My father's death happened fifteen years after that of Denise. If Denise was already rein-carnated, then her immortal Self (permanently in the HD) may have needed to keep a strong connection with the adolescent child she was by now. And since we are talking about that, one can really speculate on how, apart from exceptions, all the deceased in a family, and spanning three generations, are able to attend the arrival of a loved parent. Are they not reincarnated? The answer, in my opinion, is that one's immor-tal Self does reside permanently in the HD, whether or not we have an ongoing incarnation on Earth.

It's no wonder, given all the above, that I turned to Denise for help when I met a very thorny familial situation and no wonder either that she was able to have, from the other side, such an influence on her elder sister that she did solve my problem. We'll now turn to this specific instance of intercession.

HELPFUL INTERCESSION INTO FAMILY PROBLEMS

It is noteworthy that major changes in the social or family situation of a person provoke an unconscious change of expectations on the part of their parents and social network. It's the case for example with getting married, having a child, starting a new job, or obtaining a social promo-tion. I saw this clearly happening in my life and that of my friends as well. In the decade during which I had two long-term love relationships, my mother had no specific expectations of me. But as soon as I was married, I had to bear heavy pressure from both my mother and Mario's mother, to the effect that I *should* now have a child. As far as I was concerned, and by an equally instinctive inclination when I felt securely installed in Denise and Lulu's house in a south suburb of Paris, I also wished to have a child (house and comfort being much more important than money for our maternal instinct as far as I could fathom it).

We were in France for about two and a half years, and I'd obtained my doctoral degree in psychological anthropology with highest hon-ors. My publisher was accepting wholeheartedly any new book project I would propose to him, generally on the day I was submitting the manuscript of the previous contract. He would call his secretary and ask her to prepare a contract with the working title I'd just mentioned and, while we kept on discussing my books, she would bring it and we would sign it right on the spot. This was the way of the old traditional publishers' school in France: support your authors with empathy and give them free rein. That suited me perfectly because my domains of interest were varied. As soon as I had gotten a good grasp of a domain (in my own view) and felt I had mastered it after a few years of study, then it had no more appeal for me and I would dive enthusiastically into another one.

So the desire to have a child was filling me but I had very clear principles about it, notably that it should be a responsible decision from the two persons in the couple. So I waited for a nice moment of intimacy to tell Mario about it and ask him if that would be his desire too. He responded he would think about it. A month later I asked him again and he still hadn't made up his mind; and finally another month passed before, on asking him again, he told me that, no, he wouldn't want to have a child with me. I was past my midthirties, and thus I had also explained to him that, in order for my pregnancy to be safe and secure, it should happen within the next three years. So that was it for me: a definite and final rebuttal. I swallowed it, healed myself, and turned all my attention and hopes to my books. (Yet, I couldn't help feeling I had been too decent, though, that I should have done like so many women do—just getting pregnant when the situation is favorable, and now you've got to assume your parental role!) I, of course, had not taken anybody into my confidence about my expectations and our pondering.

About a year after that, the pressure from the hopeful would-be grandmothers became really heavy. When I tried to explain that it was Mario not willing to have a child, I was met with total semantic deafness, as if I had said nothing. Not only didn't the pressure relent, it just kept mounting, and on *me* alone. I had answered to Mario, "Well, I will respect your choice. I just hope you'll not change your mind when it's too late for me, and abandon me to have a child with a younger woman."

(Unfortunately for me, that's what happened about twelve years later.)

So that was the global psychological situation bearing on me. Now the problem became more acute with my mother whom we were seeing about twice a month, when we had lunch at my parents' flat; in contrast, we would visit Mario's parents, who had left the United States and retired to Greece, only once a year. My mother somehow must have identified too much with Denise because after the latter died, she suddenly became very judgmental and demanding vis-à-vis her daughters, as her younger sister had been. Denise and Lulu had been estranged from their two children for a decade when, after a short interlude of one or two dinners during which they made peace, the hostilities flared up again to remain such even with their father after Denise had passed away.

Things went from bad to worse with my mother. Now we couldn't even share a meal together without her directing nasty remarks at me, infinite variations on the theme: "You are an egoist and it's normal since you don't have children." It came to the point that, when we were telling them about our work and what we were doing at the moment, as soon as I was mentioning the book I was toiling on, or a new publishing or some lectures of mine, I would get slapped with the "egoist" epithet within a few minutes. Only Mario's work could be discussed; I couldn't open my mouth about my profession, despite the fact I was the one to bring most, if not all, of the money home. My mother was constantly upset about me. Her contemptuous comments were always voiced in an undertone, as if she was talking to herself, targeting me, like so many arrows, without breaking the overall interaction. Our relationship became poisoned by her projections on me, for just a single reason: I had no children. It was stifling. The saddest part for me was that Mario didn't help at all; worse still, he systematically sided with my mother. As for my father, he stayed neutral and never put forward a judgment, and even less so a reproach, on that question.

Due to this stressful atmosphere both at home with quite a womanizing husband and at my parents' place, and adding to that a heavy professional workload, I felt at one point totally drained of my energy. I needed to take a break, to make a spiritual retreat, in India and alone. I opted for spending five weeks in Pushkar, Rajasthan, whatever the bad comments I would get left and right. There, I meditated each and every day for a long time on the ghats of the sacred lake, beholding the exquisite sight, on my left, of a Mughal-style palace turned into a hotel (where I stayed), and in front and on the right, the magnificent overhanging dunes and desert landscape. It worked wonders. Indeed, I was soon reconnected with my deep Self and felt utterly rejuvenated and re-energized.

On my return, I knew I wasn't going to bear this skewed and unhealthy relationship with my mother any longer. I decided to change it drastically, back to where it had been all my life, and to put myself to the task immediately. To stand a better chance, I figured I should act on three levels at once—visualization, getting some help from the soul dimension, and of course direct dialogue. Since my mother was so deeply bonded to her sister that she had identified with her plight with her children, and since Denise was my ally in the dreamtime, she was definitely the one best able to act from this level. (But note that, at this time in my life, while I could sense or see them, and sometimes "hear" a sentence or two, I was not yet able to interact in lively discussion with the deceased.)

We were going to have lunch with my parents the next day. In the night, I got into a deep meditation, eyes closed, with the strong intent to work on the problem and solve it. First, I called Denise, visualizing her face very clearly, slightly above and in front of me. Then I talked to her, with an insistent tone: "You have to make Yvonne understand that she's not you; not only has she never been estranged from her children but she never had any problem with me before! Please, find a way to make her unconscious mind at peace with me, to make her realize she has to let me be free to live my own life." Then I made a visualization sending peaceful and loving thoughts to my mother and reestablishing the empathic relationship that we had enjoyed between us in the past. My connection to my own Self, after five weeks of meditation in Pushkar, was strong and crystal clear.

The next day, before we went to my parents' home, I prepared myself psychologically by taking on the free-spirited and humorous attitude I had displayed during my adolescence, and that both my parents had loved. At the first hint of my mother getting on her "selfish you" stance—we were alone together, setting the table—I confronted her with candid humor, looking her straight in the eye:

"What is it with you? You well know I've always been an odd character, doing things my own way. I'm NOT your 'normal' type. Be happy that I got married in the first place, that will be all I'll endorse as far as social customs go. Look, you've already five grandchildren. Isn't that enough to make you happy? Why don't you enjoy them fully, instead of longing for more?"

She looked at me, stunned but smiling—remembering that *Yes, this one is an odd one, an artist,* remembering how much she and Victor respected that trait in me when I was young and acting so freely. And suddenly that was it; she was her old self again. A mischievous smile lighted her face, her eyes sparkled. *Yes, the artist of the family, the intrepid and carefree daughter, the adventurous globe-trotter, always mysteriously gone who knows where?*

And the miracle happened: suddenly, we were the old allies again; she would let me be free, let me choose my way. I had given them no other choice—ever—since I was sixteen years old. And they loved it, to see me so free. I was doing what they would have loved to do themselves . . . At that very moment, my mother's skewed projections were shattered to pieces. The soul-link was reestablished, the flow was passing again, unimpeded, between us.

The problem never came back.

THE UNFINISHED BUSINESS CASES: CARING FOR THE LIVING

This caring of the deceased for their loved ones on Earth that allows us to ask for their help, is made evident by some cases of apparitions called Unfinished Business. In these, we see that a mother or a caretaker who died abruptly while leaving young children on Earth, will appear in order to take care of them or to see to their well-being. Here is one very touching occurrence, the Lucy Dodson case, referenced by Myers, in which the percipient had no idea that the mother of the two children had even died, and is tasked with taking care of them by their deceased grandmother.

On June 5th, 1887, a Sunday evening, between eleven and twelve at night, being awake, my name was called three times. I answered twice, thinking it was my uncle . . . but the third time I recognized the voice as that of my mother, who had been dead sixteen years. I said, "Mamma!" She then came round a screen near my bedside with two children in her arms, and placed them in my arms and put the bedclothes over them and said, "Lucy, promise me to take care of them, for their mother is just dead." I said, "Yes mamma." She repeated, "*Promise* me to take care of them." I replied, "Yes, I promise you"; and I added, "Oh, mamma, stay and speak to me, I am so wretched." She replied, "Not yet, my child," then she seemed to go round the screen again, and I remained, feeling the children to be still in my arms, and fell asleep. When I awoke, there was nothing. Tuesday morning, June 7th, I received the news of my sister-in-law's death. She had given birth to a child three weeks before, which I didn't know till after her death. [I have had other experiences, but] only to the extent of having felt a hand laid on my head, and sometimes on my hand, at times of great trouble. [Signed] Lucy Dodson. (Myers 1903, 409; 2012, 178, app. 7C)

Then she adds in response to a questionnaire: "I did not know a second baby had been born; in fact, had not the remotest idea of my sister-in-law's illness." The death happened in Bruges, on June 5, between 11:00 p.m. and midnight. Moreover, she felt the children to be still in her arms for a long time, until the clock struck midnight.

To add to this precise and stunning case, Myers states, based on Lucy Dodson's report, that "the distinctiveness with which the vision was seen is not explicable by the real light" that was coming from a street lamp. In the large body of cases, apparitions, both of the dead and the living, are seen to be glowing in the dark and appear with extremely fine detail, as clearly in an obscure room as in full daylight, and sometimes as precisely with eyes closed as eyes wide open. This fact, for Myers, is a strong element in favor of the reality of discarnate beings, as opposed to hallucinations, because a simple psychic projection would not present such detail in the clothing or gestures, or in the clearly perceptible sounds of footsteps.

We also have cases in which recently deceased persons want to give clues to their descendants as to where they have hidden money or a will. In a case, given by Myers (1903, 411; 2012, 179, app. 7D), a man underwent a violent death outside his home. On hearing the news, one of the daughters fell into a swoon and, when out of it, said her father had appeared to her in strange white and black clothes and told her that "he sewed a large roll of bills inside his grey shirt . . . and the money is still there." After another swoon she asked her brother to go get the clothes. At the morgue, they had removed and tossed his old clothes, and on recovering these they found the money. All the details about the new clothes and the stitching were correct. However, because of the swoons, which left the daughter very sick, this case seems to show, on the part of the deceased, more of an attachment to one's possessions than a real caring for the children surviving.

Alleviating a Mother's Fear of Death

This case, mostly referred to as the Scratch on the Cheek case is deemed by researchers as one of the strongest in terms of evidence for survival, and of the securing of witnesses as well. Mr. F. G. writes that his very dear and only sister died of cholera at eighteen in St. Louis. He later became a commercial traveler. Nine years after her death, he had visited some clients and got back in his hotel room around noon, upbeat after having gotten some substantial orders. Here is his report:

> While busily smoking a cigar and writing out my orders, I suddenly
> became conscious that some one was sitting on my left, with one arm
> resting on the table. Quick as a flash I turned and distinctly saw the
> form of my dead sister, and for a brief second or so looked her squarely
> in the face; and so sure was I that it was she, that I sprang forward in
> delight, calling her by name, and, as I did so, the apparition instantly
> vanished. Naturally I was startled and dumbfounded, almost doubt-
> ing my senses; but the cigar in my mouth, and pen in hand, with the
> ink still moist on my letter, I satisfied myself I had not been dreaming
> and was wide awake. I was near enough to touch her, had it been a
> physical possibility, and noted her features, expression, and details of
> dress, etc. She appeared as if alive. Her eyes looked kindly and per-
> fectly natural into mine. Her skin was so life-like that I could see
> the glow or moisture on its surface, and, on the whole, there was no
> change in her appearance, otherwise than when alive.
>
> Now comes the most remarkable *confirmation* of my statement,
> which cannot be doubted by those who know what I state actually
> occurred. This visitation, or whatever you may call it, so impressed
> me that I took the next train home, and in the presence of my
> parents and others I related what had occurred. My father, a man
> of rare good sense and very practical, was inclined to ridicule me,
> as he saw how earnestly I believed what I stated; but he, too, was
> amazed when later on I told them of a bright red line or *scratch* on
> the right-hand side of my sister's face, which I distinctly had seen.
> When I mentioned this my mother rose trembling to her feet and
> nearly fainted away, and as soon as she sufficiently recovered her self-
> possession, with tears streaming down her face, she exclaimed that I
> had indeed seen my sister, as no living mortal but herself was aware
> of that scratch, which she had accidentally made while doing some
> little act of kindness after my sister's death. She said she well remem-
> bered how pained she was to think she should have, unintentionally,

marred the features of her dead daughter, and that, unknown to all, how she had carefully obliterated all traces of the slight scratch with the aid of powder, etc., and that she had never mentioned it to a human being from that day to this. In proof, neither my father nor any of our family had detected it, and positively were unaware of the incident, yet *I saw the scratch as bright as if just made.* So strangely impressed was my mother, that even after she had retired to rest she got up and dressed, came to me and told me *she knew* at least that I had seen my sister. A few weeks later my mother died, happy in her belief she would rejoin her favorite daughter in a better world.

In a further letter Mr. F. G. adds: There was nothing of a spiritual or ghostly nature in either the form or dress of my sister, she appearing perfectly natural, and dressed in clothing that she usually wore in life, and which was familiar to me. (Myers 1903, 406–7; 2012, 176, app. 7B)

Prodding a Daughter to Learn and Succeed

Here is a last case, the Jo case, illustrating the care of a mother for the young daughter she has left behind—carrying her mother's duty and encouraging her in her profession, as if she had been still there in a body; and thus letting her daughter Jo know that she, indeed, was still there in her spirit or soul, inspiring and caring.

I stumbled on this interesting case on the internet and, despite not being referenced as to its source, found it (as the other ones in the collection) clearly authentic; this one is quite telling about the bodily contact with a deceased and objects or beings they bring along, as we have seen the dead mother bringing a baby and a toddler to her daughter in the Lucy Dodson case above. In this Jo case, first, there is the *sensation by the living daughter of being kissed on the cheek* by her deceased mother, while perceiving her half-formed apparition. Second, we have the hands of the live person literally passing through the etheric or HD objects (here books), as had been attested in many accounts. So that we have here both aspects of this intriguing paradox, that the beings in the hyperdimension can either remain as an immaterial field of energy, or else project a degree of materiality in order to be seen as a human form and recognized, or to interact with the living, or else in order to manipulate matter and objects (such as making a phone or a clock ring).

My mother contacted me a few times after death. The first time was the night of her funeral when I was sleeping deeply from exhaustion, and *I felt a soft breeze pass over me, and then a deep kiss on my left cheek.* I was so startled that I woke up and saw mist and a hand waving at me.

Another time was a few months later when I started school to get a promotion at my job. I was *very stressed out and not ready* to deal with a promotion, but felt that I had to take advantage of a good opportunity. I woke up one night and saw my mother standing over me wearing a nursing uniform. (She was a nurse's aide in life, and I was receiving a promotion as a nurse technician.) She had a few books in her hand. She sat and spread the books across the bed, and *when I reached to touch the books, I was actually touching the sheets.*

She began to talk to me and read these books. I do not remember all that she shared with me, but after that interaction, for each exam, I took in that class I did not get less than a 95%. I never remembered the questions on the tests. I graduated from the class valedictorian. Yes, I think that the spirits never leave us. – Jo. (Stephen Wagner, "Visions at the Hour of Death," LiveAbout website, April 29, 2018) (emphasis mine)

The second stunning piece of information in this case is the efficiency of the help given by the soul of the mother, and it is a two-pronged influence. First in radically changing the psychological state of the daughter, from being *very stressed out and not ready,* to obviously being up to the challenge. Second, we have to assume, from the fantastic results at exams, that a real acquisition of knowledge took place via a direct contact with the hyperdimension.

4

THE GRATEFUL DEAD

In a number of apparitions, the deceased are asking the living to do something for their own well-being in the afterlife. Sometimes they demand rituals to help them ascend to a higher state of consciousness, or that something be done about their sepulcher, or they ask for a dignified burial. In the astounding Baron Basil Driesen case below, it seems that the deceased, after becoming able to see things from a higher and more spiritual standpoint, now is eager to be forgiven by the person he has unjustly judged and wronged. Then, after being granted their postmortem wish, the dead are known to be grateful toward the persons who heard them and acted accordingly. Hence the legend of the grateful dead carried from the Middle Ages, and we'll see an ancient account from this period, the thirteenth-century Willekin case. The fact the dead could be thankful is immensely informative. It means first that the dead have a clear memory of their past lives; and second, that, in the soul dimension, they are endowed with clairvoyance about their surviving family and about earthly matters; third, it shows they are able, reaching out from the soul hyperdimension, to come in contact with the living and find ways to express their wishes. In other words, they display a supernatural knowledge and are able to cross dimensions.

In fact, the apparition at her annual birthday of their dead child to my Burgundy family (discussed in chapter 2) could be counted as a cordial and heartening response to their immense grief, which had overwhelmed her mother and nearly destroyed the couple. It was a way for the soul of the child to show them she was a living soul, caring for her distressed parents.

THE GRATEFUL DEAD: THANKING THE LIVING

The following cases all have in common that they involve the deceased making a request of the living.

The Brewer Thanking a Friend for Taking Care of His Children

This case reported by Myers has several striking and rare features. First the farmer, Karl D., a sober man, awakens some time before midnight with a funny dream about his upbeat brewer friend (who, unknown to him, died in the afternoon). Still in bed, he now hears the brewer's loud voice just outside his window, and that upsets him. But then the brewer walks right into his bedroom, "wildly gesticulating with his arms" in his usual manner, and talks to him as in a normal conversation, telling him he just died. Then, on hearing the farmer promising "I will look after your children," he comes forward to embrace him, at which point the farmer, horrified, stops him from approaching.

> About a year ago there died in a neighboring village a brewer called Wünscher, with whom I stood in friendly relations. His death ensued after a short illness, and as I seldom had an opportunity of visiting him, I knew nothing of his illness nor of his death. On the day of his death I went to bed at nine o'clock, tired with the labors which my calling as a farmer demands of me. . . .
>
> In my dream I heard the deceased call out with a loud voice, "Boy, make haste and give me my boots." This awoke me, and I noticed that, for the sake of our child, my wife had left the light burning. I pondered with pleasure over my dream, thinking in my mind how Wünscher, who was a good-natured, humorous man,

would laugh when I told him of this dream. Still thinking on it, I hear Wünscher's voice scolding outside, just under my window. I sit up in my bed at once and listen, but cannot understand his words. What can the brewer want? I thought. . . . Suddenly he comes into the room from behind the linen press, steps with long strides past the bed of my wife and the child's bed; wildly gesticulating with his arms all the time, as his habit was, he called out, "What do you say to this, Herr Oberamtmann? This afternoon at five o'clock I have died." Startled by this information, I exclaim, "Oh, that is not true!" He replied: "Truly, as I tell you; and, what do you think? They want to bury me already on Tuesday afternoon at two o'clock;" . . . I asked myself: Is this a hallucination? . . . I say to the brewer, "Herr Wünscher, we will speak softly, so that my wife may not wake up, it would be very disagreeable to her to find you here." To which Wünscher answered in a lower and calmer tone: "Don't be afraid, I will do no harm to your wife." . . . I said to Wünscher: "If this be true, that you have died, I am sincerely sorry for it; I will look after your children." Wünscher stepped towards me, stretched out his arms and moved his lips as though he would embrace me; therefore I said in a threatening tone, and looking steadfastly at him with a frowning brow: "Don't come so near, it is disagreeable to me," and lifted my right arm to ward him off, but before my arm reached him the apparition had vanished. My first look was to my wife to see if she were still asleep. She was. I got up and looked at my watch, it was seven minutes past twelve. My wife woke up and asked me: "To whom did you speak so loud just now?" "Have you understood anything?" I said. "No," she answered, and went to sleep again. . . . I must further remark that the brewer *had* died that afternoon at five o'clock, and was buried on the following Tuesday at two. (Myers 1903, 375; 2013, 162, app. 4F)

In fact I've seen only rare cases of apparitions that include some bold bodily touch, one being the handshake with a "hand, which was long and cold" when the deceased is granted forgiveness in the Baron Basil Driesen case below. Interestingly, in both cases, the behavior is a spontaneous gesture of thankfulness and gratitude from the part of the recently deceased person. However, percipients feeling light touches and strokes on the hand, the head, or the shoulder (as with my house genie) are not rare.

The Dead Voicing Specific Demands to the Living

Sometimes the reported cases don't show the dead being grateful per se but having clear demands as to their burial site, their belongings, or the care of loved ones left behind. If they can thus ask the living to carry on specific tasks, we can be confident that they will be pleased with the outcome. Here are two instances in this category. The first one is reported by Myers in his 1889 article, "On Recognised Apparitions Occurring More Than a Year after Death."

A man (let's call him the tutor) was charged by a dying man with taking care of an elderly relative; the now deceased man appears to him more than a year later, to complain that he has not kept his promise. After this stunning encounter, the tutor launches a thorough investigation into the measures he had taken at the time of the death and how they were enacted, and to his great surprise finds out that somehow they have been modified and not executed properly. He proceeds to correct them in order to uphold his promise. In this case, we see that the deceased is aware of the fact that his elderly relative is not being properly taken care of, and he will certainly be comforted when things are straightened out.

We'll also see a complex case of multiple and long-term apparition, that of Palladia (chapter 7), starting with the percipient feeling a strong invisible presence, and resorting to the Ouija to understand who is there. The dead, Palladia, is not a parent of the percipient, but the fragile younger sister of his best university friend, whom he had often helped when she was sick. Palladia's first words are a demand concerning the statue of an angel on her sepulcher. When the percipient asks

Palladia what she wants, the Ouija spells out: *To replace the angel, it is falling.* Then Palladia appears regularly, looking bright and alive, sitting across from his desk and smiling at him, her face leaning on her hand; for years to come, she'll be the ally of the percipient, giving him hints about future events.

The Legend of the Grateful Dead: A Dead Knight's Gracious Thanks

We find a trove of ancient accounts of deceased spirits' apparitions, and genies, in the books of Claude Lecouteux—a Sorbonne professor of Middle Ages literature and civilization. Here is one case taken from *The Return of the Dead* (123) called "Willekin and the Ghost," extracted from a thirteenth-century Germanic short story called "Knightly Loyalty." Lecouteux says it "provides a finished form of *the legend of the grateful dead.* The dead individual of course appears as an ectoplasm, but the text shows how the importance of the sepulcher persisted and is reminiscent of what we know about Roman beliefs. We should also remember the words of St. Augustine: 'Doing good for the dead is very useful.'"

The story, however, is deeply faulted in terms of our standard of human values, not to mention what should be Christian ones! In short, its obvious aim, beyond stating it's a Christian duty to bury the dead, is to show that these dead will reward you because they are still conscious and they have the means to tinker with reality to do so (such as to find the perfect winning horse for you). Unfortunately, it doesn't seem to be a Christian virtue (at this epoch and place at least) to give the woman the right to decide about herself, nor the right to impose or defend her loyalty toward her just-wed husband. What counts is the loyalty for a vile oath taken in order to get to win. Thus, when reading this account with a big grain of salt for its moral shortcomings and its didactic embellishment, let's nevertheless remember that Abrahamic religions hold as a dogma the resurrection in the flesh at the End Times, and also that the Christians believe in the resurrection of Lazarus of Bethany by

Fig. 4.1. Three Saints rising from the dead. Limoges artwork,
circa 1250, champlevé enamel on copper.
Photo by Marie-Lan Nguyen (2012), CC BY 2.5

Jesus four days after his burial and, as the thirteenth-century Limoges enamel in figure 4.1 exemplifies, in the resurrection of the saints.

Count Willekin von Montabur came to an inn one day and learned that a knight had died there but a short while before. Because the knight had not paid his bill, the innkeeper had the corpse thrown under a pile of manure. Willekin paid off the dead man debt's and obtained a decent burial for him. Seeking a good horse to take part in a tourney whose prize was the hand of a noble lady, Willekin saw a man in the street astride a magnificent charger. He addressed him, offering him money in exchange for the horse. The other turned down the sum and surrendered his mount in return for half the prize of the tourney.

Willekin was victorious and took the prize, thus the wedding occurred. The next day, when he shut the door of the nuptial chamber, the knight with whom he had concluded the bargain arrived, demanding his half. The count offered him money and goods, but in vain. In order not to break his oath, he left the room. To his great surprise, his interlocutor followed him and declared: "I am the dead man whose body you redeemed and to whom you provided a sepulcher; I wanted to test your loyalty." Not daring to rejoice, Willekin sought tangible proof of what he was hearing. He stuck out his hand and encountered nothing but air. The dead man thanked him again for his good deed and vanished, renouncing the price of the horse.

THE DECEASED COMES BACK TO ASK FOR FORGIVENESS

Here is an interesting related example, in which it is not the living asking the deceased for atonement and reparation of past deeds, but the recently deceased who appears to ask for forgiveness—the Baron Basil Driesen case.

The baron states in his report:

I had not been on good terms with M. Ponomareff [his father-in-law who died after a long illness]. Different circumstances . . . had estranged us from each other. . . . He died very quietly, after having given his blessing to all his family, including myself. A liturgy for the rest of his soul was to be celebrated on the ninth day. . . . On the eve of that day . . . I read the Gospel before falling asleep. My wife was sleeping in the same room. . . . I had just put out the candle when footsteps were heard in the adjacent room—a sound of slippers shuffling. . . . I called out "Who is there?" No answer. I struck one match, then another . . . I saw M. Ponomareff standing before the closed door. Yes, it was he, in his blue dressing-gown lined with squirrel furs . . . white waistcoat and his black trousers. It was he, undoubtedly. I was not frightened. . . . "What do you want?" I asked my father-in-law. M. Ponomareff made two steps forward, stopped before my bed, and said, "Basil Feodorovitch, I have acted wrongly towards you. Forgive me! Without this, I do not feel at rest there." He was pointing to the ceiling with his left hand, whilst holding out his right to me. I seized this hand, which was long and cold, shook it, and answered, "Nicholas Ivanovitch, God is my witness that I have never had anything against you." [The ghost of] my father-in-law bowed [or bent down], moved away, and went through the opposite door into the billiard-room, where he disappeared. I looked after him for a moment, crossed myself, put out the candle, and fell asleep with the sense of joy which a man who has done his duty must feel. . . .

[Then, the next day, the confessor doing the liturgy asked to talk to me and] said to me in a rather solemn voice, "This night at three o'clock Nicholas Ivanovitch [Ponomareff] appeared to me and begged of me to reconcile him to you." (Myers 1903, 415–16; 2012 181, app. 7D)

For a seasoned researcher like me, there is a rare and absolutely remarkable element in this account, which, being originally from the *Proceedings of the SPR* 10 (385–86), is as usual corroborated by witnesses (namely that of the confessor), and thus a very solid case. The deceased appearing to two distinct persons the same night at the same hour, both times with the same intent to beg for forgiveness, is already quite a feat. Note also the precise description of the deceased's clothing. But furthermore, we have quite material effects of these apparitions, namely the "sound of slippers shuffling," the walking and approaching nearer, and the most astounding of all, the actual handshake with the ghost hand: "I seized this hand, which was long and cold."

The semimateriality of the soul body and of genies is something Claude Lecouteux was keen to stress, as well as their capacity to do all kinds of actions in the matter world, thus being proficient at moving and handling objects and matter.

5
STIFLING BONDS
WITH THE DECEASED

The strong bonding that two persons have built during their lives may turn out to be a real hindrance for the one person surviving the other. The problem becomes acute if the living one is so engrossed in the relationship with the deceased that they become estranged from a normal social life.

I came across this type of problem when, in my late twenties, I got a job as a psychologist in a mental hospital in the suburbs of Paris. In fact, I had just gotten my master's degree in cultural anthropology but, due to this diploma, the post I was offered was that of a psychologist.

It was a huge public hospital with independent sections on different floors, each having its own administration and rules—something I wasn't aware of when I started working there. Fortunately, I had been hired by the Daytime Hospital, whose innovative purpose was to handle minor psychiatric cases and to facilitate the reinsertion of patients into society. This would have been a great and bold new way to deal with mental sickness, except that patients were attributed to one section or the other, not according to the severity of their case but to where their homes were located. As I was shocked to learn, the unlucky residents of certain quarters within Paris and its suburbs would be assigned to the floor above ours, and lo! the mean duration of their hospital stay would be five or six years, and all the while they would be kept in mental limbo by heavy doses of tranquilizers and sedatives, and mostly stripped of their legal rights as well. The head of that section, no doubt, must have been a ruthless and tone-deaf Freudian psychiatrist, indifferent and obtuse, more intent on being sure his hospital beds were all filled with patients than on curing them. This money-driven rationale, the real culprit and the source of great suffering for some patients, derived from the government funding being a function of the number of occupied beds.

At the Daytime Hospital, my job had been defined as setting up cheering activities and uplifting collective events, so that the mood of the patients and their social networking could improve. As I got there the first day, upbeat and full of goodwill, I was met by the head of the ward and part of the psychology team of six people. We got into a nice chat, sitting at one of the four long tables at the front of the ward used for talking or eating.

I explained to them that I was proficient in hypnosis and that I had obtained, on a few trials, a very notable and lasting improvement of diverse physical and mental problems. They were highly interested and curious, and the head of the ward gave me carte blanche to try it on individuals I thought could be cured that way. Maybe the psychologists and nurses were impressed by my position as a psychologist—most of them not having such a status. Or maybe I oversold my competence in hypnotism—my experience amounted to a period of a couple of months in Nice, during which I had studied with a professional and weathered hypnotist, while simultaneously practicing it on others, thus learning the roles of both the hypnotized and of the one hypnotizing. He would hypnotize me every day, then we would discuss the session and the method. Meanwhile, I was practicing healing with light hypnosis, free of course, on diverse members of the family and social circle of my friends in Nice, who came to me with a variety of complaints and ailments. And I truly obtained a 100 percent success rate, however on a quite small sample of four people. I was able to remove a grave type of headaches, repetitive and obsessive nightmares, and backaches; I also cured the adolescent with the headaches from fits of incoherent behavior that were cyclical and lasting a few days. My voluntary guinea pigs had ranged from a grandmother to an adolescent of sixteen years old, and for all four, the cure to their specific problems was long lasting or else they totally disappeared. However, the real feat in this healing was that, for all four persons, I never addressed any of the specific problems they had complained about but, after putting them under a light hypnosis, conducted a visualization of reconnection with their own Self. The adolescent even spontaneously remembered an incarnation in which she was struck on the head as the source of her actual headache problem. Such is the power of the ego-Self connection.

Our chat on the ward was interrupted by the patients exiting their rooms and coming to the long tables for lunch, while the meals arrived on rolling stands from the kitchen. I was impressed to see the medical team split to sit among the patients and converse agreeably with them. I followed suit, thus interacting and getting a bit acquainted with a few patients. When the lunch ended, everybody, including the team, got up and dispersed quite suddenly. I felt I had been left a bit abruptly standing on my own, with hardly any direction or advice as to what I was supposed to do.

The ward was an immense rectangle with, at one of its small ends, the two rows of large tables accommodating the twenty-five or so people in the section for meals and gatherings. Then, on the three other sides, room after room whose doors were now all closed.

I went to knock on the first door on the right side where I had seen a girl I had talked to disappear. After being welcomed in, I stepped into a neat room and faced the fifteen- or sixteen-year-old, a bit shocked at her being here at such a young age. I presented myself again, in a low-key, smiling, and empathic fashion, while moving slowly inside the room. She was seated near a table, withdrawn and shy, and I took a seat in front of her. We spent a few minutes chatting in a light humoristic tone. I was eager to set and maintain my relational style as remote as possible from that of a cold psychiatrist; to do that, I immediately used the friendly *tu* (more intimate than the formal *vous,* although both translate to "you") and initiated an affable and cozy dialogue. And only thereafter did I ask Emilie (that was her name) to tell me her story.

She started with a stern statement, saying and repeating that she was "mentally very sick." I let it pass without comment, taking it as the result of the projections of the psychiatrists and nurses in this hospital on all their patients. Then Emilie explained that she had a very dear friend, a girl named Marie, with whom she had been in the same class at the same college for nearly three years. Marie had died eight months earlier, but she was still with her, at her side, day and night.

"How's that?" I asked. "Do you see her in your room, for example?"

"Yes, of course. She's sitting next to me and we can speak together. If I walk and go somewhere, then she accompanies me. It's just like before she died. We were always together, inseparable . . ."

After a moment of silence, she added:

"You see, I'm very sick. I've schizophrenia, hallucinations."

"Look Emilie, you have to know that, in about three-quarters of the world, if you were to tell your story to people or even to doctors, everybody would believe that you are indeed communicating with your dear deceased friend. It's solely in most of Europe and North America that our Western science has decreed that only matter and your body are real and that there's no survival of the soul after bodily death. Everywhere else, in the ancient cultures, many individuals have the gift of seeing their own deceased loved ones and quite a number like you are even able to communicate and discuss with them."

She looked at me briefly but intensely, pondering my words but not quite ready to believe me.

Knowing that "walls have ears," I was careful not to express anything about my own experiences. About the fact, for example, that due to my practice of meditation since I was eighteen, I was able to see the spirits of the deceased moving around and flying in the air; that I had sensed them in Brittany, in Africa, even in my own workroom in

Fig. 5.1. A Vietnamese altar for ancestors, with the Buddhist altar to Kwan Yin, bodhisattva of compassion, set higher in the upper-left corner

Photo by Thang Nguyen from Nottingham, United Kingdom, CC BY-SA 2.0

Bièvres, a south suburb of Paris. Instead, while talking to Emilie within the hospital, I was keen on making various references to Eastern religions, to the worldviews of shamanic and ancient cultures, and my own academic competency regarding these subjects that I had covered as part of my cultural anthropology studies. Indeed, I didn't linger on that subject with her, but the rituals of connection and thanks to the ancestors, the existence of ancestors' altars in the house, the possession cults in which the initiates are said to impersonate some deities or ancestors, are a worldwide and timeless phenomenon. Ancestors' altars are widespread across the world cultures. See figure 5.1 for a Buddhist one in Vietnam.

One of the most original cults of the ancestors is the Day of the Dead (*Día de Muertos*) in Mexico, on November 1 and 2. Here is coverage by Norma Schafer, who is, in her own terms—"a contemporary record-keeper of Oaxaca art, culture, history"—of this remembrance feast in one village. "On November 2, in Teotitlan del Valle, the low-key

Fig. 5.2. Offerings of copal and incense while spending
the night with the ancestors in Mexico
Photo by Jordi Cueto-Felgueroso Arocha, CC BY-SA 4.0

ceremonies of honoring the dead begin with a mid-afternoon meal at home to ensure the dead return to their graves with full bellies. The villagers then accompany the spirits to the cemetery (around 6 p.m.) and sit with them through the night to be certain they are cared for and rest in peace" (see fig. 5.2 and plate 6).

I went on explaining further to Emilie: "Indeed, if we were to take any religion seriously, then, since they all posit a survival of the souls in full consciousness, there would always be the possibility that some human beings could have the gift of seeing these departed souls."

Now she was positively hooked to my story, even if she still didn't make any straightforward eye contact. I went on, slowly:

"So, in brief, about three-quarters of the people on Earth would readily conclude that you have this gift yourself. And in some cultures you would be highly respected because of this gift. I myself believe that you are really seeing and talking to Marie. However the problem isn't your gift or even your mental balance. The problem lies in the fact that you're putting your life and your freedom at risk by being constantly with her. Look, if she died it's because she has something to do on the other side. And if you're still here, alive in your body, it's because you yourself also have something to accomplish in your life. Do you see my point?"

"Yes! This sounds right . . . But then what? What shall I do?"

I was glad that I had succeeded in shifting her viewpoint on her own experience, and that she was now eager to learn more. But I wanted her to share more of her experience, to express herself, and to start trusting me as a friend and ally.

"But first, why don't you tell me how you got in this hospital exactly?"

"It's my parents. I told them about my experience and they thought I was crazy. They took me to a psychiatrist who then told them I had to be sent to a mental hospital. And he sent me here."

"Oh my! Such stupid shortsightedness on his part! Well, now you know better. But let's get back to what I was saying, that your problem, Emilie, is that you're still sticking together with Marie, despite the fact each one of you has something very important to accomplish alone and by oneself—Marie in the Beyond, and you here in France."

I felt so much empathy for her plight, I was so anguished at seeing a young girl's future screwed by bigotry and stiff Freudian dogma! She could feel it I guess. I was speaking low and softly, directly to her heart and soul, with loads of implicit thoughts. "Do you understand that this relationship has gotten you in deep trouble? And that it could become worse?"

She hummed and rasped her throat, knitting her fingers.

"How could you possibly go on with your own life and accomplish something if you only stick with her?"

She nodded her assent.

"You sure don't want to stay in this ward for months, don't you? You have your own life in front of you! What about pondering the important accomplishment you have to do here in this world—which is why you didn't die like Marie. And it's the same for Marie: she has to start focusing on why she died, and what is it she has to do on the other side. Surely, if she loves you so much, she would prefer to see you happy and not secluded in this place . . . don't you think?"

All the while she had kept her head down looking at her hands crossed over her knees, giving me a quick and shy side glance once in a while. But she nodded again and I felt that I had pulled her out of the psychic knot and brought her mind to a more global yet more essential point of view, where she could mull over her actual predicament in a more strategic light.

I had wholly sided with her and made her aware that the hospital and psychiatrists' stand was something that could be questioned—a definite mental leap to a more global worldview. Also, I had made her take some distance from the situation she was in, and from them. The grip on her mind was broken. She was now thinking along new lines, more in accord with survival tactics.

After a long moment of silence, letting her follow up her line of thought, I suggested:

"Look, I really want to meet and confront your parents and talk about all this with them, because, in my psychologist's view, they have acted in an abnormal and cruel way. I really want to make them understand that they have to protect you and try to empathize with you, instead of sending you away. Do you like the idea? Anyway, I'm going to go and face them with what they did to you . . . Would you like to come with me?"

"Yes I would," she looked as if she was receiving a breath of fresh air.

"Then we'll do that as soon as I ask for an appointment with them, in two or three days, okay?" She nodded. "Now listen, here is what we are going to do right now: You'll talk to Marie and explain to her that your sticking together is harming you right now. That she has to focus on her own life Beyond, and that you yourself have to focus fully on your life here. Explain everything to her and tell her she has to take some distance for a while and let you breathe . . . Will you do it today?"

She nodded again, this time with a hopeful expression, while she looked at me still a bit shyly but now straight in the eyes.

"So look, I'm going to leave you now. Do that and you'll see that your situation will greatly improve . . . And don't speak about it around here. I'll tell you when I've an appointment with your parents—the head psychologist will make it for me, and we'll go the two of us only. See you later then . . ."

Meanwhile, the very night I came back home after my first conversation with Emilie, I got into meditation and, once in a deep state, I summoned the spirit of Marie to come and talk with me. Indeed, I had the capacity, while Emilie was talking about her friend Marie, to perceive the psychological and mental imprint of her soul—her *semantic field* (or syg-field in short). And this allowed me, that night in meditation, to call and summon the spirit of Marie and keep her in my sights while talking to her.

For about half an hour, I conversed with her, being aware that she must have sensed and followed our exchange that afternoon, but nevertheless explaining what I had already said to Emilie and what Emilie would certainly have also told her. I was especially careful to let her know exactly the fate Emilie would have—locked in this cuckoo's nest for an indefinite time—if she, Marie, didn't let go of her relationship with her friend, at least for as long as she needed to be taken out of the hospital. At that time in my life (in my late twenties), I was not able to really "hear" a spirit talk back to me apart from a few words, but I could sense their presence precisely and sometimes even see them. Having hour-long dialogues with them was something I was to develop along the years, with sudden drastic leaps such as the conversation with the quantum physicist Wolfgang Pauli. And then I had to wait for more than three years for such a feat to occur again in my life, and when it did, it was a new leap and I could hold hour-long daily conversations with my group-Self (the core mind of a constellation or family of souls). In my late twenties, I could, however, assess the result of my talking to the deceased via the events that would follow—a much better personal proof, as it was, of the effectiveness of the technique! Yet, to be clear, in terms of scientific assessment, the result didn't prove in itself the reality of the spirits nor that an exchange had taken place. However, in that specific case, the combined effect of both conversations with Emilie and Marie (and certainly of Emilie's demand to her friend as well) turned out to be extremely positive, beyond my wildest dreams in fact, given that neither Emilie, nor I, had explained to anybody else what had happened and what we had decided between us that afternoon.

Indeed, the next day, when I arrived at the hospital for the afternoon shift, again I sat at the long tables with the head psychologist and two nurses. I had the surprise of my life when I was told:

"Look, Emilie's state had not budged since she was sent here two and a half months ago; but she improved dramatically after your session with her. So we decided that you are *her* dedicated psychologist and she is your patient—that's how we work here—and only you will deal with her. You alone will make all the decisions concerning her."

"Very fine," I responded, extremely astonished, "I'm glad she has improved so quickly and in such a way that you could remark it."

"Yes indeed."

Then I pushed my point that an appointment for me to discuss her case with her parents, in front of her, was essential. To which they agreed.

"Thanks a lot, I really think it's crucial for her full recovery and even more so for her future well-being."

Meanwhile, during the meals we shared together with all the patients at the long tables, I started to speak to most of them, introducing a much more direct and humoristic way to interact between the medical team and the patients. Also, during the afternoons, I started to organize artistic and fun activities for whoever was interested. What I was trying to launch was a true group interaction among the patients, a team spirit. Not so many showed up the first day but their numbers grew over the week.

Sometime later, encouraged by my results with Emilie and the positive backing I had received from the hospital staff, I went to knock at the door of another patient—a young man in his thirties. As I had done with Emilie, after he let me in his room and agreed to have a discussion, I casually closed the door behind me and we took our seats on the two chairs in his room.

He was a very learned, if convoluted and walled-up, man who expressed his problem as being mostly intellectual: he was torn between an atheist reasoning and hard-core Catholic beliefs. Being cognizant of both frameworks, their sets of assumptions and worldviews, I had no problem making my way into his intricate, labyrinthine, and split mental structure. It was going to be tough to make openings between the two encysted semantic constellations, but I was up for the challenge.

That day, we talked for nearly two hours about atheist philosophy, such as that of Jean-Paul Sartre, versus the Christian one. And then I went back to the large common space. There, I was called by the head of the ward and a nurse, both female, to sit with them at a long table. I was told, first, that I was not allowed to close the door of a male patient's room while being inside and, second, that it didn't behoove women in the medical staff to say *tu* to male patients.

I was flabbergasted.

How can they, in an age of social liberties, stick to such moral antics? I thought to myself. But I had the good sense to accept the rule, telling them that, on seeing things from the outside, I had failed to remark such gender restrictions. Yet, to be honest, I could have understood why a male psychiatrist wouldn't be allowed to stay behind a closed door in a young girl or woman's room. But the inverse situation was really farfetched. Moreover, as regards the staff's safety, we had absolutely no aggressive patient in the ward. I understood, then, that I wasn't going to be able to help this patient. On the one hand, if our iconoclast and rebel discussion, even in a free thinking and secular society such as the French one, could be heard by anybody in the place, I knew the patient wouldn't feel secure enough to talk openly and reveal his innermost thoughts. And that would apply to any male patient—the great majority of the patients here. On the other hand, if I was not allowed to initiate a deeply empathic relationship (and, for this to happen, the use of *tu* was essential), then I would fail to reach the core of a patient's psyche and to arouse confidence in me. No healing process of the kind I could provide could ever occur in these conditions.

At that point, I focused on group activities, on infusing a team spirit, and on restoring their interaction with the outside world. It was painfully evident to me that after months of seclusion, they had become more and more estranged from it. The head was giving me free rein on that, and so my idea was to make them mingle a bit with the summer crowd in Paris and lead them to behave as if they were normal citizens.

This is how, one weekday in the early afternoon, at a time where shops and streets are mostly empty, I took them to *Le Bon Marché,* a department store set not far from the tiny park—called *Le Vert Galant*—at the western tip of *Ile de la Cité,* the most central Parisian island on the Seine River.

In the meantime, I had gone with Emilie to visit her parents. From the outset I presented myself in a somewhat harsh and inquisitive stance, serious as befits a psychologist, and asked them some hard questions. Then I scolded them the way a schoolteacher would talk to their students, belittling them with my knowledge. I explained haughtily that Emilie was nowhere near being crazy or unbalanced and that they had themselves acted in a malevolent and harmful way toward her by agreeing to send her to the mental hospital. And I informed them that she would soon be out of the hospital, but would live, from now on, in her own flat, because the whole psychiatric team had judged that they (the parents) could only have a very negative and constraining influence on her. She needed to breathe freely, to be out of this unwelcoming and unsupportive family. And for the *coup de grâce,* I warned them, with the sternest look I could assume, that if they ever tried again to call on a psychiatrist to take care of Emilie—especially the one who had demanded the hospitalization—they would be hearing from me. At that point, the two mean parents, in their dirty gray and malevolent auras, bent their heads as if they had been reproached by a priest. And I left with Emilie who had not said a word but had seen her parents being put in their place, their authority over her pulled out from under their feet.

It felt good when we walked through Paris in the sunny afternoon and then took the bus back to the hospital. Emilie was basking in a newfound freedom. A dire weight had been lifted from her.

The last leg of the healing process with Emilie was when she tried to prove to me that she was indeed mentally unbalanced and ill. As I understood it, this was how she acted upon the numerous projections of "fool and psychotic" placed on her by the first psychiatrist, and then by the mental hospital staff and their basic assumption of sane psychologists versus mentally ill patients.

That confrontation happened on the day I took a group of seven patients to Le Bon Marché. This traditional department store was indeed the first one to have been built in 1838 in Paris. Émile Zola made it the theme of one of his novels, *The Ladies' Paradise,* a critique of the early consumerist trend and an analysis of the working class, mostly women, in such stores. Zola was the famed author of "J'accuse," the thundering pamphlet he wrote to oppose the unjust and unfounded condemnation of a Jew in the *Affaire Dreyfus* that shook and tore the French society from 1894 to 1906 until the real culprit of the leaking of military secrets to the German Embassy in Paris was unmasked. Zola's role was crucial in the reopening of the case that turned the tables and ended with the officer Dreyfus being cleared of all suspicion and reinstated in the army.

The interesting thing about this department store, and why I chose it in the first place, apart from its opening on the Seine River and its (finally, maybe due to Zola's critique) lenient and good-boy attitude, was that it had a large bookstore section on the ground floor, as well as a huge do-it-yourself and artwork section displaying any tool and material needed to make paintings, drawings, clay molding, macramé, knitting, ceramics, and the like. And it was a sheer delight to walk amidst colors and paints of all types and size. Curiosity and creativity could be aroused and, on top of that, my protégés could buy whatever they felt like.

I was intending to leave them full freedom to wander by themselves, while setting a protective boundary to help them stay grounded and safe. So that, first we came by the great entrance on Rue de Sèvres, and once inside, I pointed out the engraved name of the gate, the section we were in, and where to regroup later. Then I set the appointment to one hour later precisely. I was thus treating them like adult citizens, yet within a clear boundary. And we parted.

I went myself to the books section, picked an art book and dove into it. When I came back for our appointment in front of the main entrance, everybody was already there, forming a group talking in a hushed fashion among themselves, except for Emilie. It was nice to see them at last as a group and not as a collection of too reserved and shy individuals.

I approached them with a large smile and asked them if they had seen interesting things around. Then I pretended to look around and threw entertainingly:

"So are we all here? . . . Oops . . . apart from Emilie. She'll come!"

And I kept the conversation going nicely. No rush, no anxiety, everything is perfectly normal. Let's put out some jokes and appear really cool and easygoing.

After a good ten minutes, here was Emilie coming, crossing the large space toward us, shyly and with a worried look.

"*Alors?* So what?" I said half-jokingly, half-scolding her. "You couldn't check your time right?"

She looked at me, her face pink and eyes feverish:

"I told you I was mentally ill!"

So, this is it! I thought quickly to myself. *She is trying to prove to me, by any means, that she is what her parents, and then the psychiatrist and psychologists said she was—a crazy girl needing to be in a home! Sticking to their projections that she has interiorized. Checking how I'm going to react.*

"Look," I said, not even answering her, but taking the schoolteacher stance instead, "if you ever do that to me a second time, I won't take you on our trips out anymore! Got it?"

And now she moves into another frame of reference: she's expected to behave responsibly, like all kids; she's treated like all the other adolescents, like normal girls and boys. And if she is treated normally, she'll now behave normally.

And indeed it worked wonders. She never again thought of herself as mentally ill, nor tried again to persuade me of it. She had gotten rid of the interiorized projections and she now could relate to herself as a whole *I,* an *I* who had to behave and get smarter if she wanted to get free and run her life the way she wished.

Then we walked a bit toward and along the Seine and I took them to a café with a terrace overlooking the quay. We brought two tables together and sat all around (acting as if everybody is behaving normally, as if everything goes smoothly). When the waiter arrived to take our orders, I felt a wave of panic spreading among them, and they all froze, looking dismayed.

How long since they have been immersed in a casual social situation such as this one?

The panic was voiced aloud by a very shy boy in his early twenties.

"Wait!" he burst out; and, looking at me with pleading eyes, "What am I supposed to drink?"

"Whatever you want!" I answered as insouciantly as I could. "Whatever you like!"

And when some of them started to order lemon soda or Coca Cola, then he remembered what he liked.

We started to talk and joke about our trip to the Bon Marché. Yet, they just couldn't relax and take it easy. The authoritarian persona of the psychiatrist had been deeply internalized—now their superego— and I could sense they kept asking themselves: *"How should I behave?"*

I then understood the extent to which I had been right, how much they needed to be plunged back into casual social situations outside of the ward. And, even more crucial, they all needed to be addressed as adults and as individuals responsible for themselves.

Sometime in the third week of my work at the mental hospital, the news filled the ward that they were busy looking for a flat to rent for Emilie. I couldn't contain my joy! As soon as they could find the perfect place with a decent rent, Emilie was to be accompanied and helped with moving her stuff from her parents' home. That meant that, without telling me this, they had broken a deal with her parents to the effect that they allowed their daughter—despite still being a minor—to live by herself. This was fantastic! They had followed my lead all along in deeming the parents responsible of an abuse of authority; and, moreover, of having such a nefarious influence on their daughter that she had to be kept away from them.

I knew the hospital staff would make an array of welfare aids available to her, such as funding part of the rent and a monthly subsidy. She was going to be free and yet supported from all sides. Any help she needed, she just had to go visit the ward and she would get it. I was overjoyed! The healing process had taken less than three weeks. When I saw her, she was beaming!

Shortly after, by a meaningful twist of destiny, the hospital's administrative center found some problem with my status of psychologist there, and I was discharged of my job. I couldn't care less. Especially since they had barred me from helping any other patient make a decisive recovery. By now I was convinced I had gotten the job just in order to get Emilie out of her predicament and free her from her parents' malevolent clutches. I had done it, and there was nothing more for me to achieve, let alone to learn, in that place.

I said goodbye to everybody with a light heart.

SHAMANS AND THE INTERCESSION WITH SPIRITS

In the above instance, materialists would argue that Emilie's breathtaking healing could be explained solely by the change I prompted in her mindset. This is of course an undeniable factor in her recovery that I intentionally set up to work. But it was not the only one by far, nor the decisive one. The two-pronged demand on her friend's spirit to let go of the stifling bonding and continuous presence—made by Emilie and by me the first night—was, in my view, the crucial factor at play.

In all ancient shamanic and animist cultures, the shaman or healer used to communicate with spirits in order to ask, pray, or command them to effect a cure. Although this action in the spirit world was often made conjointly with the use of medicinal plants and effective suggestions and magic via rituals, the shamans claimed it was the core of the healing process (see plate 7).

In contrast with my spur-of-the-moment method—asking Emilie to make a new deal with her deceased friend—the interceding with spirits was done solely by the healer/shaman, supposed to be the only person able to interact with spirits and see them in the first place. But Emilie was seeing her friend and interacting with her continually; on purely psychological terms, she had to create for herself a new relationship with the departed friend, and demand from her friend that she do the same.

Of course these ancient rituals of intercession exist in all religions, in the form of benedictions of houses and objects, and in Christianity with the use of holy water and rituals of exorcism. For example, in cases of haunting or poltergeist—in which a lot of psychokinesis (PK) happens, such as displacement and levitation of objects, a priest is often called by the family to make a benediction or an exorcism, with mixed results.

ARE THE SPIRITS ABLE TO MOVE OBJECTS?

Psychokinetic events of the large-scale type are mostly studied in poltergeist and haunting cases. Moreover, these cases are centered on a specific place, where they happen regularly over a period of months, thus making their study extremely precise, allowing one to draw statistics.

Let's see first an outlandish case, that of Sisir Kumar from Bengal, in which the haunting entity, creating havoc in the house, was revealed by the deceased father—appearing repeatedly in the role of a protective spirit—to be the desperate wife of Sisir in his previous incarnation. This case was studied by Dr. Ian Stevenson who interviewed the witnesses in the Bengal home and reported it in his 1972 article "Are Poltergeists Living or Are They Dead?" Sisir was the son of an engineer and was sixteen when the events started.

> Kumar and his young friends were chatting and playing games in a room. They heard a sound as of falling objects in an adjoining room. Rushing in there, they found brickbats lying in the room. . . . Bottles inside rooms flew out. Once a pewter vessel which had been on a table in the house flew out into the compound. . . . Police were stationed around the house to catch a possible mischief-monger, but no one was found and brickbats came flying into the house even when the policemen were on duty around it. . . .
>
> Some herb roots . . . appeared in Sisir's hand one night and . . . he received a communication from his deceased father instructing him to attach the roots to his arm with a copper band to save him from the evil designs of a female spirit. The family . . . attached the roots to Sisir's arm with only a thread or tape. Shortly afterwards . . . the tape was mysteriously cut. . . . Some others present heard a female voice say: "I have taken it away. How now?" . . . Sisir . . . stretched his arm under a bedstead and recovered the roots which were there. He said his father . . . guided him to find them under the bed. A smith was then called in, and he riveted an iron band (with the roots attached) to Sisir's arm. The metal band was 5–6 mm. in diameter. . . . Soon after this was done, witnesses sitting around to encourage Sisir heard a sound as of metal being cut through and the iron band fell off his arm. It was found to have been cleanly cut as if by some instrument. . . .
>
> Sisir then heard his father saying that he had advised using a copper band and the smith, called again, attached the roots this time with a copper band around his arm. This band remained undisturbed. (23738)

The havoc lasted two months and Sisir's health had deteriorated.

The deceased father advised that Sisir be taken to a Kali temple and a ritual be made. The poltergeist ceased totally after this ritual.

Several individuals had seen apparitions of a woman in a red-trimmed sari; and this figure appeared on several occasions to Sisir, very clearly so; she used to talk and complained that, when she was his wife in a past life, he abandoned her, and she killed herself. From that moment on, she said, I search for you and now I'm going to take you with me. She gave him the address where they had lived in Benares, some twenty years prior. Stevenson did an inquiry, but new owners were there.

Poltergeists: Research Data

William Roll, in his 1974 article, did an analysis of 116 cases of poltergeist, haunting, and apparitions dating from the seventeenth century to 1974, and sorted out seven characteristics: (1) they are focalized on one person; (2) yet with a spatial focus; (3) the movements of objects are sometimes purposeful with unusual trajectories; (4) objects may pass through walls or matter, without damaging them; (5) many cases show some means of meaningful communication (apparitions, voices, knocks); (6) exorcisms and rituals seem ineffective; (7) generally, perturbations cease when the central person or family leave the place.

Roll found that in 79 percent of cases (92 out of 116) one or two persons were directly connected to the poltergeist, this percentage reaching 85 percent in the 1950–1974 period. And when the agent would travel, the phenomena would move with them 42 percent of the time. Only in two cases did the perturbations start after the death of a loved one, and only in eight cases after the family moved into a haunted house or after a spiritualist séance. Lastly, 53 percent of agents had had medical or neurotic problems (epilepsy, hysteria). Roll in his 1978 article thus states that numerous cases suggest that poltergeists could be triggered by tense interpersonal relationships. The typical agent was around thirteen years old, at the period of puberty, and implied a boy or girl separated from their parents and/or with grave and stressful family life.

Teleportation, Apparitions, and Attacks

According to Roll, among 105 cases showing repeated movement of objects, 18 (17 percent) presented some teleportation—that is, objects passing through walls or ceilings. In the Nickhleim case studied by Hans Bender (with a thirteen-year-old agent), stones were hurled at the house from the outside, then would penetrate inside totally closed rooms, and would later disappear as mysteriously; objects inside the house were flying around, sometimes turning around corners. When a priest came to bless the house, with all windows of the room being closed, a stone fell from the ceiling very slowly and landed softly on a plank without rebounding. On touching it, the priest found it hot. Now, in the famously studied Rosenheim case that happened in the attorney Adam's office, the latter made some experiments, and placed bottles containing perfume and medicines on the kitchen table, then asked everybody, including himself, to go outside. After a short while, first the perfume bottle, then the medicine bottle appeared in midair and fell in a zigzag fashion to the ground (Roll 1978; Bender 1969).

As for apparitions, they happened in 46 cases out of the 116. Roll lists 27 cases with human or animal figures, hands, fingers, devils, formless shapes; 13 cases with intelligible voices (with or without apparitions); 8 cases with sound effects; 5 cases during which one or several persons were either hurt or struck, or stigmata appeared on their bodies (he notes that the agents themselves would often be the victims); in 5 cases, fires broke out. Finally, among the 27 cases of apparitions, 17 times these were observed by several witnesses at the same time, and in 8 instances, by a group of people. Roll also notes that if objects are often thrown with rare violence at specific targeted persons, they rarely hurt them; in fact, they often change direction at the last moment.

Most researchers who studied poltergeists on site leaned toward explaining them in terms of a real capacity of the mind to influence matter, that is, psychokinesis (PK); and they fathomed some sort of psi energy; whereas those who studied micro-PK (computerized experiments showing mental effects on a random number generator) leaned toward a psychological explanation, or a receptive psi one (clairvoyance, telepathy, precognition).

To explain these poltergeist cases, Roll proposed the concept of *rotative fields*. He first analyzed the distance of PK events to the agent, and didn't find that it followed the electromagnetic law of a decrease of strength as an inverse function of the distance. But he found a decrease of strength similar to that of a wave penetrating a substance (as in a sunray penetrating water). Next, with colleagues, he discovered that movements tend to show a rotative motion (clockwise or anticlockwise) and thus proposed they were caused by rotative fields. However, to better fit the observations, the rotative field was to be generated by two sources out of sync. In an interesting 1975 paper, "A Wave Theory of Psi Energy," W. Joines (a co-author of the theory of rotative fields) remarked that we can expect that if the psi energy were a totally different type of energy, that it would nevertheless present a wave behavior, and thus follow the laws of wave theory. That concept fits well with the syg-energy as forming and filling the hyperdimension.

6

MY HOUSE GENIE

I was nineteen and had undergone—in the past year that took me from the diploma at the end of high school to my first year at the Sorbonne university in Paris—a sudden and rapid spiritual awakening. It all started when I decided to settle in the country house of my parents in Igny, on a tall forested hill that stood at the edge of Verrières-le-Buisson forest, south of Paris, and just at the boundary of Igny village. I was so eager to stay at Igny (as we called the house) that, before I could legally own a driving license, I was hitchhiking back and forth to this place when my father couldn't drive me.

Strangely, the piece of land in the forest had originally been bought by an author of Catholic saints' biographies, Gabriel Ledos, around the oak tree where he used to meditate in the forest. Then Ledos had a house built according to specific esoteric plans, as was apparent in many features. For one, the house of traditional Meulières stones of the Bièvres valley, was surrounded to the north and the east (where the forest extended) by a half circle of five oak trees, with the meditation antenna one overlooking a lawn at the main entrance.

Indeed, there was much more to this man than the devoted Catholic revering the faith of outstanding persons such as Lacordaire and Saint Gertrude, and possibly reveling in the kind of anomalous phenomena and blissful miracles that sprinkle the lives of holy men and women, some duly ascertained by numerous witnesses, as in the case of Francis of Assisi.*

First, here was a man who had made of this place his creative den and writing house where he would retire all by himself, regularly leaving the Parisian ebullient social life and his wife and children, in order to focus on his work. Second, even before buying the land, he had come to the forest by himself, climbing the high hill to find a perfect oak tree under which to sit and meditate, and probably to write—something I was going to do myself with another oak tree farther up in the forest some forty years later. That was noticeably more like an Eastern meditation practice than some sort of Christian prayer or philosophical meditation. Third, as my father heard it from his widow and saw the sign when he purchased the property from her (after his death in 1939 and before WW2), Ledos had called the house Montjoie—which was no less than the rallying cry of the Knights Templar, and whose esoteric meaning, as I was to be told by an alchemist, is "the Mount of Jupiter." *Mont* in French being a mount, and *Jovis* in Latin meaning "of Jupiter," which would show an evolution toward the French *joie* (or joy). Thus both a Mount of Jupiter and the Mount of Joy. (As I was to find out while checking the internet for this book, Ledos was a deputy librarian at the Bibliothèque Nationale, Paris' national library, as well as an expert in the writings of the Greek philosopher Plato, highly regarded by ancient secret societies.)

Could this Templar knighthood have been definitely anchored in a much deeper Celtic soil, in order to revere sacred mounts and trees? Indeed, as goes the mystic transmission from the Celts priesthood—the Druids—to the Roman religion, and then to the Christian era, the precise locus chosen to establish sacred sites always persists through time, the religion of a given age constructing its own temples over the foundations and ruins of the ancient ones. As I have unraveled in my book on the megaliths' grid—*The Sacred Network*—megaliths and ruins

---

*Ledos wrote *Lacordaire* in 1902 and *Sainte Gertrude* in 1901.

of Gallo-Roman or Egyptian temples exist under several Christian churches. Thus, according to trustworthy notary reports, there exists a megalithic astronomical temple underneath Chartres Cathedral, consisting of an arc of twelve menhirs or standing stones, with runes carved on them. In Paris, *Notre-Dame de Paris Cathedral* is erected above the ancient foundations of a temple to the Roman goddess Diana and *Saint-Sulpice Church* above a temple to Isis (the church was the seat of the Priory of Sion, a secret order that founded the Templar Order). As Jean Markale, one of the most knowledgeable French experts on esoteric knowledge and sacred sites, writes in his book *Cathedral of the Black Madonna,* "the Christian sanctuary *Mont-Saint-Michel* stands at the location of an old Mithras temple, itself situated where a Gaul sanctuary dedicated to the shining god *Bélénos* was" (154–55). This shows, says he, that St. Michael has this same "shining light" attributed to Belenos (in my opinion, they are the same transdimensional entity). Mont-Saint-Michel (St. Michael's Mount) is one of the most sacred sites of France and stands on the boundary of Brittany and Normandy (see plate 8).

Then Gwen Le Scouëzec, another eminent expert on Celt sacred sites and Druid religion underlines that there were megaliths at the tip of Mont-Saint-Michel, and he shows that this high site had been dedicated in the pre-Celtic times to the Megalithic god of light Gargan, then to the Celtic god of light Bélénos, and then to the Christian Saint Michael (St. Michel). This Sacred Network transmission is even more mysterious since, according to Le Scouëzec and Court-Payen, the sacred mount sits on the Saint-Michel line—a sacred line featuring many high sites of the Druids and eight sites dedicated to St. Michael, all of them on hilltops open to all directions. It crosses all of Brittany from Mont-Saint-Michel to Quimper Cathedral (about 130 miles), and then extends far beyond France (see fig. 6.1). Eastward, it is aligned with the rising sun on May 1 (the Celtic feast of Beltane), and to the west, with the setting sun on November 1 (the Celtic feast of Samhain, at the end of summer).

Furthermore, the Celt-period Mont-Saint-Michel high site presents very ancient sculptures, predating the Saint Michael cult, which show a

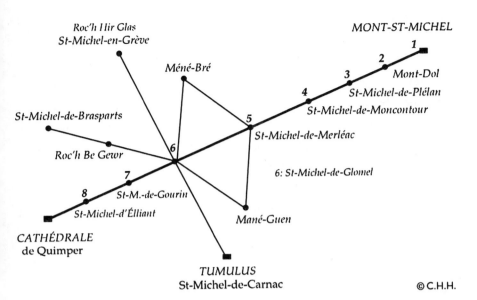

Fig. 6.1. The St-Michel sacred line in Brittany, by Gwen Le Scouëzec.
Courtesy of Gwen Le Scouëzec and Le Corps à Vivre Association.
Digital artwork by Chris H. Hardy (from Hardy, The Sacred Network, p. 145)

warrior riding or overcoming a dragon without slaying it. As we know, Saint Michael overpowering the dragon (or the devil) is a widespread Christian symbolism, as we see, for example, on the magnificent Saint-Michel Fountain in front of the Seine River in Paris (see plate 9).

To get back to the house in Igny (whose root is *ignis,* "fire" in Latin), the property was set high on the hill, on a gentle slope above a steep incline, and surrounded a large half circle of five venerable oak trees—obviously a nemeton, the Druidic sanctuary in a clearing within a grove of trees, where the Druids held their spiritual rituals. Ledos, who sliced the piece of land from the forest, was indeed the first modern "dweller on the mount." The group of houses is called *Le Vaupereux.* This is a linguistic evolution from *Val Preux*—a term meaning the "Courageous Knights' Valley"—given that the plural of *val* is *vaux;* this is corroborated by Valpreux being the name of the castle residing at the hill's base. Moreover, the dirt road climbing the hill to the house is *Allée du*

Bel-Air, a name that would just evoke a "beautiful-air alley" if it was not for the above mentioned Belen, Bel, or Belenos, the Celtic god of light, the Shining One. Interestingly, I was stunned when I stumbled yesterday on this very name "Bel-Air" in my just delivered Jean Markale book on *The Druids,* while I'm making the last-ditch work before submitting my manuscript in a couple of days—with the helpful hand of the angel of libraries no doubt! (especially since, pressed for time, I allowed myself only the reading of a few pages on Belenos). And Markale does state that the "Mountain of Bel-Air" (Côtes du Nord, France) is an ancient site of worship to Belenos, and Tombelaine (the older name of Mont-Saint-Michel) or "Tum-Belen, is none other than the Mound of Belenos" (70–75).

But then, what could be the "Air" referred to in Bel-Air? Here is a possibility—the goddess Airmed. Belenos (Bel, Belenus), "the Shining One," is the most ancient and widely worshiped Gaul and Celtic deity. His feast being Beltane "the Fires of Bel," on May 1, he is the god of youth, beauty, and renewal (spring), and has been associated with Apollo. As Belenos-Grannos—a god of medicine, health, and curing waters—he has the same healing powers (and knowledge of curative plants) as the Irish Diancecht, the god of medicine and healing magic of the ancestor gods of the great north (Hyperborea), the Tuatha Dé Danann. Only Diancecht, and his daughter Airmed working with him, had both such knowledge as to be capable of reviving the dead warriors in a Fountain of Health that Airmed had filled with medicinal herbs (in the Battle of Mag Tured).

Thus we see Airmed, the healing ancestor-goddess, as a daughter of Belenos-Diancecht, and essential in working with him, and thus, a Bel-Air place of worship and healing would be quite appropriate! Belenos is often depicted in Gaul with a mysterious goddess called Belisama: Could she be his daughter and Belenos be the Celt or Gaul name of the ancestor Diancecht?

But there is more: Belenos was thought to ride the sun across the sky in a horse-drawn chariot, and his emblem is the wheel. Now, Bel is definitely known in ancient Sumer (Mesopotamia), as in Babylonian and Akkadian languages Bel is an ancient title meaning Lord or God, and it became the sole epithet of Bel-Marduk (when he became the Lord of the Gods). Marduk is the god Ra in Egypt, and Ra, as the sun god, indeed crosses the sky above earth during daytime, and the immortal realm at night, giving regeneration and life to the dead. We thus have a link between Ra and Airmed, reviving the dead.

As I was to experience it in meditation, this hill in Igny was a beautifully tuned antenna of the Earth, with a clear earth-sky axis, that, with certainty, had been used as a sacred hill by the Celts. And soon I was going to have my own oak tree higher up the hill in the forest, under which I would sit to immerge myself in the living and conscious tissue of nature to write poetry.

To digress a bit further into this line of thought—this is of paramount importance to get a glimpse at the kind of immaterial spirit who dwelt in this specific house—my atheist yet sensitive father changed its name and called the house *Le Bouzou,* an odd phoneme in French meaning "the kid" in his ancestors' Indre region dialect. However, given the underlying currents running in our collective unconscious, and flooding our creativity and archetypal dreams, it's no wonder that *Buzur,* in Sumerian, means "The Initiate" and is one title of the god Enki as "The Knower of Secrets."

Thus we see in Igny multiple references to the Celts and the older Hyperborean ancestors, marking a sacred mount. The Celtic nemeton within the half circle of oak trees; Igny (fire) and *Belenos* as a god of light feasted with fires. *Belenos-Diancecht* and *Airmed* and sacred healing; Bel-Marduk as a sun god and his father Enki as Buzur-*Bouzou.* And the more recent names *Valpreux* and *Montjoie* signifying the valley of the Knights Templars.

Another symbolic link with Igny-Buzur is between Enki, Shiva, and meditation to gain knowledge. Enki's initiatic title was "The Serpent" while his emblem and blazon were the blueprint of Hermes's caduceus, Hermes/Ningishzidda being his son. Enki is the root of the symbol of

Fig. 6.2. The Nagaraja protector of the Buddha, Mucalinda, sheltering Gautama Buddha. Statue at the Pagoda Wat Phra That Doi Suthep in Chiang Mai, Thailand.
Photo by Takeaway, CC BY-SA 3.0

the Serpent as supreme initiatic knowledge, and thus the emblem of great yogis and initiates—such as the Hindu god Shiva (the ascetic and meditative knower) and Kali the Great Goddess with magical powers; likewise, the Great Minoan Goddess (in Crete) is holding snakes in her two hands. The Naga king (Nagaraja) called *Vasuki,* and the Naga queen *Naga Yakshi,* knowers of tantra and yoga, are both initiating and protecting the Hindu gods and the Buddhas, and the sacred sites in the Khmer, Buddhist, and Hindu civilizations* (see fig. 6.2 and plate 10). Vasuki was also the divine serpent used as a rope around the pillar of creation (Mount Mandara) on which Vishnu sat, in the churning of the

---

*See the archetype of the Serpent in my book on the Sumerian tablets, *DNA of the Gods.*

ocean of milk. The king of Nagas, Vasuki is a yogic ally of Shiva, and stays always around his neck. At Thiruvananthapuram in South India, is a temple of Serpent Wisdom, Thuppanathu Kavu, where Vasuki and his wife the Naga queen Yakshi are honored.

I started to write poetry when I was sixteen, and Igny (where I would accompany my father to water the garden or pluck fruits) was like a magnet, attracting me more and more until I longed to spend any short school holidays there alone, to walk in the forest and write. I would then evoke the pretext of having to study for some exams, and be driven there by my understanding and compliant father . . . until I settled there. Of course my father knew well that I was writing poetry, because at sixteen I was part of a small club of poets in Montmartre, and he (who, as a hobby, was a painter and had been a violinist) would have done anything to encourage this talent and vocation in me, including leaving me blissfully alone in Igny.

And it was precisely when I began spending days and nights there alone that I engaged in meditating. With my eyes closed, I tried the basic yoga position I had seen in a simplistic book, and immediately experienced high states of consciousness, which were simply the extension of the kind of immersion in a poetic stance, empathic with nature, in which I dove so easily.

Simultaneously, I plunged into the Upanishads, the core of the Advaita Vedanta (or philosophy of nonduality) . . . And I was swept into tremendous changes that happened very suddenly: starting with the first lines of the first Upanishad I read, it was like opening a gate in my memory; I exclaimed to myself: *But of course, this is the profound reality—the oneness and the web of interconnection underlying all material reality! I knew it all along! Something deep in me knows it already! This text seems so familiar, as if re-evoking a whole spiritual landscape, a lifetime!*

And now, as soon as I took the classic cross-legged posture in lotus, I found myself immersed in this Oneness field. Then the learning process was easy: I just had to meditate and wait until the opening of a new level of the state. My Self was teaching me; the Oneness field was guiding me. And the process finally blossomed when—after my bachelor's degree three years later—I reached first Iran where I stayed with my Sufi master, then India.

Of course, anybody with a background from an ancient Eastern religion culture—Hinduism, Buddhism, Taoism, Jainism, Baha'ism, and the like—would readily understand my experience as the reopening of a knowledge and a state of consciousness I had attained in the far past, a memory springing forth from one or more past incarnations. (And indeed I came to later remember several incarnations in Eastern cultures, one as a learned yogi in India, and one as the head of a Khmer temple in the Angkor Vat complex.)

For me, the trigger to the opening of the memory gate had been twofold: first, the text of the Upanishad (and its syg-field) driving my mind back to accessing the deep reality; and second, the lotus yoga posture taking me back into the specific consciousness-energy field—the specific syg-energy frequencies and aura—that could best nurture states of Oneness or samadhis.

Being alone, writing and meditating... wasn't it exactly what Ledos had been doing in this very house? In fact, it was as if the house itself had a memory of what Ledos had experienced there. Sometimes, I had the clear feeling that the house itself was teaching me. And in any case, it was the perfect node or niche in which my own spiritual aptitude could blossom. The house was an ally. But I soon discovered there was more to it, beyond the spiritual imprints of syg-energy that were pervading the air (the prana), the land, and the walls of the house.

And what was more than this specific syg-energy that Ledos had left in his writer and sage's house, was indeed his own presence as a familiar benevolent and guardian spirit. Indeed, specific events revealed to me the presence in this house of a guardian spirit, a house *genie,* who acted intelligently as an immaterial protector spirit for my own sake and that of the house.

But before I get into this, let me explain why I never reacted to anomalies and dire events with fear, something that has its root in my inner path; also, my lifestyle at the time will show the context of these interactions.

As I mentioned it, my spiritual path was nurtured by a great deal of reading, mostly focused on the main spiritual and mystical treatises of the world's religions. Given my propensity for poetry, stemming from states of fusion with nature, the high states of consciousness I experienced—after a period of attunement to my deep Self—were states of oneness, and all of them very blissful. When visions occurred, they were from a peaceful and wise quality, some of them from heavenly places—astonishing, because they were quite at odds with religious clichés of paradises. Furthermore, I was guided by my own Self, and have been all my life, and this inner guidance has given me an unshakable trust in the process of learning and discovering a new level of reality, because, no matter what, I felt totally protected. And that fed my self-confidence and impeded any fear from arising. Whether hitchhiking in Germany or France at sixteen, or across the Sahara Desert and two rain forests in Africa at twenty-one, without money or even shoes, or whether sensing strange spirits or beings in sacred Celtic places, or even when confronted with the most dangerous situations alone on the road, I've always been devoid of fear. If a situation was putting my life at risk, or if it could create great trouble for me, my instant reaction was to merge with my higher Self who would then dispel the immediate danger and turn the situation upside down in a matter of seconds. At the time, the shift to a higher consciousness level seemed to happen in a split instant, and I must add, it could happen precisely because I was devoid of fear and in sync with my Self. (However, to be true to myself, I must confess that, while it remained the case for a whole cycle in my twenties, especially when wandering alone without money across Asia and Africa, in later cycles of professional activity and married life, interferences to this process occurred, yet never in life-threatening situations.)

The awakening to a new level of reality happened very suddenly when I started meditating. I was now perceiving the etheric layer of

Earth, as it is called in theosophy. I could see not only the deceased but the auras of people, of sacred objects, the energy fields of monuments or places—what I call now the syg-fields and the syg-dimension of reality. And of course, many a time an experience would come with its own solid proof, even if the proof was delayed in time, as we'll see in the occurrence of the household spirit in Igny. Because of these solid cases, I came to trust my perception of the semantic dimension. Whether perceiving nature spirits in sacred springs (such as in Thailand) or in the sacred fire of a sweat lodge (in New Jersey), or else communicating with the consciousness of sacred trees in India and Africa, hiking to the top and talking with the Great Spirit of the Tamalpais Mountain (the Sleeping Lady) in the Bay area (sacred to the Native Americans), any novel encounter and any totally unexpected event was a learning experience. Says the "mountain runner" Peter Holleran in his web article "Mt. Tamalpais the Sacred Mountain": "Tam was so sacred to the Miwok that they would not climb to the summit, [because] Coyote, their name for the God who created man, resided at its peak. . . . Many of the plains Indians, such as the Lakota Sioux, are said to have made the long journey west carrying their tribal leaders on litters for burial on the slopes of Mt. Tam. Difficult-to-find burial mounds still exist." He recounts a Native American legend saying that Mt. Tam is the sacred right eye of the Great Turtle forming the North American continent.*

For me, it could also take the form of sensing malevolent spirits in specific spots, or wild nature spirits that wanted me out of *their* place— such as at a cairn at night in Scotland. Add to that a lively stream of inner experiences in meditation, dreams, visions, and OBEs that may have taken different forms but hasn't stopped to this day. A part of my mind was always keenly focused on memorizing each detail with accuracy for later analysis, while the greatest part of my mind was immersed in fully experiencing the anomaly or the weird event.

---

*Article available on Peter Holleran's website, mountainrunnerdoc.com, under the Adventures tab.

This digression was to explain that anomalous phenomena were and are still part of my daily life, maybe because I always had an open-ended capacity to meet the unexpected, the "impossible," and the anomalous—what is called in psychology cognitive dissonance. It's not that I readily understand anomalies on the spot (even if I often do), but rather that I commit their strangeness to memory and wait for other similar occurrences in order to come up with a working hypothesis. Thus, it's more an ongoing process of welcoming the unknown and the anomalous, and pondering them at length. Where the great majority of people could and would certainly freak out, I'm observing and experiencing any eerie and supernatural event with interest and a dose of humor.

This is how I reacted to the weirdest and most astonishing manifestation of Igny's house genie—whom I quickly recognized as being no less than the sole previous owner and resident of this house, the one who had built it as a writing cove, Ledos himself.

A year before I left for my first eighteen months of travel to India, I had reorganized the second floor with its two rooms and large landing as my living quarters—one room for sleeping, writing, and meditating, the other as a reading corner that also featured another bed for friends (all at ground level with carpets, Eastern style). This top floor under the roof was my inner sacred place, where only soul brothers and sisters were welcome. The house being so large and furnished with beds on the first floor, a larger network of friends could be accommodated during the occasional gatherings I was organizing. For about fifteen years, this house was the anchor of my soul and of my writing oeuvre. I would come back to it after long travels or, at one point, after my three-year relationship in Paris with Pat, with whom I went to Mali and Ivory Coast.

Now for my first full-fledged encounter with Igny's house genie . . .

One night during the year before my first travel to India, I was, as usual, alone in the house; I climbed up the staircase after dinner to go back to my workroom. This was a funny double-spiral wooden staircase: large, angular, and turning counterclockwise up to the first floor landing, then a narrow spiral moving clockwise up to the top floor. I was climbing the first volley of about fifteen steps in the deserted and deeply silent stone house when, hardly at the fifth step I became aware of a tall presence following me, whose regular pounding on the wooden and creaking steps was in rhythm with mine but slightly retarded, just one step below me. Moreover, I sensed a regular breathing on the back of my neck, a bit to the right (nearer to the wall). Astonished and curious, I kept climbing up with the same pace, my attention now wholly focused on the two distinct phenomena—the sound of somebody climbing just behind me, and that person's regular breathing on my neck. As I honed my senses, I sharpened and confirmed my first impression: climbing behind me was a perfectly clear and precise manifestation, though invisible and quasi-immaterial, of a human being, yet one who was breathing and making the wood creak. I recognized the invisible host—the good genie of the house that I had often sensed evasively—and kept going to my sacred space. After reaching the first landing, the sensation and perception stopped. I was extremely puzzled, yet amused, by this manifestation that had a clear-cut, even if light, effect on matter reality. How was that possible? How could the spirit of a deceased person have energy and physical components? Were not they supposed to be perfectly immaterial—as we imagine souls to be? (We will see the excellent research of Claude Lecouteux on this point, at the end of the chapter.)

As a reflex when confronted with straightforward anomalies, my mind had registered the whole unfolding event and my sensations in such precise and subtle detail that, to this day, I can re-evoke and replay the exact sensation on my neck.

OUT-OF-BODY EXPERIENCES AND LUCID DREAMS

During the same period, in Igny, I received the visit from an immaterial being from a higher dimension who had sat next to my bed to converse with me, or rather, I should say, with my hyperdimensional Self. As I will recount in detail in chapter 10, this being had an immaterial human appearance, yet he also displayed very tangible energy effects. Not only did he make the wooden floor softly creak while crossing the room, but when he passed right through the closed door while exiting, its wood emitted strange creaks and screeches.

In contrast, the (live) friends and persons who came to visit me during their astral travels or OBEs, didn't produce any sound or weight effect on the furnishings. They usually appeared in the daytime in my living space and could sit around me on the cushions. My level of perception, at that time in my twenties, was to sense precisely the mindset and emotions of the person (and generally to recognize known friends), their energy field, and where it was located exactly (posture, height, movement, or stillness); the exchange of thoughts was still very basic on my side.

The Etheric Body Makes an Advanced Visit (a Vardoger)

In one instance, while I was driving in Paris toward l'Etoile and caught in a traffic jam on Champs Elysées, the etheric body of someone flew right in my car, through the door, and in the same sweeping movement sat cozily on the passenger seat. I was flabbergasted and began to laugh, while trying to sense better the tall presence next to me that felt familiar, and to perceive it more keenly using the (pyramidal) side cells of my eyes, much more tuned to the etheric dimension; I was still doing that while driving at the slow and intermittent pace of the traffic, when, a good fifteen minutes later, I caught sight of my old friend and spiritual brother Christian, at the same moment he spotted me as well, with a look of surprise on his face reflecting the one I must have had myself. Then of course, he came forward to get in my car, as being such great friends, we were all too happy to share a moment and a ride together. Yet, when I saw him with his hand on the door knob, then opening the door, I had a moment of confusion, a mix of alarm and mad laughter, thinking: *Wait! Is he really going to sit on top of the etheric someone next to me? What's going to happen?* And he got in and sat of course very naturally, and the etheric body was just gone it seemed.

Christian had been my boyfriend a year before I went to India and it was together that we discovered an Orthodox-Druidic monastery in Brittany; he had, from then on, lived with the community there, for a few years already, and his short visits in Paris were very rare. It took me a while to understand that the etheric body had been his own, and that he had just fused back with it when he sat in my car.

Indeed, this case belongs to the category of apparitions of the living in which the etheric body (or the double, the dreambody) of a person is perceived well in advance by the people they are supposed to meet, or at the location where they are planning to go or are already traveling to. It has been named *vardoger* in Scandinavian mythology (from the old Norse language signifying guardian spirit). The vardoger is a spirit predecessor, similar to the double, and is defined as "premonitory sound or sight of a person before he arrives." According to the definition on Wikipedia, "a spirit with the subject's footsteps, voice, scent, or appearance and overall demeanor precedes them in a location or activity, resulting in witnesses believing they've seen or heard the actual person before the person physically arrives."

The Double or Doppelganger

This is, in my opinion, the same dreamtime or etheric body that is known as the double (or doppelganger), and the same also who can exit the body and move around at thought-speed in OBEs and astral travels. Guy De Maupassant, a French poet and novelist, frequently saw his double, and related a specific confrontation with it in a short story called *Lui?* In it, the main character perceives for the first time his double sitting in his own armchair in front of the fire, seemingly asleep in it; at first the silhouette is so neat, despite having its back to him (and thus its face hidden from him) that he thinks a friend is visiting. But on reaching to touch the shoulder of the said friend to wake him up, his hand touches only the back of the armchair, and the supernatural body disappears. As for William Roll, the famed poltergeist researcher, he recounts the striking experience that happened to his son: "About a year ago my 11-year-old son, William, said he saw himself seated cross-legged at the foot of his bed" (Roll 1974).

The Etheric Body in OBE and Lucid Dreams

An individual may travel in an out-of-body state (such as, in a dream-time or etheric body) either during sleep or as a conscious psychic feat.

We naturally get in the OBE state during our dreams, as a way to reconnect to the dimension of our Self and also to stay in touch with our loved ones on Earth. Yet, when this happens, the ego (the ordinary consciousness) is generally unaware of having shifted to another dimension, or of having traveled to a distant place to visit some friends. The sole remembering is a more-or-less clear dream about having these encounters.

The exceptions are the practitioners of either lucid dreaming or astral journey. In astral journeys, meditators and psychics are able to exit at will from their bodies and travel to wherever they want in an energy body that the Tibetans call the illusory body of dreams; this feat was also a cornerstone of the shamans' skills. In lucid dreams, the dreamer becomes abruptly aware of being in a dream (and of their body lying asleep), and they can thereafter control the unfolding of events within the dream. There are techniques to master this type of mental capacity, both modern ones and ancient ones.

In Tibetan Buddhism, traveling in a subtle body and developing this skill was the stuff of the yoga of the dream state and the yoga of the Clear Light of sleep. Moreover, the yoga of the transference of consciousness (or *Phowa*), shows not only the capacity of the Self to intentionally exit one's own body at will and to travel in one's subtle (illusory) body but, for specific Mahasiddhas and avatars, to transfer one's Self into another body at death. These yogas are part of the six yogas of Naropa, the (first generation) disciple of Tilopa, who initiated the great tantric line of transmission (see plate 11). Tilopa, Naropa, and his own disciple Marpa the Translator, were Mahasiddhas, eminent tantric masters (literally "great psi-power").

Fig. 6.3. Ruins of Nalanda University, India
Photo by Prince Roy, CC BY 2.0

The disciples of Tilopa taught at the University of Nalanda in Bihar, India—the cradle of Buddhism in India and Tibet, which was a prominent center of learning in the spiritual paths of both Hinduism and Buddhism, and for sciences as well, from the fifth century until the thirteenth century (see fig. 6.3). Marpa translated into Tibetan the ancient Sanskrit books concerning tantric teachings and thus launched the Tibetan doctrine and yoga. Naropa's teachings, codified by the line of disciples, form the core of the *Tibetan Yoga and Secret Doctrines,* translated by the Orientalist Walter Evans-Wentz and the Lama Kazi Dawa Samdup in 1935. These two scholars gave us the translations of the most fundamental books of Tibetan Buddhism, such as *The Bardo Thödol* (1927) (see fig. 6.4).

There is a large body of research on lucid dreaming in both psychology and parapsychology, with the main researchers, such as Stephen

Fig. 6.4. Walter Evans-Wentz and Lama Kazi Dawa Samdup, photographed circa 1919

Laberge, having themselves developed techniques to produce lucid dreams (see Laberge and Rheingold 1990). Regarding controlled OBEs while meditating or concentrating, or during a lucid dream, the experiencers are by definition aware and conscious of the events, and they suffer no break of consciousness and no loss of memory when getting back to their usual state of consciousness.

Now, introducing the hyperdimension in the picture allows us to explain some really weird occurrences: for example, I've experienced quite a few times meeting people whom I considered "old friends" in the dreamtime (including conscious meditations), and yet, on reflecting later on their names and facial features, I had to admit that they were complete strangers to my ordinary conscious mind.

THE SOUL AND SPIRIT DIMENSION

Let's now draw some conclusions from my two encounters in Igny with immaterial beings. My house genie (a deceased entity) following me climbing the staircase definitely made a display of his reality in etheric body. It means that he willfully made me aware of his presence in a tangible way, by sound, energy form, and breathing on my neck.

These two cases show that human entities have an etheric or dreamtime body; this body is devoid of gross matter but nevertheless displays a higher-dimensional form (espousing the biological body silhouette and social clothing and hair style); this higher-dimensional form has an energetic component since it interacts with matter by disrupting or perturbing its atomic and cellular organization, even temporarily so. However, it's probable that this noisy perturbation is not produced by the weight itself of the etheric body (since it's quasi-immaterial) but rather by the specific energy field of the being clashing with, or forcibly penetrating, the energy field of a wooden staircase (or a door in the transdimensional-being case).

Allow me to make some theoretical assessment on that topic. Any theory that intends to posit the reality of souls and of the spirits of the deceased dwelling in an immaterial dimension, has to account for these conative (intentional and willful) processes, and grant these spirits a full self-awareness and self-control, as well as memory of their earlier biological life and family. These above cases also make it necessary to account for the energetic component of the etheric body (yet an energy of an unknown type, linked to the hyperdimension rather than to spacetime). And lastly, such theory would also need to address the evidence of a whole layer of reality that is not matter, and yet has its own energy systems and processes. The psychologist Carl Jung was the one to elaborate the concept of *synchronicity* as meaningful coincidences expressing deep connections based on meaning and triggered by significant links (just as hyperlinks); for Jung, synchronicity was a totally new order of laws in the universe, beyond time, space, and causality.*

As Jung began working with quantum physicist Wolfgang Pauli, they envisioned a layer of "deep reality" below the quantum level and beyond space and time, which would be a mix of matter (energy) and psyche. It

---

*On *synchronicity*, see Jung 1960; Combs and Holland 1995; Peat 1987; and Hardy 2004.

is in this deep reality that would exist the archetypes as living symbols, but also as beings (such as cosmic guides), and the Selfs of humans (see Pauli and Jung 2014). Allan Kardec, who launched spiritism in the nineteenth century, stated in his 1868 book, *The Genesis,* that there was a third substance besides matter and energy, which he called the "fluids," that was immaterial, invisible, and yet capable of acting upon both matter and energy, being also responsible for most phenomena in spiritism. Another hint at a hyperdimension of souls or spirits!

I myself have posited a hyperdimension of the universe that would be triune, with hyperspace and hypertime entwined with cosmic consciousness (or syg-hyperdimension). I developed it in two theories over the years, the first one in cognitive sciences (*Semantic Fields theory*) and the second in cosmology called the *Infinite Spiral Staircase theory* (or ISST). We'll delve into the hyperdimension in chapters 11 and 12; but let me say briefly here that, in my view, we have to grant both the deceased and the living humans a higher dimension of being; or, to put it differently, we have to posit that human beings—and all beings as well—do exist simultaneously in biological matter form (our body) and in a mysterious higher soul dimension that allows them to have not only an energy body, but intelligence, free will, conscious and intentional behavior, and higher spiritual and psi capacities as well.

MY HOUSE GENIE ACTS AS A GUARDIAN

Now there is a follow-up to my story of the deceased Mr. Ledos appearing as a specter climbing the staircase behind me.

A few years later, I was living in this same house with a soul sister, Annick. She had taken over the second room facing south and the valley. Together, we were sharing our quest and meditating, each one having a creative work, as she was herself drawing and painting, while I was of course writing.

One evening that we had gone to the Quartier Latin in Paris and enjoyed a late dinner in some *crêperie,* we met a very odd character,

Roland. He was an artist traveling around France, with a very sympathetic and funny outlook on life. We got into a fascinating discussion over a glass of Brittany cider and were moved when he explained he had just arrived in Paris and had no place to stay. So I offered to let him stay at my house in Igny for a fortnight.

And back to the Bièvres valley we went, the three of us in my old car. On arriving there late at night, I set the rules of his staying with us clearly. With Annick, we were working at the time on designing a Tarot deck (the initiatic Tarot), part of a larger project I had started, comprising a half dozen different decks. I was myself writing the texts accompanying each card, while she was drawing the cards—and we didn't want to be disturbed in our concentration; Roland had to fit like a roommate, by himself. So I showed Roland the sitting room—a medium-size room furnished with a table, armchairs, and a one-person bed, that was on the ground floor next to an oversized living room. I told him his quarters were to be strictly limited to this room and the ground floor, where he had access to the kitchen and a bathroom. I emphasized that he was forbidden to climb the staircase to our own living quarters. And he agreed heartily, too happy to have a cozy place to stay with free meals for a while.

Of course the fortnight extended into another one and so it happened that, one evening, we went together with Annick to visit some friends north of Paris. Around 2:00 a.m., when we parked the car outside and got into the garden, we saw, through its large bay windows, that the kitchen was fully alight, as well as some other ground floor rooms. Something strange was going on, since Roland, unlike us, wasn't usually going to bed so late. As I pushed the entrance door and, more and more intrigued, made my way to the kitchen with Annick following me, I discovered a weird scene. Roland was sitting at the large round table, all curled up, his face white as a sheet, his body shaken by a nervous trembling, and surrounded by all the lights he could muster.

"What the hell happened to you?" I asked him, while we took our seats around the kitchen table.

Roland looked at us with imploring eyes—he was really scared beyond his wits.

"You look like you've seen a ghost!" joked Annick, who, one day, had asked me about the strange "old man" she had seen in the basement's wine cellar, and was reassured when I told her he was Ledos, protector and ally. She had thereafter sensed him each time she would go down there. Apparently, Ledos's predilection room was this wine cellar.

Roland gave us his story, stuttering:

"I wanted to go to the f-first floor and, w-when I st-started to climb the staircase, I f-felt (suddenly, he shuddered and trembled all over his body) there was a ghost climbing on the steps just be-behind me, and-and I could feel he was b-breathing on my neck, and I could hear his footsteps behind me . . ."

I mustered a rolling laughter.

"But look, I had forbidden you to climb upstairs! You've met the guardian of the house! You've no business to poke your nose upstairs! So he stopped you and barred you access!"

As often, it was so surprising for me to hear someone else, to whom I hadn't spoken about Ledos's presence, stating they saw or sensed him. But what Roland was describing was the exact replica of the experience I had had some years back. And in my mind, I thanked Ledos for having so convincingly protected our sacred space on the second floor, which was, no doubt, the real focus of Roland's curiosity.

The poor guy must have been waiting for us for hours in the kitchen, not daring to get out of the perimeter of the brightest lights in the house!

Given that all my circle of friends at the time were on a spiritual quest and most of them also artists, it's no wonder that so many of them, when visiting me in Igny, had some kind of encounter with Ledos. An Iranian poet saw a ghost passing on a large antique mirror. Annick saw him repeatedly in the wine cellar. But another hilarious feat of

Ledos-Le-Guardian took place a few years after the just mentioned case of the specter climbing the staircase.

But first, let me explain that one of my favorite hobbies, since my first travel to India, is to play drums (ethnic rhythms), and that two of my early love relationships were with a guitarist (Pat) and the other with a flutist—both also keen on drumming. And consequently, my inner circle of friends were the ones with whom we could have jam sessions, such as a very dear couple of friends, married and working, Hughes and Sylvie. Hughes in fact was the head guitarist of a band he had pulled together, and he had a job on the side to earn their living. Whenever we would meet, six or seven friends together, to have a jam-session night in Igny, we needed so much space for the amplifier, speakers, and all the musical instruments, that the best place was the large room in the basement. Not that we would disturb anybody around even with loud drumming all night—the two neighboring houses were too far; but rather, that room was the best in terms of sound quality and coziness. And so we would meet regularly at Igny and Hughes would bring all his *mathos* (the slang for the sound equipment), entering through the large double-door gate at the bottom of the property, which allowed to bring the car right up to the basement door and bring the equipment in easily.

The year I left for two and a half months, in order to tour all the labs and researchers doing work on psi (starting with the Rhine lab in Durham), I left my keys with Hughes and Sylvie, so that they could come spend some weekends with his band, making as much noise as they cared—something that was a sore point in the suburban flat they rented.

At some point during my trip (I had been gone for at least three weeks already), I was visiting a friend of mine, a French author and her husband living in a plush house on the West Coast, for a few days. Of course I had no previous knowledge of the specific weekends chosen by my friends to go to Igny. And we had no way to keep in contact (no internet and no cell phones at the time). It was a weekend, and during a short nap, I had the enigmatic flash of the statue of a meditating Buddha with a broken arm. Pondering on it, I started to feel telepathically that my friends were indeed in Igny. I could sense Sylvie in the kitchen and Hughes in the living room and then the basement. But then, I began to sense that something was wrong there, and getting worse. And now that I thought about it, the broken arm of the meditating Buddha—an obvious symbol for my sacred writing space—reinforced that impression. I went to ask my friend if I could use her phone to give a short call to France, and she was agreeable. So I called my phone number in Igny. And, as telepathy would have it, Sylvie answered the phone (something you generally don't do when staying in another person's place).

"Ah! Christine! It's so neat, so great that you're calling! Look, we're in full crisis here—one problem after the other. And Hughes is so scared he retreated to the garden and won't step inside the house anymore! It started from the moment we opened the garden gate; we wanted of course to get the car full of mathos all the way to the basement, but there was no way. However hard we tried, again and again, the car wouldn't pass the threshold of that gate: it would freeze and stop dead in its tracks just before crossing it. So, one, we had to park it outside and carry the mathos all the way to the house. But then we got another series of problems, electrical, when we got inside the basement and wanted to plug in the electric guitar and the amplifier. Each time we tried, the whole electrical grid of the house would crash. And finally Hughes saw a ghost and now he is sitting in shock on the lawn and refuses to get back in!"

"Whoa! I see! Some problems with the Guardian Spirit for sure! Look, I'm talking to him while we are on the phone. He will know, through that contact of ours, that I gave my permission for your getting inside the house while I'm not there. Now there shouldn't be any disturbance anymore. Ask Hughes to come in to talk to me."

She went outside, and only when she told him I was on the phone did he gather the courage to step in the house. I told him to go and plug in the mathos again, and this time it worked fine. As I had predicted it, the Guardian was now appeased and allowed them to play music. When

I hung up after hardly twenty minutes, Sylvie had told me she could hear some guitar tunes coming out of the basement.

I recounted the whole story to my friend who had overheard some of the exchange, and she was amazed both by the occurrence and by my sensing it.

As for myself, I had had time, over the years, to get fully acquainted with the kind of protector spirit that Ledos was. At the beginning of the fifteen or so years that I spent—in between travels and else—in this house, I would rarely have appointments, and I was so focused on my own work, that I would just forget about them. On two occasions, while I was sitting on my workroom mattress reading or thinking, I felt a hand lightly tapping my right shoulder three or four times, startling me out of my reverie. *What is it? Oh! Of course, my appointment! . . . Just enough time to get ready and leave!* I'm not sure I would also remember to thank the household spirit. The fact is, I was *very* casual with him, as with all my allies from the syg-dimension, totally unencumbered by superstitious beliefs and self-imposed duties and chores toward them, treating them as equal and friends, and only in times of dire necessity asking for their friendly help or counsel. For the great majority of the occurrences of communication, they themselves were the ones to initiate the contact. That way, I was sure of two things: One, that I didn't make up the interaction, or the sensing of my interlocutor (by wishful thinking or imagination), and two, that I remained the sole master of my own life, self-responsible, because they were only friends and allies, and not any unseen power to bow to or, even worse, to obey. Even when asking them for some advice, I behaved as I would with human counsel, pondering and weighing it and being the one to make the final decision about it.

From these early encounters, I knew Ledos was an ally and my protector in the house he had built on a sacred hill where stood his meditation oak tree. I was totally at peace with him, happy in fact that he would still be in touch with his ancient abode and that he so nicely welcomed me in it. The house, esoterically oriented, was itself conducive to meditative and creative states, due to the syg-energy he had imprinted in the stones, the trees, and the walls. I had no doubt that, given his highly spiritual energy, Ledos was a great spirit in the Beyond dimension.

I came to think, early on, that my father's Self and my own Self had decided all this in the syg-dimension, well before I was born, and that we had together selected this house to boost my awakening in a totally safe way. It's a bit like saying: You inherit or find the house you are worthy of, with a distinctive syg-field and eco-consciousness that's in sync and attuned to your higher Self; so that your soul and the soul of the house can merge and blossom together—each on its specific plane of consciousness. This is why my Igny house was my best ally for the whole time I lived there—until I moved to the States to work as a researcher.

I'm not sure what nonsensitive people can really sense about the grid of energy lines that a person in meditation, or in a creative state, is weaving over the years around themselves, and is de facto imprinting in the walls. But a great percentage of human beings will feel some unease in a place or house where dramatic and violent events have taken place. As I came back one day to visit, with a great pang of sadness, the Igny house that my father had sold while I was living in the States, it so happened that the new owner was there in the garden and he let me in for a short chat. I explained I had been drawn to the place out of pure nostalgia, and he responded to me, as if shy and awed:

"You know, I didn't touch anything on the second floor—it's exactly as it was, painting and all!"

I was dumbfounded that he had sensed anything at all in the first place! It thus seemed the house had found a new soul worthy of the antenna place!

HOUSEHOLD SPIRITS IN VARIOUS CULTURES

In many a culture, people have a cult (a belief system and its specific rituals) to propitiate spirits protecting their houses, and another one to honor their family ancestors—believed to be still very influential in all

Fig. 6.5. Family altar in India
Photo by Jorge Royan (www.royan.com.ar), CC BY-SA 3.0

matters pertaining to the family, to the larger community, and even to the country and its government. We find these cults in Hinduism, in China's Taoism and Confucianism, in Buddhism (Tibet, China, Japan, and Southeast Asia), in ancient shamanism (Africa, Asia, Southeast Asia, Australia, Siberia, and Mongolia, the polar regions), in possession cults (Southwestern Africa, Haiti, Brazil), and in many ancient Western polytheist religions as well (such as Ancient Greece and Rome) (see fig. 6.5).

In contrast, my communication with Ledos was totally spontaneous and carefree, and rather humoristic as a general style of relationship. It didn't carry any type of obligation on my part, and nevertheless, he showed that he was, over the years, dedicated to my protection and that of the house.

In traditional Hindu families in India and in Bali, a part of the altar is dedicated to the family ancestors in each house, next to the goddesses or gods venerated by this specific household. In Bali, the beautiful and so enchanting morning ritual is performed by a woman of the household, sometimes a young one, who goes with a basket of flowers and fruits first to the elegant garden altar to pray to the gods and the ancestors. Then she will stroll around the property and draw a sacred *yantra* design with colored chalk and place some flower-petal offerings in front of each door—something that will delight all the tourists residing in a bungalow hotel! As you wander around market streets in Bali or in India, you may remark, on entering any shop or office whose owner or director belongs to the Hindu religion, such flowery OM or yantra design arranged on top of the door or/and on its threshold, with fresh flowers hanging in collars, or set in a banana-leaf basket (the *canang sari*) on the pavement in front of their shops, or else in front of the sea, or at a temple altar (see fig. 6.6). Then, in a corner of the room, or in the entrance hall, will be a small or large altar with the

Fig. 6.6. Balinese flower offerings (canang sari): (a) women perform a morning offering in front of their shops; (b) and on the beach, in front of the sea, Kuta Beach, Bali

(a) Photo by Okkisafire, CC BY-SA 4.0;
(b) Photo by Chezumar at English Wikipedia, CC BY-SA 3.0

statue of a venerated god or goddess, surrounded by flowers and half-burnt incense sticks. Same with cars, and especially taxis and trucks, that display sophisticated mini altars for the owner's god, goddess, or guru, complete with statues and photos, incense holders and flower collars, arranged and glued right on the dashboard.

When, after writing the experiences I had had for this book, I made some larger research into domains I wasn't familiar with, namely the household spirits, I discovered a real trove of information in the books of Claude Lecouteux—a Sorbonne professor of Middle Ages literature and civilization—that dealt with ghosts, spirits, and cults of genies during the Middle Ages, mainly in the whole of Europe including the Baltic countries.

I was astonished at finding precise parallels to my own experiences, especially in his 2013 *The Tradition of Household Spirits.**

According to Lecouteux, the belief in household spirits and divinities, and their rituals, was widespread in all ancient religions and cultures. His scholarly theory about genies is that "the [ancient] divinities have settled and became the dwellers of specific houses" (117). In Europe, as Christianity expanded, the grand cults to the ancient gods gave way to more familial cults, such as to the household genies, to the spirits of the land and place (*genii loci*), and to the ancestors—mostly derived from older Greek and Roman cults. Lecouteux explains further that there are indications that speak in favor of an interaction between the dimension of the gods and that of the dead. One such indication is "the offerings and sacrifices that fall on the same dates on which the deceased and the gods are conjointly venerated" (117). Indeed, we have one clear-cut example in the Christian religion, in which All Saints' Day, now tied to the Day of the Dead, has become a remembrance of the deceased and the visiting and adornment of the tombs of deceased family members. Now, in my view, this coupled veneration of the dead

---

*My citations, to the end of this chapter, are taken from the 2000 French edition, *La maison et ses génies*. The translations are mine and page numbers refer to it. For other books by Lecouteux, I'll specify the work, and citations are taken from the English editions.

and the saints or gods does reveal a knowledge transpiring from the collective unconscious about a dimension of ascended souls and immortals, or cosmic masters, being one and the same as the dimension of the deceased—namely the syg-hyperdimension I'm postulating.

But let's see the ancient roots of the household spirits. In Greek antiquity, specific deities were venerated as guardians of the house, and were believed to bring riches and luck to the household: thus Zeus as *Herkeios* (the protector, with his altar in the courtyard), Zeus as *Meilichios* (or "the generous Zeus" with a serpent body, a chthonian Zeus), and the *Dioscures* (sons of Zeus, also with a serpent body) (see fig. 6.7).

For the ancient Romans, the generic term for house deities is *Penates,* and the *Manes* are the protector domestic divinities—and there were specific rituals to venerate them. The goddess Hestia, as *Vesta,* is the goddess of the sacred fire in temples and in the house hearth, whose ritual was performed by women. The *Lares* (plural of *Lar*) were revered as the protectors of the family lands, and evolved into the cult of the *Lar Familiaris* (the household spirit), whose sanctuary was the hearth

Fig. 6.7. Zeus as Meilichios, with snake form
Illustration no. 27 in Martin P. Nilsson's 1940 book Greek Popular Religion

fire (see fig. 6.8 and plate 12). This house genie was "linked to the whole family and its destiny" (98). Many household spirits, in many cultures, are said to reside near the hearth, and offerings are made for them to the fire. Of course, most ancient religions were venerating gods of fire such as Agni in the Vedic times, or in ancient Greece, Prometheus—the Titan god who stole fire from the elder gods and gave it to humanity. In my anthropologist view, this is because the cult of fire honored our essential civilizing leap as humans—the control of fire, leading to protection from wild beasts, warming the house, and cooking. The traditions of Lithuania speak about a domestic god (*deus domesticus*) called Dimispatis, considered to be the god of fire, who protects the house against destructive fire, and also an immaterial Mother of the House who has the same guardian role.

Fig. 6.8. Lar Familiaris (household protector spirit), tutelary deity of ancient Roman religion, bronze, Madrid Museum *Photo by Luis García, CC BY-SA 3.0*

The class of household spirits who have the appearance of human beings are called revenants or ghosts, and nowadays are mostly experienced as hauntings (with visual manifestations), or even as poltergeists, with disturbances and effects on matter systems, noisy and bothersome physical manifestations. It's not rare for the revenants to be recognized by their appearance and clothing as being an ancestor or a previous owner. A number of ancient village stories speak about revenants who manifested themselves in a noisy and harsh manner to the household until a specific favor that they asked from their descendants was met. Thus, as recounted in Lecouteux's *Return of the Dead,* one demanded with insistence that his brother, who had been buried in the same tomb, be buried elsewhere "because he can no longer tolerate his violent nature" (82).

Now there is another interesting category, that of the genius loci—the genie of the place (*locus* in Latin, plural *genii loci*). The site could be a forest, a lake, a tree, a mountain, or a mountain pass. As I have mentioned earlier, such spirits or *devas* of nature are said to inhabit these natural systems in Asia and Sub-Sahel Africa and are called by their locus; for example, the spirit of the mountain or the *génie du marigot* (small lake) in Western Africa. In Lithuania, these genies of the place (called *Barstucci*) are considered lower entities under the god Putscetus, the divinity of the locus and of sacred trees (161). People would invite them to settle in their houses in the hope they would get richer.

Common Traits of Igny's House Genie and the Literature

I will now list the characteristics of my own experiences with my house genie and genies of the land that correspond to some given in the literature, as presented by Claude Lecouteux (with my own experiences or comments preceded by ▶).

In some European cultures, the house genies of the human type are historically linked to the ancestors and therefore to their cult

(*La maison et ses génies*, 123). And indeed some of them look like a recognizable deceased person and display the latter's psychological profile. And in this respect, for some researchers, the domestic spirits represent the collective soul of a family.

Thus in Finland as well as in Scandinavia "the genie is the one who started a fire for the first time in the new house, the founder of the farm, . . . or *the first dweller of the place* to have died there" (119, 121, my emphasis). But it could also be a genie of the land that had been tamed when the new construction occurred. In Bulgaria and Germany, the souls of the ancestors inhabit the house, and specifically near its hearth, stove, or kitchen range and, while being honored during the All Saints' feast, are addressed as "Master of the house" (121). "In Russia, each inhabited house possesses a spirit called *domovoj*, who is often the first deceased person" (120).

▶ Ledos was clearly such a first dweller and founder, highly bonded to the place where he used to meditate under an oak tree before buying the piece of land around the tree.

Furthermore, this part of the forest, when I started living there, was still very pristine, with lots of flowery undergrowth, such as garnet heather, white lily of the valley, wild mauve irises, and lots of bramble thickets, making it a delight of colors and shapes at all seasons.

One day as I was strolling in the forest just above the house, in a poetic creative mood, I was suddenly surrounded and accompanied by a group of six or seven dwarfs. While I couldn't see the detail of their clothing and faces, I could perceive their energy fields as silhouettes of specific height; they were about two and a half to three feet tall, and rather stout. I could sense as well their mindset—welcoming, playful, joyful. They took me to an old fort, which was their dwelling, in a part of the forest I had never ventured to before; it was an old fort left over from the wartimes and totally invisible on three sides. There, we sat in a circle over the flat top of the fort, covered with three feet of soil, for a good twenty minutes. I couldn't hear the exchange of thoughts clearly, but I know my Self was in such good-humored conversation with them.

It is said that human-type household spirits like to reside in isolated and dark places in the house, such as the attic or the cellar.

▶ It's funny that the spirit of Ledos would have chosen to reside in the wine, alcohol, fruit liquors, and spirits cellar—the latter we call in French *eau-de-vie* (literally "water of life"), and *spiritueux* (literally "spirit-full") from which is derived the adjective *spirituous* in English, meaning "strong in alcohol."

The domestic genies are known to benefit the household, offering their services and carrying out many tasks in the house, as well as taking care of domestic animals, the stable, and the fields. One knows that a *Sotré* (the domestic genie of Lorraine in France) has been riding his preferred horse because he has plaited its mane in a braid in order to grip it while riding; the Sotré takes care of the horses and also of the cows but cannot always be trusted. In the Basque country in France, the *Mamarroak* "help people in their daily chores and protect the family with which they live." In the Alps, "the women, when going out, were entrusting the care of their children to the *Sédètes,* the home fairies, for short periods. The feminine house genie is indeed considered in several regions as a fairy who does the household's work, feeds the children, spins, manages the cowshed, and takes care of the cows, in return for receiving some milk to feed herself" (142–43).

Lecouteux cites a 1586 book by the German author Jean Weier describing household spirits; the "good ones" are "very lenient, good-natured, and docile. . . . They stroll about the house, especially at night, and make themselves heard . . . as if they were very busy, *walking up and down the staircase,* opening doors" (126, my emphasis).

▶ Here we have some details concurring with my experience: not only house genies walking up and down the staircase, but making themselves heard!

An interesting piece of information from a twelfth-century author was about household spirits talking and communicating: "the spirit was in the habit of conversing with humans, and was openly blaming those who clamorously asked—most were doing that for fun—that he tell them what he had been doing since his birth" (103).

But the most surprising detail was in a thirteenth-century text cited by Lecouteux, called *Dit de Thorvald le Grand Voyageur* (108–9). Around 981 CE, Thorvald visits his father Kodran in Iceland, who was known to have a cooperative house genie. He is accompanied by a bishop to hopefully convert him. "Kodran misidentifies the bishop for a diviner and replies to his son that he already possesses one [house genie] who is of great benefit to him: he predicts the future, guards his cattle, *reminds him what he is supposed to do,* and what he should beware of" (my emphasis).

▶ If you remember, that's what Igny's genie, the late Ledos, was doing: he would tap gently on my shoulder three times, and then I would remember something I had to do urgently, like going to an appointment.

In fact, apart from their well-known tendency to play tricks on people, the good genies are said to be of great advantage to the household. Some of the dwarf type, called *kobold* or *drache* in German, derive their names from the riches they bring to the family who has welcomed them—as those genies need to be willingly introduced into the house—such as the money-drache. Other ones, while also bringing riches and prosperity, may become rather bothersome and one can't get rid of them.

A rather astonishing, but quite widespread, quality of these genies is their sense of ethics. They don't bear coarseness, swearwords, quarrels, dirtiness, and when irritated make noise and punish the offender. Says Lecouteux, "In the whole of Europe, the genie oversees the behavior, the morals, the manners, the lives and actions of the dwellers; . . . he is thus a conservative and a defender of morality; in this respect, his function overlaps that of the revenant" (164–66). Finally, he is a good counselor and able to make correct predictions, and he would then appear of his own will, to offer some advice.

▶   In the traditions gathered by Lecouteux, we thus find many traits of Igny's genie being well known and widespread: the house genie, especially of the first dweller or revenant types, will protect the house: Ledos doesn't allow my musician friends to even enter the property without me, the host, being present. But with his super-normal means of knowing, he's able to understand, during my phone conversation, that I had given them my permission to do so. And from then on, he will cease to harass them and disturb their sound equipment. Also, while Ledos made himself known to me through facetiously climbing behind me, he uses the same trick to scare the hell out of an untrustworthy guest and to impede him from trespassing on my sacred space on the second floor.

Another trait was of great importance to me, and it's something that Lecouteux was keen to underline: genies (whether human or dwarfs) are able to interact with matter (objects); one can hear them walk, talk, make noise. Two funny instances mentioned by Lecouteux exemplify this point. In the first one, we have a genie that resides during specific hours of the night on the bench next to the stove; whenever somebody wants to sit or lay down on this bench during the genie's hours, they are roughly thrown to the ground. The other one concerns the *Follet* (a French genie): "Each time a new loaf of bread was started, one had to put one mouthful of it under the table for the genie, otherwise, one would receive a slap in the face" (148).

▶ Reading this was so hilarious to me, because during my first travel to India, I had received a slap on the top of my head from an immaterial goddess whom I had offended . . . But this will be for another book.

To conclude, genies are immaterial beings, and yet they also display material aspects; for example, they can go through closed doors or walls, and yet it seems they prefer to adhere to their old living habits and walk through an open door or take the staircase when it's convenient. Also, according to Lecouteux, they are able to change their own shape and appearance at will, appear in an instant, or disappear into thin air. They definitely are beings belonging to another dimension, their body is an etheric or dreamtime body, and yet it is able to move and affect matter. In our last two chapters, we will explore the 5th dimension or syg-hyperdimension, which is no less than the divine cosmic realm pervading the universe; this is the dimension of cosmic consciousness where dwell the immortal souls of the deceased, divine entities, and cosmic guides, and yes, to which our own Selfs and souls belong.

7

A Ouija Experiment

After having approached a half dozen publishers in Paris to no avail, I had the chance to be received in his office by Jean-Paul Bertrand (JPB), then financial director of the renowned Laffont publishing house, who had just bought a tiny publishing house for one symbolic franc, Le Rocher. He was frankly uninterested in my master's thesis on "psi-energetics" but more by my stories, and offered me a deal on the spot to write a book on my strange spiritual and psi experiences during the previous ten years, spent mostly meditating and traveling all over the world. I was still writing the book (published later as *L'outre-monde*) when the Ouija session occurred. In fact, this book was supposed to be the first one published by Le Rocher, but then things unfolded otherwise. JPB, in hardly a decade, was going to become one of the three most prominent publishers in France, practically launching the new spiritual trend. Soon afterward, he started to invite me to dinners where I was to meet his wife and other newly co-opted authors, and this is how I became close friends with him and his wife Sylvie.

That period, at the very start of the 1980s, also saw the rise of a group of scientists intent on developing a spiritually inclined science, yet fully independent from any religious creed or dogma. As it happened, the seed of this regrouping was a book of interviews highlighting novel theories in science with a spiritual outlook and moving beyond the materialist paradigm. The idea of a book of interviews about the approaching great scare of 1981 (one of those astrological end-of-the-world affairs) fell into my lap through a series of astounding synchronicities. The three purported authors had just gotten JPB's okay to interview not only scientists but eminent spiritual and artistic figures, and they were looking for a knowledgeable person to carry on the scientific interviews. I hadn't been in the loop at all on the book project, but JPB had recommended me, and so the main author, let's call him A, contacted me by phone to explain the project and make a deal. I had such a strong sense of humanity's future, the great leap in consciousness I always felt we had to undergo, that I couldn't care less about the alleged coming catastrophe—nor would I buy any of the subsequent waves of scares, whether the Y2K bug or the 2012 Mayan-end-of-the-world one; the latter I understood as being a leap in consciousness to the new cycle. In contrast, I was more than eager to approach the greatest and most innovative scientists in France! Yet, I slammed down the phone sharply with a sarcastic insult when I was offered a disgraceful 1 percent out of the 10 percent given to all authors—because that amounted to giving 3 percent to each of the three contracted authors, and only 1 percent to the one, me, doing three-quarters of the interviewing job and text writing, furthermore the only known researcher and soon-to-be published author in the pack!

The next instant, still fuming, I was calling JPB at his office and recounting to him the vexing deal proposal. Says he:

"Oh! If that's so, then I'll scratch their contract and give it to you."

"Come on, Jean-Paul, I can't foil the chances of somebody else just because I know you. That won't go."

"Hum . . . then here's the idea. You write a book of interviews of scientists, and they make a book about the 1981 scare interviewing anybody else they want."

"Ah, now that's a deal!" And we fixed a rendezvous to sign the contract at his office. (Needless to say, I scrapped any mention of the 1981 scare in my own book.)

In the same sweeping movement, I hung up and then called back A, explaining excitedly that we now had two separate contracts. Thus the three of them still had their full 10 percent royalties (and I would do some interviews of spiritual leaders free for them), and I had my own 10 percent. "Isn't that great? We should drink to our success! Give me your address, I'm coming to meet you guys this evening!" And being the penniless, hopeful authors we were, we toasted with an instant coffee.

The regular meeting and interviewing of scientists became a kind of way of life during the following months. JPB was as anxious to meet notorious potential authors for launching his new book collection "Spirit and matter" as these scientists were to find a publisher, so I started to hold great dinners—caterer-level quality cuisine thanks to my father, served with half-century-old wines taken from his Igny cellar. One by one, couple by couple, all the scientists I had interviewed were to meet my eager publisher and get together to talk. Meanwhile, Jean-Paul and Sylvie would in turn invite me and my boyfriend of the time, Paul the flutist, to their Paris home, sometimes with other authors or scientists, and we came to develop a close friendship.

As often in groundbreaking epochs, a new magazine in the same spirit was just being launched—*Le 3ème Millénaire*—that was soon to become the media hub in France for all researchers in the new domain of "science cum consciousness." This was a harbinger of the New Age movement of the 1980s and 1990s that suddenly pulled most publishing houses worldwide along these new spiritual trends. Needless to say, I was the youngest of all these innovative thinkers . . . Among them, Druidic-bearded biologist Étienne Guillé, with whom I was going to co-author a soon-famous book, *L'alchimie de la vie* (The alchemy of life), and who became the figurehead of the movement; the media-savvy ethologist Rémy Chauvin—the first renowned professor and scientist to endorse psi research in France (and who became my first thesis director, making the opening for me to visit Rhine's lab); physicist Jean Charon, who was mostly teaching at Stanford University, and whose theory was a pre-Chalmers panpsychism, stating that electrons (born with the Big Bang) had a form of consciousness; Jacques Donnars, a preeminent psychiatrist who, moving beyond Freud, heralded trance states as a healing process for both body and psyche; also, Stéphane Lupasco, a logician postulating a novel three-term logic; and professor Bassarab Nicolescu, a bootstrap-theory physicist who initiated later the Center for Transdisciplinary Research.*

In these times of great changes, such as the turn of the century or right now, events are happening at groundbreaking speed, the minds undergo tremendous shifts and mutations, totally novel paths of knowing and self-discovery open for all sensitive individuals.

In this high-gear context, the event I'm going to recount now is a bit pale in comparison, but it brings its own little stone to the understanding of the Beyond.

One afternoon, at Jean-Paul and Sylvie's place near Val-de-Grâce, we were with Sylvie and a visiting French-American writer, C, who was also an expert on Ouija (or spirit board) and had brought a board with her. It had a large round piece of cardboard with all the letters of the alphabet inscribed and spaced regularly, and a place in the middle where C put an upturned glass from the kitchen. We were only the three of us sitting at one end of the dinner table, and C showed us how to put, each one, an index finger lightly on the glass. The glass was supposed to move by itself on the board and point to specific letters in turn, thus composing sentences in answer to questions, and our fingers were just meant to follow or accompany its movements, and in no way whatsoever to push or drive it. First, a communication with a spirit would be queried, and a question asked aloud, and the words and sentences forming would reveal the answer.

Neither Sylvie nor I had ever seen a board, and we were both curious and rather doubtful about it. Having understood how it worked, we now wondered who was going to ask the first question. I volunteered to call "my Sufi master from Iran" without conveying any more detail than the assumption he had died. When I had stayed at his *Rhonerah* (or ashram

---

*Centre International de Recherches et Etudes Transdisciplinaires (CIRET), Paris

Fig. 7.1. Shahab al-Din Suhrawardi, philosopher of illumination

in Farsi) in Teheran, to learn and become a Dervish (in Farsi, pronounce it *Darvichi*), I was twenty-one years old and on my way to India, on my first eighteen-month journey to the East. He was the archetypal wise old man, already ninety years old, and was addressed as *Azra Darvichi* or Venerable Darvichi, the head of a whole Sufi sect of philosophers and poets—in the spiritual line of the twelfth-century philosopher and angelologist Suhrawardi who launched the Philosophy of Illumination or *ishraqi* philosophy (a quest for Inner Light and mystical enlightenment) and the mystical poet Al Hallaj (end of ninth century) (see fig. 7.1).

So with Sylvie and C, we all set our right index finger on the upturned glass, and I called to him in French:

"Azra Darvichi, I would like to communicate with you; please answer me."

To my own and Sylvie's great astonishment, the glass started to slide quite quickly toward the round of letters, pointing to some of them one by one.

The first two words made great sense to me, but were totally at odds with anything known about Eastern gurus or spiritual masters and moreover, it was totally awkward in French, even for a parent, to call somebody *fille* (the right term would have been "ma fille"). However, this was a name the master of a Darvichi sect would use extremely selectively himself.

"Oui, fille . . ." (Yes, daughter)

Indeed, that alone was enough to let me know for sure that I was talking to the soul of Azra Darvichi, because I had not told them anything more than "my Sufi master" when I got the idea in the first place. "Daughter" (in Farsi) was in truth the name by which he was addressing me back then in his Rhonerah, or else "Christ" (and not Chris or Christine). Whoever was the Daughter or the Son of the master among all his disciples was the one singled out to be the next master in the line of Tradition—whether male or female. (Let's note that he didn't demand that I become a Muslim to be initiated, since the Sufi path is an inner one—something I would have refused anyway, because my Self-driven path has been to explore many paths of old.) But I didn't make any comment, so as not to interrupt the flowing movement of the glass, since it was working so smoothly.

The glass went on, pointing to the letters: "mais pas au . . ." (but not on the)

So far so good: the letters were forming common words in French. But then came the beginning of a word *parl* that made no grammatical sense in the French sentence appearing so far. It's the beginning of the verb *parler,* "to speak," whereas the *au* called for a substantive and couldn't precede a verb whatever its tense, and moreover *parl* isn't the beginning of any substantive. In brief it couldn't turn out to be grammatically correct. I started to frown and tension gripped me when the next letter was even more distanced from any French word whatsoever. *Parlo* (speako); and now *parlogr* (speakogr). I thought the glass had lost it!

Now, something is really amiss, I thought, while the letters kept coming, each one removing us further from any sensible communication . . .

until the whole word made us all erupt with laughter: "pas au parlo-gramme" (not on the speakogram).

The spirit of Azra Darvichi had in fact invented a funny derisive name for the Ouija, constructed on the model of the word *telephone,* from the Greek roots *phon,* "speaking, sound of voice," and *tele,* "at a distance"; the *telephone* meaning the device to speak at a distance. Now *gram* in Greek is like a graph—a design, as in the French *diagramme* or English *diagram.* Thus the *parlogramme* was the graphic device enabling to speak: the Ouija board!

Thus, not only were we able, using the Ouija/parlogramme, to tran-scribe the real thoughts of a spirit, but furthermore, the device conveyed the language puns of this alive mind! This was for me a double proof that none of us had cheated—by, for example, leading the glass to some insipid and guru-esque "message" as would emanate from a purported "master." Firstly because no one but me knew the specific name Azra Darvichi used to call me, and secondly because the pun-intended word didn't exist in French. And if no one had cheated, then the device was working: the communication with a deceased person could indeed be established.

Of course, the fact that my Sufi master did refuse to speak to me through such a crude mechanism is perfectly in line with the depth of communication and the mental sophistication of the mystical arts and knowledge of Dervishes. Moreover, the light humor was also a vintage expression of Azra Darvichi, because more often than not, following an age-old Sufi tradition, he used jokes and stories to convey his teachings and deep wisdom.

So the way he addressed me, the pun, and the refusal to communi-cate via the Ouija—all was in perfect agreement with both his psycho-logical profile and his level of consciousness.

The three of us gathered that day were now convinced that it worked and that we had received the thoughts of a deceased Darvichi master. Yet, Azra Darvichi's warning and his refusal to use the board as a means for communicating made us stop short of trying to invoke other spirits.

The Ouija was working, but it was too crude a way to talk to spirits of a high order with whom a telepathic exchange should instead be developed and refined until it reached enough fluidity to allow the empathic communion of two higher Selfs.

It has been my experience and understanding that people able to communicate with the syg-dimension and transmit messages from the deceased are still rare enough that, were they to allow it, they would be crowded and hard pressed by spirits just willing to talk—most of them not worth our time.

When our psi capacities start blossoming, we need to keep to high sources of contact and knowledge, and silence the noisy sources. That will help us advance quicker and will definitely protect us from unwanted disturbances.

You may then wonder how this fits with the fact I was visited by so many spirits without me specifically calling them. Here is my secret: when you are on a spiritual quest and work on yourself in meditation or inner attunement, you create around yourself a potent syg-field that has a specific range of frequencies, that of your soul, and your field of research. And this syg-field is also imprinted in the room, the walls, the whole place where you're living. And the only souls or minds who can penetrate this field are either in that frequency range or higher. But you may also intend it that way from the start, or visualize it, and it will take effect. The only secret is to have, in your home, such a sacred personal spot that is yours only, and where you can get in inner communication with your own Self, and reinforce it. As I mentioned, the whole syg-hyperdimension is made of, and working through, frequency links and resonances.

RESEARCH ON SURVIVAL
WITH TRANCE MEDIUMS

Let's turn now to some data accumulated on trance mediumship, and see an astounding case of recurrent communication over the years with the soul of a young woman, which happened to start with a medium-ship séance.

The Palladia case involves multiple apparitions over several years, in the tsarist Russia of the 1870s. Palladia was the daughter of a rich landlord, who, having lost both her parents in the first two years of her life, was raised by her aunt, a superior nun in a convent. The percipient is Eugène M., friend of the deceased's brother, both studying at Moscow University; on a few occasions, he had helped the young and often sick Palladia, who died of a stroke at fifteen, in 1873. Eugène writes his report to the SPR in French; the following summary is mine, as the translation.

Two years after Palladia's death, says Eugène, he attends a spiritualist séance for the first time, hears knocks on the table, and thinks it's a trick. "On my return home, I wanted to see if the same knocks would happen in my own place; I took the same posture, hands on the table. Soon knocks started to make themselves heard. Imitating the procedure I had just witnessed, I began reciting the alphabet; the name *Palladia* was shown to me. I was stunned, nearly scared; unable to pacify myself, I sat again at the table, and asked Palladia what did she want to say? The answer was, 'To replace the angel, it is falling.'"

Eugène only knew that Palladia was buried in Kiev, where he was staying temporarily at the time. He couldn't sleep anymore and went to the cemetery first thing in the morning. "With great difficulty, with the help of the custodian, I finally discovered the tomb heavily covered with snow. I froze, bewildered: the marble statue of an angel with a cross was actually crooked on its side."

After a first apparition of Palladia, with a distinct perception of her clothing "with the same dark dress that she had on the day she died in my presence," and during which "all the time, I was looking at her in the eyes," Eugène starts to see her regularly. One morning, six years after her death, while finishing some work at his desk "suddenly, in front of me, seated in an armchair, I saw Palladia; she had the elbow of her right arm on the table and her head resting on her hand." To check his own mind clarity, he looks at his watch and the seconds pass; but Palladia is still there, in the same posture. "Her eyes were looking at me with happiness and serenity; and for the first time, I decided to talk to her: 'What do you feel at the present?' I asked her. Her face remained impassive, her lips, as far as I remember, remained unmoving, but I heard distinctly her voice pronounce the word *quietude*. 'I understand,' replied I, and effectively, at that moment, I understood the whole meaning she had put in that word. . . . She was starting to fade away and disappear. If I had thought of writing down on the spot the significance of the word *quietude,* my memory would have retained all that was new and strange in it." Another time, while a mother and her two daughters were guests at his parents' house, Palladia appears. "She stood in front of me, about five steps away, and was looking at me with a joyful smile. As she approached nearer to me, she told me two things: 'I went, I saw,' and still smiling, disappeared."

"As soon as I had seen Palladia, my setter dog had his hair stand up and he jumped on my bed while barking; pressing himself toward me, he was looking at the direction where I could see Palladia." Eugène says nothing to his parents about his encounter, but that same night Sophie, the eldest daughter of the guest, expresses that something strange happened to her that morning. "Having awakened early morning," she says, "I felt as if someone was standing at the foot of my bed, and I heard distinctly a voice that said to me, 'don't be afraid of me, I am a good and loving person.'" It so happened that the daughter was to become the wife of Eugène, but both had no idea at the time—yet the deceased knew about this future fact, and she had acted like an ally of Eugène. In another encounter, at the house of a friend, his and Sophie's son, now two years old, enters a well-lighted room, where he is sitting when Palladia appears. The toddler "didn't take his eyes from Palladia; turning toward me and pointing to Palladia with his hand, he pronounced 'the aunt.'. . . His face was perfectly tranquil and joyful" (Myers 1903, 400; 2012, 173, app. 7A).

The marble statue of an angel, which we saw described on Palladia's

Fig. 7.2. *Angel of Grief,* the Story monument in Rome, Italy
Photo by Carptrash, CC BY-SA 3.0

tomb, is also a customary heartening presence in American cemeteries. The Angel of Grief adorns many tombs, as a heartbreaking expression of the grief and sense of loss felt by those mourning. In 1895, the sculptor William W. Story was so devastated by the loss of his wife Emelyn that the only sculpture he did before his own death a year later was that of the *Angel of Grief* for her grave, at the Protestant Cemetery in Rome. Story said of the angel: "It represents what I feel. It represents Prostration." Since then, the Angel of Grief has been represented in many cemeteries; however, we also see lovely smiling angels guarding tombs (see fig. 7.2. and plate 13).

Cross-Correspondences

I studied the overall trance-mediumship material for my first doctoral thesis subject on psi and the afterlife, and covered what experts in the field consider one of the strongest evidences of the survival of a full personality, the *cross-correspondences* phenomenon. Looking at it now with a larger understanding, I truly believe that this great endeavor was concocted and launched directly by some great ascended minds, namely that of the deceased researchers of the SPR in London, or the ASPR in New York, who aimed at creating a bridge between the two dimensions. In fact, some researchers, such as Myers, had promised their colleagues that, once on the other side, they would try to communicate. And indeed, isn't it interesting that the bulk of cross-correspondences started after the three main researchers of the SPR had died, Myers, Gurney, and Sidgwick, and were predominantly linked to Myers's spirit? They consisted of using several mediums, such as the famed Mrs. Piper in Boston, and Mrs. Willett in London, working at the time for the ASPR or the SPR. These mediums would each receive regular messages (mostly from Myers) as pieces of a puzzle that, when patched together by the researchers, pointed to a coherent overall theme—one being a scholarly literary piece, a poem of Roden Noël, another one was steeped in Greek mythology. These cross-correspondences went on for years and it seemed that the puzzles were so complex, and the pieces of information so exotic and meaningless by themselves, as to exclude the possibility that the mediums could exchange the information by telepathy.

As we can surmise, the spirits of the deceased researchers didn't relent in finding novel complicated ways to try to prove their point: that of their existence in the syg-dimension! But no amount of research or evidence will ever convince a skeptic. Of course only researchers should be bothered by that! But even as a researcher myself, I've never been interested in convincing skeptics, especially by rational means. In contrast, I've been eager to recount real psi experiences for the benefit of whoever has an open mind, because I believe in experiencing and on experimenting on oneself. Then you'll just know for yourself. Psi capacities are on the rise, everywhere, and we are definitely bound to get somewhere soon. Let's make the most of the opportunity, each one of us, to get there.

8

SPIRITS CROWD FOR A BARDO READING

Eastern religions—Buddhism, Hinduism, and Taoism among them—state that human souls undergo a series of incarnations in a biological body on Earth, until each person (their ego consciousness) reaches a state of fusion or oneness with their own Self and thus with cosmic consciousness. This Oneness state is called nirvana in Buddhism, *moksha* (or liberation) in Hinduism, Clear Light and *thödol* ("liberation") in Tibetan, and in our terms, illumination or enlightenment.

This is of course a stupendous notion! First because it views life as an ongoing learning process, called the wheel of karma, not only for human beings but also for animals and consequently for all the living beings.

Let's note that the karma—the seeds we plant by our actions and decisions—can be either negative or positive. It is only a check and balance of all our deeds, with two columns, credit and debit, just like our usual accounting. Yet, Hindus believe that one instant of pure consciousness, such as a peak state in attunement, prayer, or meditation, is able to burn a pile of bad karma, and we find the same notion in the Bardo teaching of the Tibetans. In fact, one of the greatest yogis and Mahasiddhas (meaning endowed with *siddhis* or super-psi) of the Tibetans—Jetsun Milarepa—who lived in the eleventh century in western Tibet, started in his adolescence on the left-hand magical path when he was asked by his mother to take revenge for their family being bereft of their wealth; he sought a left-hand sorcerer to teach him and killed many people (see Evans-Wentz, *Tibet's Great Yogi Milarepa*). Yet, he learnt at tremendous speed the sacred science of consciousness and high meditative states, and thus opened his mind to a larger world vision and values that finally blossomed into a highly spiritual and ethical path of knowledge. And that meant that a moment of Clear Light in meditation, while still engaged with his tortuous and malevolent teacher, had been enough for him to leap to a higher state of consciousness, and to a contact with his own Self—bringing on him sufficient understanding to abruptly discard his previous path and open a new one by himself. He then found a new right-hand guru in the famed Marpa the Translator, disciple of Naropa. (As we saw, Marpa taught at Nalanda University in India, the cradle of Buddhism, and then he traveled to Tibet and brought the doctrine there.)

Marpa put Milarepa under extreme duress in order to build his endurance and will to attain enlightenment. And the common-sense morality of Milarepa's life is that he certainly paid a huge price for his past mistakes. However, there's a deeper message in this teaching. And it's the fact that even a murderer (however sound or shallow his motives to thus act) can readily achieve Liberation and Enlightenment, and furthermore, in the course of *one* lifetime or incarnation. This is because the light and wisdom of the Self dwells in cosmic consciousness, and the Self of a person cannot be sullied by what the ego undertakes but can only be more and more separated and estranged from it. The instant of a true connection with one's Self endows the embodied mind such intense reception of syg-energy (soul and consciousness energy) that the "light of understanding" fills it and provokes a huge leap and a merging with the collective soul (or cosmic consciousness). The ego is brought back in line with the Self, the aim of the path shines clearly, and past karma, due to ignorance, is just instantly dissolved. (And if we remember the healing using hypnosis I recounted in chapter 5, the real healing force was such ego–Self connection.)

Now, what happens to the enlightened beings who have reached the end of their incarnation cycle? According to the Hindu and Tibetan convergent worldviews, they will now move to a higher dimension of consciousness; they will still be in a learning process, but at a whole new level.

We meet here the extraordinary Eastern concept of multiple dimensions in the universe, beyond our material world—the 4D spacetime manifold. Another manifold, comprising several spiritual or immaterial dimensions, is said to exist beyond our matter region. This is above and beyond the fact that there exist a number of universes.

Astonishingly, physics and cosmology are now forced to admit the existence of what they call extra-dimensions or a hyperdimension in the universe, such as hyperspace (4th dimension of space) at the very least, but maybe a hypertime too. What has led to this necessary admission is the discovery of dark energy and dark matter—the first being non-matter and the second being non-ordinary matter—that together make up 95 percent of the total energy of the universe, leaving ordinary matter to be a meager 5 percent of it. And ordinary matter—this 5 percent—comprises everything we know of, namely stars, galaxies, and our whole material, spacetime, region. (We'll dive into this in more depth in chapter 12.)

Physics is still in the process of determining the nature of this non-matter stuff, yet, the simple admission of the existence of an *energy* that's not matter is of crucial importance for any quester on a path. Since Carl Jung coined the term *psychic energy,* we have had the grounds to argue for such a spiritual, mental, and semantic energy (syg-energy)—something all sensitives are able to detect, to feel as it is exchanged during our daily interactions, and to control in meditation. This soul energy (*psyche* means "soul" in Greek) is no less than the kundalini energy that we sense in our chakras and that is rising through them while in high meditative or altered states. And Carl Jung had definitely pointed to this fact in his book on yoga and kundalini called *The Psychology of Kundalini Yoga*.

Thus science is now at last stalking the nonmaterial dimensions and getting disengaged from gross matter; the materialistic paradigm, which has ruled science for nearly four centuries, is a punched bag of air, reduced to only 5 percent of the reality of the universe.

However, all mysticisms and religions speak about a spiritual or soul dimension in which dwell the divine beings, inorganic spirits, and the souls of the dead. It is, indeed, in the essence of most religions to state that the souls survive the death of the body, and that the good and worthy souls will access the divine realm or paradise. If we translate these concepts in physics terms, the main religions posit the existence of a hyperdimension (beyond the spacetime or matter region) populated by higher-dimensional beings. And the miracles of the saints and the feats of shamans are brought forth by the privileged access of their mind to this hyperdimension beyond space, time, and matter. And in this context, a remark by Henri Corbin (2019, 65) (the great philosopher of the inner path and of Sufi theology, and friend of Carl Jung), in his chapter on the Bardo Thödol, is as funny as remarkable, "Along with Jung, we must recognize that the old lamaist sages may well have thrown a glance in the direction of the fourth dimension and lifted off a veil from the grand secrets of life."

IN BETWEEN INCARNATIONS: THE BARDO STATE

The state the souls are in between incarnations, or, in between an incarnation and a state of pure enlightenment as ascended souls is called by the Tibetans the Bardo state—the Bardo itself being the in-between dimension. Let me tell you in this section my view of this Bardo state, based on my experiences and despite its being a bit divergent, in some respects, with the Tibetan teachings.

The Weighing of One's Own Life and Actions

In this Bardo state, which can have any duration in terms of our Earth time, the souls reflect on all their actions in their previous incarnation, and weigh them in the light of their overall spiritual aim in the long journey toward full enlightenment. The Self (soul) will ponder what their last life added, as knowledge and experiences, to their previous incarnations, and how the ego has met the challenges the Self had selected for them to meet in their lifetime (before they were born, that is, in the previous Bardo state). The Self of a person is the oversoul, the guiding spirit both in their earthly lives and in the Beyond; and the Beyond—the Bardo or in-between dimension—can be viewed as a lower layer of the cosmic consciousness. It is my understanding that the Self is assisted, in its weighing of its ego's past deeds, and in all its decisions regarding the next life experience, by other Selfs, some of a higher order, and some belonging to the same group-soul—a group-soul being a higher oversoul that comprises and guides many egos in incarnation, impervious to time and space.

Of course, the soul of a departed who has just accessed the Bardo (and who generally took some time to realize its body was dead) is often still clogged and perturbed by all the emotions and events pertaining to the person's last months on Earth. To this soul, its own Self will appear like an angel, or a guru, or a divine being; this is made apparent in the NDEs in which a being of light (often called an angel) will appear at the end of a tunnel to speak with the consciousness in its etheric body, and give it guidance.

Depending on the soul's recognition of one's own mistakes in life and its desire to use the Bardo state as a springboard to hasten one's spiritual evolution, a soul may want or agree to make a thorough review of its own past incarnation. The soul will now be able, while playing back the unfolding of crucial events, to observe clearly the scene not only from an outside and detached perspective, but also with an inside grasp of the inner experience of all other persons involved. The impact of one's own actions on the others becomes clear and their consequences inescapable. The souls who undertake such a dire learning process, and who suddenly become aware of what they have left behind for their family and friends to carry on, will try anything to alleviate those consequences and to help their loved ones avoid getting entrapped in these psychic knots. Doing so, if successful, will simultaneously alleviate some of their own bad karma. For this in-depth review, the guiding "angel" or "wise one" will be always at the side of the beleaguered and striving soul, offering help, guidance, comfort, and insight. The spiritual and psychological understanding thus gained by a soul—and which will be part of its personality and endowment in the next incarnation—can be groundbreaking. Of course, as the deceased soul is now in a beyond-space and beyond-time hyperdimension, this review of one's past life can be observed as it really happened, by simply focusing on the past time and place, yet from a more global and spiritual perspective. While carrying this self-chosen task, souls are also watching what their loved ones are doing on the earth plane, and may decide to appear to them or help them in some way, thus triggering an apparition. Let's emphasize here that the souls are never charged with this task or judged or exiled anywhere, but (in the better light of this realm) act according to their own spiritual desires or else the beliefs they want to cling to.

It's only in a second phase that the soul and its Self are going to figure out what would be the best conditions and context for their next incarnation: What type of experiences and what gross lines of destiny would give them the greatest challenges, would prod them to develop their potentials and be a trigger for spiritual evolution? (We can right away understand that a linear, happy, and uneventful life won't offer such a trigger!) And having thus decided on several aspects of the most fecund life experiences, the search for the suitable culture, family, place, and time will start. Eventually, the soul will make contact with the minds of the chosen mother and father, and their family. The future parents would have themselves agreed, from within the higher dimension of their souls (in the dreamtime) to accept and welcome this child for their own spiritual benefit—including that arising from dire tensions and suffering.

Let me pause here to recount a dream that showed this teaching we get from our own Self. In the dream, I am standing along the wall of a fast-food restaurant with my companion of the time, Paul the flutist. We are both observing a raucous scene happening in the middle of this room, where Paul, this one in flesh and bones, is having a quarrel with a friend that quickly degenerates into a dogfight. We are obviously in immaterial form, both of us, and analyzing the psychological impulses leading to the brawl, and how he was unable to control himself, in a scene that happened in Paul's life a few years earlier. At one point, I turn to Paul and ask him, with a soft and cool voice: "So, have you got it now?" My interpretation of this dream is that we were both in our Self consciousness, and Paul was reviewing some of his subconscious drives.

To get back to the Bardo . . . In the opposite scenario, that of a soul unable to extricate itself and disentangle from its strong impulses and emotions (such as hate, violence, fear, helplessness, and the like), then it won't recognize and listen to its Self, and will tend to reincarnate swiftly. As we'll see in depth further on, *The Tibetan Book of the Dead*—one of the most sacred books of the Tibetans' Mahayana Buddhism—shows precisely, in its third phase, the sitpa Bardo, how the departing soul will be either intending to access a higher consciousness or attracted to a specific soul-sphere according to its desires and emotions.

As drawn on paintings of the Wheel of Life (see fig. 8.1 on page 182), a person can make of their personal life a paradise or a hell (the six possible states of incarnation), depending on their willingness to learn and be in accord with their Self—here represented by the bodhisattva Avalokiteshvara present in each of the six realms of existence.

Fig. 8.1. Wheel of life (Bhavacakra) with Avalokiteshvara present in each realm
Photo by Stephen Shephard, CC BY-SA 3.0

DEVAS, ELEMENTALS, AND TANTRA MASTERS

According to most ancient religions, there exist different extraphysical dimensions in which dwell sentient and intelligent entities. Many entities of a more or less ethereal substance (generally in the invisible spectrum of the subtle energy of the hyperdimension) populate the Earth. There are spiritual and highly evolved spirits, gods and goddesses of a higher order—such as Buddhas and Dakinis (the male and female Buddhas of Mahayana Buddhism in Tibet and Japan). Apsaras as winged and dancing angels (Southeast Asian and Indonesian Buddhism and Hinduism), and angels in the Christian and Muslim religions. There are also lesser spirits of natural systems and elements, called, to name a few, (little) Devas in Hinduism; spirits, genies, or inorganic beings in shamanism; and genies, elementals, or fairies in the West (see fig. 8.2).

Fig. 8.2. Apsara appearing to a meditating yogi, bas-relief, Borobudur temple (Java, Indonesia), ninth century
Photo by Gunawan Kartapranata, CC BY-SA 3.0

We have the spirits of trees, places, mountains, lakes, and the like. They can range from being wise guardians and guides (such as trees and mountains), to being tricky and even malevolent, such as the spirits of dangerous mountain passes in Tibet, who need to be propitiated by prayers when crossing the pass on a journey. In the Yaqui Indian lore, as recounted by the cultural anthropologist Carlos Castaneda, these elementals are called inorganic beings and are clearly visible to the shamans and sorcerers.

Very old trees are revered and temples erected around or next to them in predominantly Hindu, Taoist, and Buddhist countries. Our Western lore on genies, fairies, and elementals—mostly stemming from the ancient Celtic religion, and still found in Irish legends and fairy tales—describes the Little People as behaving in a manner that remains rather mysterious and incomprehensible to us, ranging from tricking people into hardships, abducting some to live with them for very long periods of time, or else bestowing on babies wondrous gifts.* Yet, the diverse fairies are said to have great knowledge, specifically about magic, and to be allied with the most powerful magicians. A magus such as Merlin—who lived between Brocéliande Forest in Brittany and the court of Avalon (ancient Glastonbury) at the time of King Arthur, in the late fifth century CE—was renowned for his ability to command them.

In the East, and especially in Tibet, the accent is put on the capacities of great gurus and yogis to communicate with initiatic masters who are often nonhuman entities such as Dakinis, or the King and Queen of the Nagas (the royal cobras). Dakinis (enlightened female entities), according to Judith Simmer-Brown's 2002 study (139) can be of different orders, from an emanation of the cosmic consciousness of the void, to an enlightened Buddha guiding the yogi, to an initiator and tantric guide, to a yogini (female yogi) in physical form and consort of a yogi in the rituals of the sacred sexual tantra (see fig. 8.3).

---

*On fairies, or the Little People, in Ireland, see the classic works of the Irish poet William Butler Yeats, *Fairy and Folk Tales of the Irish Peasantry*, 1888, and *The Celtic Twilight*, 1893.

Fig. 8.3. Tibetan Dakini statue, early nineteenth century,
Georges Labit Museum, Toulouse, France
Photo by Didier Descouens, CC BY-SA 4.0

Thus the Great Guru Padmasambhava (said to have lived for a thousand years before his arrival in Tibet) was teaching the science of Tantras—the knowledge of how to raise one's consciousness into the highest states of fusion. To do so, the yogis use the influence of postures and gestures (mudras), of specific geometric figures and colors (mandalas), of magical designs (yantras), as well as the power of sounds and letters (mantras).

A part of the teachings of tantra is the science of kundalini—the syg-energy in our energy body that, when arising along the spine, is able to awaken the chakras one by one up to the head chakra, called the Thousand-Petal Lotus. And one set of techniques is sexual tantrism. Padmasambhava (Guru Rinpoche), during his lengthy travels in Asia, had five tantric consorts who were supraconscious *wisdom Dakinis,* the first and most knowledgeable one was Yeshé Tsogyal (see plate 14). In fact, two of his Dakinis achieved the Buddhahood state, Yeshé Tsogyal of course, and Mandarava. Both of them were Mahasiddhas—powerful tantric and psi-masters—among the eighty-four Mahasiddhas in the whole of Hindu and Tibetan Buddhist traditions.

Each Mahasiddha master is said to have developed his or her own specific *siddhis,* or yogic powers (*maha* means "great" in Sanskrit). There are a few women, the most stunning and original ones being the two Headless Sisters, *Mekhala,* the elder, to the left, and *Kanakhala,* the younger to the right on plate 15.

Both sisters were abused for years by their respective husbands and seized the chance to take off when a wandering yogi passed by their village. Having received some tantra teaching from him, they practiced for twelve years alone in the wilderness, being directly taught by the immaterial *Vajrayogini,* the most advanced of direct wisdom-teachers of Tantra (see plate 16 and also 22). They became able to control matter, that of material things and the environment, and their own biological body as well. (Note that their tantra path at the time didn't comprise a sexual practice.) Then, on meeting their former guru, they suddenly reached the highest illumination, power, and knowledge. As sky-dancers, they were now able to slash their own heads with a sword without losing their human form, and then they ascended to a higher dimension while dancing in the rainbow body. They are considered specific avatars of Vajrayogini.

In their peak state, the two yogini sang their enlightenment:

> Prajna is the all-pervasive light of phenomena,
> The essence of space,
> And space itself.

From the non-dual union of space and awareness,
The unborn bindu [point] of blazing luminosity
Illuminates totality.
In shadowless complete surrender,
This is the vajra dance.
AH

(Penick 2011, 71)

In some secret knowledge of tantra, the Mahasiddha Ghantapa and his Dakini would be able to conjoin the sexual bliss attained by rising the kundalini energy in all chakras during sexual intercourse, with a flight in their subtle bodies, as shown on plate 17.

Padmasambhava also made a pact with the Naga Queen to ensure peace and protect Buddhism in Tibet, and obtained great magical knowledge from her. The Nagas are supraconscious entities and, beyond their immense spiritual and magical knowledge, are able to take a human form at will.

TIBETAN WISDOM OF THE BARDO THÖDOL

The *Bardo Thödol* (or "Liberation through hearing during the intermediate state") was given as a teaching by Padmasambhava in the eighth century, to his consort and disciple Yeshe Tsogyal, who wrote down and buried the text in central Tibet, where it was discovered in the fourteenth century by the *terton* Karma Lingpa. A terton is the chosen discoverer of hidden ancient texts, or *terma*, that had been buried until humanity becomes ready to have this kind of initiatic teaching. Karma Lingpa discovered other ancient texts, including the *Self-Liberation through Seeing with Naked Awareness* (see Reynolds 1989).

The Many Dimensions of the Beyond

Tibetan Buddhism, as mentioned, conceives of a number of regions, beyond the physical one, ranging from paradises to hellish ones.

In the highest and most spiritual ones, we have the paradises—or *Buddha-fields*—manifested by numerous Buddhas. In fact, there are thousands of Buddhas, male and female, because a Buddha is any being who has achieved the Clear Light of understanding and the liberation from the Wheel of Incarnations. At this point, the yogi may choose either to move beyond the earth plane into Nirvana (creating their own Buddha-field or paradise world), or to remain on Earth until all beings are liberated, thus taking the oath of the Bodhisattva. It is on the eve of enlightenment that a yogi intends to create their own Buddha-field. Padmasambhava is said to have attained the highest state of liberation, *the Rainbow Body of great transference*—an enlightened and light body that allows great masters to remain on Earth for as long as they want. In this specific Rainbow Body, "the master dissolves his or her body into rainbow light and lives for centuries in order to benefit others."*

The Hindus view the animal and vegetal kingdoms as also in process of learning, until eventually they reach an incarnation in a human body. They deem the human life as priceless in terms of opportunities for learning and advancing, a great gift we should be aware of. There are for us so many challenges, strifes, and obstacles that these will make us rise to our best potentialities. In comparison, souls in the paradises, they believe, and even gods and goddesses, hardly learn and evolve because these realms lack the disorder, obstacles, and dangers, as well as the intense and fast-moving time, that make us surpass ourselves and leap forward.

The Psycho-Spiritual Dynamics of the Bardo Thödol

The state of the Clear Light (Liberation) is the state in which the yogi attains a fusion with cosmic consciousness (Buddhahood, Great Body of Radiance), which we find in all Eastern religions (such as brahman, Tao), as the highest state of consciousness and the aim of all yogic spiritual quests. As expressed in Evans-Wentz's *The Tibetan Book of the Dead:*

---

*See the article on Padmasambhava in the Rigpa Shedra Wiki page, an online encyclopedia of Tibetan Buddhism.

Thine own consciousness, shining, void, and inseparable from the Great Body of Radiance, hath no birth, nor death, and is the Immutable Light—Buddha Amitabha.

Knowing this is sufficient. Recognizing the voidness of thine own intellect to be Buddhahood, and looking upon it as being thine own consciousness, is to keep thyself in the [state of the] divine mind of the Buddha. (8)

It follows that all Buddhas and Dakinis (all the innumerable people, men and women, who have achieved this realization) dwell in this same Buddha-dimension (despite having created their own paradise, or Buddha-field, as a sub-space in it). The wisdom of this text is that becoming aware and experiencing one's own consciousness as being one and the same with cosmic consciousness is in itself the gate to, and the core of, the liberation state. If we equate this cosmic consciousness with the syg-hyperdimension, then it means recognizing that our Self consciousness (syg-field) is of the same nature as the cosmic hyperdimension itself, and part of it—an extraordinary knowledge, yet one that infuses all Eastern spiritual philosophies. It is also the main thesis in ISST—all syg-fields, from personal to cosmic, being infused with hyperfrequency syg-energy, and forming, all together, the hyperdimension of consciousness (more on this in chapters 11 and 12). Of course, this is a state of fusion that allows the knowledge of cosmic consciousness to pervade the yogi. Reaching that state during one's lifetime demands intent and yogic meditative practice.

Now, the most astonishing thesis of the Bardo Thödol is that, based on a kind of law of attraction (which governs also the karma, good and bad), the entry into the Bardo state after bodily death is one of the greatest opportunities of our life to leap to a higher dimension. If we fathom how it works, we'll simultaneously understand why the confession in Catholicism (true regrets and atonement for one's own wickedness), as well as funerary rituals in most religions are the enactment of such a psycho-spiritual law of attraction. (When I use this *law of attraction* term, I'm not binding it or myself with any school of thought, just with the dynamic process.)

The *Tibetan Book of the Dead* describes how, when the soul is leaving forever its temporary body, a process is triggered, by which the departing soul will be attracted to a specific soul-sphere—according to its own spiritual, emotional, and intelligent capacities, the ones most activated and energized at the moment. The Bardo process offers the best opportunities first, such as the highest and purest Buddha-fields or dimensions of paradise. If the soul, starting to be detached from its social and physical bonding, experiences a pure instant of love for, or resonance with, any of these paradisiacal realms, then a spark will be lighted—like an electric arc—and in a split second the soul will be merged with this dimension of being. In other words, the soul will find itself relocalized in this soul-dimension of high frequency, as in a new home, among souls of the same soul-family.

If the spark of recognition and attraction hasn't happened, the next lower dimension will appear as a vision to the departing soul, and so on. A number of opportunities and soul-families and realms are thus appearing to the detached soul in the Bardo state. If it cannot recognize itself (in its own spiritual energy, aspiration for beauty, or light, or music, heightened states, love, or values) in any of these high realms, then another suite of human-style, earth-style dimensions will open up one by one. And if it still isn't able to desire or like or recognize itself in any of these, then a new suite of hellish realms will be displayed, in a decreasing quality order. The law of the Bardo works in the sense that the soul is pulled toward a dimension that corresponds to its own vibratory level—whether harmonious and spiritual, or else a harsh purgatory, an animal life, of a hellish sphere.

So how is this law of attraction really working in the Bardo state? At a superficial layer, it seems to posit that like attracts like, so that, if your thoughts are filled with love and benevolence, you'll attract in return love and gifts to yourself; and if they are full of hate, you'll attract hate and obstacles. However, the Bardo teaching adds greater complexity and depth to the process, fortunately so, because our lives and psyches, in the modern world, have become increasingly complex.

Indeed, for the great majority of people on Earth, our psyches and minds are not a harmonious and unified stuff. Quite the opposite, we house in ourselves a great number of what I call *semantic constellations,* that is, clusters or networks expressing and managing different functions, actions, values, knowledge systems, and the like. One such constellation could be a childhood trauma that has developed into a pocket of hate and aggressivity. But next to it is another constellation reflecting an experience of true love and positive emotional bonding.

Let's say, for the sake of the example, that in Bob's short life, the two most energy-laden constellations have been hate for his father and love for his wife. At the moment he enters the Bardo, if his love constellation can resonate with one of the loving-type soul dimensions, and if he's able to desire to be fully in these love relationships, then his soul will immediately create a bridge to that realm and merge with it. From that moment, still in the Bardo but in a paradisiacal dimension, he will keep on learning and preparing his next life. In contrast, if, at the moment of death, it is his hate constellation that is the most strongly activated and energized by emotions and thoughts, then, unfortunately, this will not allow him to express his love and his soul will connect with constellations of disorder and hate, where it will be much more difficult for him to learn and progress.

We are, each one of us, a psyche-mind full of diversity and of contradictions—a variegated landscape of constellations. We should then, if we want our Bardo process to be a springboard, do as the Hindu wise men and women have devised: at a senior age, when their children are able to take care of themselves and they have no more professional or hard-pressing obligations, they will now devote themselves fully to their spiritual and peaceful realization. For example, the Rama-Sita path is a specific path of knowledge that is trodden by a senior couple, and whose model is the harmonious couple formed by Rama and his wife, Sita. The Rama-Sita couples totally retire from the social sphere and even from their family, leave all their possessions behind, and move to a holy place where they will build a hut for themselves. They will from now on devote their life to meditation, accessing high spiritual states such as samadhis. I have met such couples in beautiful holy places, such as Omkareshvar, on the Narmada River, the sacred river of Shiva. They had given up their houses and belongings, were estranged from their previous families and social networks. They remained in meditation all day long, and even performed a dream yoga to remain in a clear consciousness during their sleep. Whatever bad deeds they had done in their early life, the last few years of their life, strongly focused on their spiritual realization, would redeem them. According to the Bardo teaching, given that their thoughts and souls were constantly attuned to their Self and spiritual path, they would perforce get in resonance with a spiritual realm.

Of course the same would befall an atheist who would have devoted his/her life to helping or healing others, animals, or even the planet, to any artistic, environmental, or societal cause, or community welfare. It would also befall a philosopher (lover of Sophia/wisdom), an artist seeking to develop their potentials, any being on a path of self-development. The essential ingredient, it seems, is the priority focus of our life, the kind of future that we project for ourselves and our loved ones, or even for humanity and the planet as a living organism—Gaia.

MY TEACHING OF THE BARDO TO SPIRITS

Now to my story, which happened at a time I was mainly meditating, writing, and reading, and before my first travel to India, where I was to live the life of a saddhu—a wandering ascetic.

One day that I was as usual in my study on the second floor, I got what felt like a great idea. I was going to help the souls of the deceased who were still roaming around our earth plane, still hooked to their past social and familial surroundings, because (I thought) they didn't know how to raise their consciousness. I was going to read them the

Bardo Thödol, one or two dozen pages at a time, so that they could go through the detachment and extrication process and access higher realms.

Totally in character with myself, as soon as this idea crossed my mind and I found it really great, I got into action, preparing the room for my first Bardo teaching session.

I lighted a candle, then an incense with which I made a quick purifying gesture of the whole room and set it on the altar in the center of the room, next to the candle. Then I sat cross-legged on the couch that was, at this period, facing the southwest and the valley.

Then, after a short meditation to clear my mind, I opened the book with great respect to the first page of text, and disposed it in front of me on a small low table.

Then I entered a deep state again, with my eyes closed, and called out telepathically:

Come, oh you souls who are wandering, not having found a proper realm to ascend with your souls . . . Come to me and sit around me. I'm going to read you the Bardo Thödol, so that you may rise to a higher realm.

I felt I had gathered, instantly, a small audience of four souls. And I started reading, slowly, while my mind was providing them the explanation about the process involved and described in the text.

I read about a dozen pages, and my audience was as serious and concentrated as in a church. When I stopped reading, a good forty-five minutes later, I performed a meditation to rise the energy of the souls present, and to open the access to higher energy realms. Then I told them that I would do this ritual and keep reading them the treatise every few days, and would call them on—just as I had done that day—when I would be ready to do it . . . and thus ended the session and dispelled the assembly.

I was happy with myself; four souls had answered my call and had been an avid audience to the teaching of the Bardo's secret knowledge. That proved it was a good thing to do, I mused, and that it could help some roaming and restless souls.

A few days later, when I felt that I was in the right mood to make a new session, I again prepared the room, cleared my mind, and called on the roving souls to gather and sit around me.

Now that was strange: I had now about twenty souls eager to listen to the Bardo teaching! My expectations of course had been that, if I could help them open a bridge to a higher dimension, they would then transfer themselves there; and basically, if my active meditation was working, then obviously they should depart for good from the earth plane, and consequently, I would have fewer souls around me. I started doubting my action had any of the intended effect, but, true to my aim and respecting my audience, I started reading the text where I had left it, for about a dozen more pages. My audience, despite the number, was dead still and religiously concentrated. Twenty minds eagerly drank each word of the text, while my mind elucidated the process of intending to create a bridge with higher realms; and meanwhile, in my higher Self or consciousness, I did open a pillar of light toward a higher dimension.

After I had read the text, just like the last time, I meditated on them rising to a higher-consciousness state and realm. And thereafter I dispelled the assembly, telling them I'd do it again.

Then afterward that evening, reflecting on the whole performance, I became perplexed and not sure at all of the results and whether I had met my aims. I decided to keep going in any case.

And a few days later, again I started a session and called on the souls in need to come and gather around me.

Now that was stupendous!

My small thirteen-by-sixteen-foot room, with its slanted low ceiling under a pointed roof, suddenly got crowded by intense and fixed pairs of eyes in a way I couldn't even fathom: as if the souls were represented by their heads only, and they were lined up along the walls on three levels vertically, taking most of the volume of the room around me. There was something like a hundred souls who had responded instantly to my call! They must have passed the word around and waited for me to utter my call.

Again I read the next dozen or so pages. There was an unearthly silence—souls don't move, don't sneeze or cough; wherever they had set themselves, one on top of the other, eyes wide open and their minds eagerly absorbing the teaching, they remained absolutely immobile up to the end. Strangely, no one departed, rising like a liberated soul the way I had anticipated it. Even after I stopped reading and engaged in an active meditation to open vertical paths of enlightenment for them, no one moved even a quarter of an inch; more bizarre still, no one ever got into visualizing or sensing the energy path toward higher realms that I had built from the room upward.

Second thoughts erupted in me that I couldn't suppress. *Maybe it's just like a movie for them!* or *What the hell is happening? It sure isn't working the way it should!*

That time, while thanking them for their presence at the end of the ritual, I omitted saying I would perform it again. Everybody disappeared as instantly and silently as they had earlier appeared neatly aligned on three levels.

Once I was alone, I tried to make sense of it all, but couldn't really. The ritual was working . . . as far as they were eager to listen and that meant it was definitely important for them. And yet the practice wasn't reaching its overall aim since they didn't rise in ecstasy toward a dimension of joy and peace. Worse, the pattern seemed set: there would be a constant increase of listeners. Could they gather themselves in a cubic pixel and still be there with their whole consciousness?

I figured they didn't really need any space to be there, they could just as well have two eyes in one cubic inch and extend their rows beyond the walls and ceiling!

And so I decided to stop the experiment right there.

The way I understand it now, with some more experience, is that my listeners were not the desperate souls roaming on earth's plane and not having found the gate to the Beyond (as goes the popular belief about ghosts).

Most probably, the teaching itself was what got their interest and utmost attention. They were souls of the departed just eager to learn something new and intent on self-improvement. Now, as I don't see why they wouldn't have access to any book ever written and be able to read them in the Beyond, there must have been an added element that made the gathering interesting for them.

One possibility was that they were interested in the way I had meditated on the Bardo and understood the book, which amounted to a sort of commentary of it—because, while uttering a text one is always simultaneously projecting one's thoughts and interpretation—something that was definitely easily readable or graspable for them since they use telepathy proficiently. A second possibility, very likely because I've seen it and it was also explained to me, is the out-of-the-ordinary chance of building a communication between the two realms. They are very eager to answer any occasion to create and reinforce such a realm-to-realm contact—with mediums, sensitive individuals, and of course scientists (because science is such an important part of the global evolution of minds and of society). In fact, I came to the conclusion that it was one of the axes of development for the future of humanity (and more) that the two realms had to be communicating and exchanging information, as a side effect of the rising in frequency and high states of consciousness among humans and all the living, that is, Earth as Gaia.

MUSIC-LOVER SPIRITS SURROUND A PIANIST IN ROYAL CHAPEL

Erik Pigani, a notorious former journalist for *Psychologies* magazine in Paris, is also a talented classical music pianist and composer who, after studying under the virtuoso Georges Cziffra for more than twenty years, became involved in the concert-organizing Cziffra Foundation. In 1999 he published a book that assembled several dozen interviews he had conducted over the years with famous artists, asking them about any anomalous or psi phenomenon they had ever experienced.

Plate 1. Egyptian Book of the Dead: The weighing of the heart. The ba (soul) of the deceased Ani (represented as a bird) attends the weighing of its life deeds (as a heart). The god Thoth (with an ibis head) records the weighing performed by the jackal-headed god Anubis. From the Book of the Dead of Ani, papyrus from the Tomb of Ani, Thebes (nineteenth dynasty, ca. 1275 BCE). *British Museum*

Plate 2. Hermes (holding his caduceus) brings back Persephone from Hades to her mother Demeter; *The Return of Persephone,* oil on canvas by Frederic Leighton, 1891 *Leeds Art Gallery, U.K.*

Plate 3. The philosophers' stone represented as a hermaphrodite, or Rebis (double nature)

Cover page for De Alchimia Opuscula Complura Veterum Philosophorum, *collection of alchemical treatises, published by Cyriacus Jacobus, 1550*

Plate 4. *Astronomer Copernicus, Conversations with God,* oil painting by Jan Matejko, 1872
Jagiellonian University Museum, Kraków, Poland

Plate 5. Hieronymus Bosch's *Ascent of the Blessed*, oil painting on panel, ca. 1502 *Palazzo Ducale, Venice, Italy*

Plate 6. Tidying and decorating gravesites for Day of the Dead (*Día de Muertos*) at a cemetery in Almoloya del Rio, Mexico
AlejandroLinaresGarcia, GNU Free Documentation License

Plate 7. Siberian woman shaman (either an Altai-Kizhi or a Khakas) with drum, calling on spirits
Photo by S. I. Borisov, 1908 (Tomsk museum)

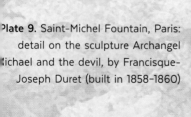

Plate 8. Mont-Saint-Michel, a sacred
site through time—
Druidic, Gaul, and Christian,
northern France

Plate 9. Saint-Michel Fountain, Paris:
detail on the sculpture Archangel
Michael and the devil, by Francisque-
Joseph Duret (built in 1858–1860)

Plate 10. The king and queen of Nagas, interlaced; stone relief, Hoysala era

Plate 11. Mahasiddha Tilopa practicing Mahamudra (The Pith Instructions)—known as the Ganges Mahamudra, in tantra meditative practice using hand and arm gestures (mudras)
Courtesy of Thouktchenling.net

Plate 12. Lararium (house shrine to the Lares) at the House of the Vettii in Pompeii. Two Lares flank an ancestor-genius holding a libation bowl and incense box, with a snake, symbol of the land's fertility and prosperity. Before 79 CE, when the city was destroyed by an eruption of the Vesuvius volcano (Italy).

Photo by Patricio Lorente,

Plate 13. *Angel of Grief* on the Pool Monument, Cypress Lawn Memorial Park, Colma, California

Photo by Seattleretro,

Plate 14. Yeshé Tsogyal: Padmasambhava's first disciple and main yogic and tantric partner
Bibek45, CC BY-SA 4.0

Plate 15. Avatars of Vajrayogini, the great secret teacher of Tantra: (a) Mekhala, the elder of the two Headless Sisters; (b) Kanakhala, the younger

a

b

Plate 16. Vajrayogini (also called Vajradakini) in the form of Nāropa's Ḍākinī; Nepalese thangka

Plate 17. Mahasiddha Ghantapa flying in tantric embrace with his Dakini; from Situ Panchen's set of thangka depicting the Eight Great Tantric Adepts (eighteenth century)

Walters Art Museum, gift of John and Berthe Ford

Plate 18. Erik Pigani playing piano in the choir of
the Royal Chapel of Saint-Frambourg, Senlis, France
Courtesy of Erik Pigani

Plate 19. *Ecstasy of Saint Teresa,* by Bernini, marble sculpture,
basilica of Santa Maria della Vittoria, Rome (ca. 1647–52)

Photo by Alvesgaspar, CC BY-SA 4.0

Plate 20. Carl Jung's
Bollingen Tower on the
shore of Zürich Lake
Photo by Andrew Taylor,
CC BY-SA 2.0

Plate 21. *The Birth of Venus* by
Sandro Botticelli (detail), tempera
on canvas (ca. 1484–86)
Uffizi Gallery, Florence

Plate 22. Vajrayogini mandala: the Vajradakini (in her red form) stands at the center of a red Sri Yantra—two entwined equilateral triangles—a rare basis-6 mandala, expressing the most powerful female Mahasiddha and immaterial teacher of Tantra

19th c. Tibetan mandala of the Naropa tradition, Rubin Museum of Art

Plate 23. Sainte Chapelle in Paris, a jewel of Rayonnant Gothic architecture, consecrated in 1248: the 139-foot-tall nave and gothic arches and its famous stained glass

Photo by Michael D. Hill Jr., CC BY-SA 3.0

Plate 24.
Notre-Dame de
Paris Cathedral:
the North Rose
Window, Rayonnant
Gothic style,
designed by
Jean de Chelles,
ca. late 1240s
(with mandala
1-8-16-32-32)
*Photo by Krzysztof
Mizera,* CC BY-SA 4.0

Plate 25. *St Jerome in the Wilderness,* by Albrecht Dürer, oil painting on pearwood (ca. 1495)
National Gallery, London

Plate 26. Confucius meets Lao-Tzu (Laozi), in the sixth century BCE; Shih Kang, Yuan dynasty (1261–1368)

孔子見老子圖・扛史 元

Shih Kang (Yüan)

Plate 27. Sankaracharya meditating and teaching, painting by Raja Ravi Varma (ca. 1900)

Plate 28. (a) Muir Snag, oldest redwood tree in the world (3,500 years old), about 140 feet (43 m) tall, base diameter of 35.9 feet (10.9 m), Giant Sequoia National Monument; (b) Methuselah Grove, home of a 4,850-year-old bristlecone pine (White Mountains, eastern California) *Photo by Oke, CC BY 3.0*

a

b

(As the research data has shown, artists are much more gifted in terms of psi than the general population.) And in this book called *Psi,* Erik Pigani inserted some of his own anomalous occurrences, notably a series that occurred in Senlis' Royal Chapel, and implied groups of spirits gathering there to listen to live music.

The Royal Chapel of Saint-Frambourg, in Senlis, France, was built at the end of the tenth century by Adelaide, queen of France and consort of Hugues Capet; then a gothic church was built at the end of the twelfth century. Georges Cziffra, the renowned pianist of Hungarian ancestry, acquired it in the mid-1970s to be the seat of his new foundation, and started its restoration, which includes eight new stained-glass windows designed by Catalan artist Joan Miró. Archaeological excavations, in the process, revealed the remnants of the Royal Chapel.

Erik Pigani recounts playing piano on the superb concert piano that occupies a place of honor in the choir of the church redesigned as a concert hall, every morning until lunch and every night until about midnight, whenever he was staying at the Foundation. When night had fallen, he was the only person in the chapel and there was only one big spotlight projecting its light on the piano (see plate 18). The following is my translation of the story Pigani relates, in French, in his book *Psi* (252–55).

"As soon as night had settled, steps were pacing up and down the alleys; there were also the sounds of chairs being moved around more or less smoothly, voices, whispers, knocks on the walls, and more. I had decided I would keep on playing whatever happened, without ever trying to peek at who could be there. Anyway, obviously nobody would be there."

One night, some time before midnight, he hears some footsteps coming from the porch of the chapel, and slowly approaching, as usual. But this time, the invisible presences climb up on the podium, then make a whole turn around the piano. "I identified the 'presence' of three persons. All by hearing, of course, since I couldn't see anything. Then they stood just behind my back. I was feeling them, so near, a few centimeters from my back. And 'it' began to whisper! Very clearly so." At which point Pigani becomes afraid they would touch him, and he bangs on the keyboard and says aloud, "If one of you ever touches me, I'll howl and I'll never come back. For one, I'm working, and also, it's disturbing me. Everything stopped. Total silence. About ten minutes later I left to go to sleep, extremely troubled." When he recounts the events the next morning to Cziffra, he is dumbfounded to learn that the great pianist had exactly the same experience when playing at night, repeatedly so, including the talking behind his back, and similarly sometimes he had to bang on the piano and call for silence.

Sometimes a group would come to visit the chapel and the crypt, accompanied by a guide, and Pigani would hear and see them enter and walk up the central aisle with his peripheral vision (the piano being set diagonally to the church). One Saturday morning, he wakes up with an imperious desire to play Mozart's Sonatas, a music wholly outside his normal repertory and he comes with the sheet music in two booklets. And when a group of about forty visitors comes in and walks toward the choir, he is just astonished not to have been told beforehand of their venue. And he follows them through the corner of his eyes while still playing. "That's when—a highly unusual behavior for such a group— everybody took their seats on the first row of chairs, some ten feet from the piano . . . I wasn't happy at all." At the end of the sonata he was working on, he stops so that they can leave, but nobody moves, and so he resumes playing one sonata after another.

"I was seeing and feeling the attention of this improvised public on me, and so was trying to play as best as possible. This Mozart recital must have lasted at least three quarters of an hour. Suddenly, the phone rang. As it was set near the entrance, the other side of the chapel, each time somebody called me I had to run to answer it. So I stopped playing, got to my feet, and, turning to the audience, I started to say: 'I'm sorry, the phone . . .' *There was nobody! Nothing.* This group I had perceived all along had abruptly disappeared. Just like that! I got my head all mixed up. I ran toward the phone, which was still ringing, grabbed it . . . Nothing. Not even a tone: it was not plugged to the landline." Then he goes to the main house, and Mrs. Cziffra, on opening the door, tells him she was just going to call him for lunch. Furthermore, that morning, no group had visited the chapel, and the phone had been left disconnected.

What we see in this account is such a remarkable perception of the human silhouettes, both auditory and visual, that the pianist believes that there are real people sitting on the chairs. I have presented in this book several instances of this phenomenon—the fact that spirits in etheric bodies are making sounds while walking, are able to open a door, knock on wood (as on the tables in séances), strike a bell, or make the phone ring. According to my ISS theory, we have to view these etheric bodies as consisting of hyperdimensional energy; and consequently, these effects on matter are not caused by a body weight, nor a muscular force, of course, but are simply the effect of the very potent HD energy, that of the syg-field of the souls of the deceased.

JUNG'S *SEVEN SERMONS TO THE DEAD*

In *Memories, Dreams, Reflections* Jung recounts that, on a Sunday in mid-January 1916, he received the extraordinary visit of a large group of ascended souls with whom he would communicate. Two weeks later, he would write the *Seven Sermons to the Dead* in a creative spree in just nine days.

> It began with a restlessness, but I did not know what it meant or what "they" wanted of me. There was an ominous atmosphere all around me. I had the strange feeling that the air was filled with ghostly entities. Then it was as if my house began to be haunted. . . .
>
> Around five o'clock in the afternoon on Sunday the front doorbell began ringing frantically . . . but there was no one in sight. I was sitting near the doorbell, and not only heard it but saw it moving. We all simply stared at one another. The atmosphere was thick, believe me! Then I knew that something had to happen. The whole house was filled as if there were a crowd present, crammed full of spirits.

They were packed deep right up to the door, and the air was so thick it was scarcely possible to breathe. As for myself, I was all a-quiver with the question: "For God's sake, what in the world is this?" Then they cried out in chorus, "We have come back from Jerusalem where we found not what we sought." That is the beginning of the *Septem Sermones*. (*Memories, Dreams, Reflections,* 190–91)

Jung further explained in his memoirs that this numinous experience with the ascended souls triggered his fourteen-year-long "confrontation with the unconscious" and was a prelude to his later exploration of the psychic and archetypal dimension, an introduction to all of his further research and books.

MEMORIES OF PAST INCARNATIONS

The belief in reincarnation—that an individual soul, living in the soul dimension, takes on a new body in our matter dimension and resides in it until bodily death—is rooted in the idea of the soul's continuous existence and learning. This worldview is widely shared in the world, as it exists in most Eastern religions (Hinduism, Tibetan Buddhism, Jainism, Sikhism, Baha'ism) and some Shiite creeds of Islam, such as the Lebanese Druses and the Turkish Alevis. It exists also in some American-Indian people (such as the Tlingit and the Haida of Alaska). We find it also in Eastern and Western Africa, in the South Pacific, in Central Australia, and among the Ainu in Japan. As for the West, surveys have shown that 18 percent of people in Europe (Gallup poll 1968), 20 percent in the United States, and 26 percent in Canada (Gallup poll 1969) believe in reincarnation.

Ian Stevenson conducted a wide range of studies in several cultures and had already accumulated more than 1,600 cases, with witnesses dutifully investigated on site, by 1977, and reported on them in his three-volume *Cases of the Reincarnation Type*.

In most cases, children start making spontaneous remarks about their past lives between age two and four, sometimes giving such precise information as to their name, family members, city and profession, circumstances of their death, and the like, that the investigators could actually find the family house and confront the child with some family members in blind tests of recognition. A stunning fact is that in some cases a birthmark corresponded to a blow received in their past life, often the one that killed them. The child would show the mark to their parents and claim that's where they were hit "before."

Here is my summary of the complex Sujith Lakma case, issued from Sri Lanka and detailed in Stevenson's second volume, *Ten cases in Sri Lanka*.

Sujith, born in Colombo in August 1969, started at two and a half years old to speak about his life in Gorakana (about seven miles from his birthplace). He stated he was then called Gorakana Sammy; that his father, called Jamis, had a damaged eye; and that he knew a monk named Amita. Then he mentioned his wife Maggie, with whom he had violent quarrels, that he had worked in railway stations and also sold Arrack alcohol; he described how he was killed by a truck while he was drunk.

A monk from a nearby temple wrote down all the declarations of the child and went to investigate in Gorakana. He found evidence of a Sammy Fernando, killed in January 1969 by a truck when he was drunk (thus seven months before his birth). Fernando's father, Jamis, had a damaged eye and his wife was called Maggilin or Maggie. He had indeed trafficked Arrack after having worked in the railways. Sujith had given many additional names and details on his past life, and practically all of them were verified. Stevenson in 1973 found both Sujith and the monk and, fortunately, there had been no interaction whatsoever between the two families before he started his own investigation.

Reincarnation cases sometimes implied xenoglossy, the anomalous capacity to speak a foreign language without having ever heard about it, which is a stunning feature of trance states (especially during possession rituals, such as in Voodoo). For example in one case, the child could sing ancient songs of the totally different language and culture of her past life; in another Stevenson case, Uttara Huddar, as a young adult, experienced episodes of quasi possession by her past personality as a Bengali, and couldn't even operate whatever household appliances had been invented since then. In these periods, generally lasting about two days, she would speak and write Bengali and couldn't understand a word of her Marathi native language; she gave a lot of information about her past life to Bengali-speaking people.

Altogether, the strength of the reincarnation cases gathered by Ian Stevenson amounts to a strong corroboration of the apparitions of the deceased cases, all giving weight to the existence of a dimension in which souls dwell as free and evolving, self-conscious and self-driven personalities; it also underlines the reality of intentional and repeated incarnations on Earth, with an intermediary period between them.

9
DIALOGUES WITH PAST GENIUSES

The way spiritual and psi capacities evolve in one's life (as far as I've experienced it) is through abrupt leaps, and these leaps in both domains—spirituality and psi—happen at different times and cycles, despite the fact they are linked.

In fact, this has been the major difference between the East and the West. The East has always pursued an inner path toward spiritual knowledge, relishing the experience of high states of consciousness and yoga, each master bringing his or her own original stone to make it a millennia-old scientific body of knowledge. Conversely, due mainly to a dogmatic or literal reading of the scriptures and biblical texts and the moralistic bent inherited from it—as well as the inflexible and pitiless repression of any departure from dogma in Catholicism—Christianity has mainly developed exercises to achieve higher morality and strict, unconditional faith. The exceptional and rare individuals to have attained states of fusion with God, such as Teresa of Ávila or John of the Cross (both reformers of the Carmelites order in Spain), left us with magnificent poems and descriptions and techniques to develop these states. They were the rare witnesses of blissful ecstatic states in Christian mysticism, as we see it so finely expressed in the splendid *Ecstasy of Saint Teresa,* by Gian Lorenzo Bernini (see plate 19, and fig. 9.1 for a detail of the face).

Fig. 9.1. *The Ecstasy of Saint Teresa,* marble sculpture by Bernini, detail of the face (ca. 1647–52). Basilica of Santa Maria della Vittoria, Rome. *Photo by Nina Aldin Thune, CC BY-SA 2.5*

Teresa had entered the cloister of Carmelites in Ávila, Spain, of her own volition at age twenty (in 1535), and soon became very sick; yet she experienced the four stages of the ascension of the soul and described this path toward ecstasy in her own writings (notably her *Autobiography*). After the stages of "mental prayer" and "prayer of quiet," the mystic attains the "devotions of union" and then the "devotion of ecstasy"—the union or fusion with God, while all awareness of the body has disappeared. She had also been observed levitating during Mass on several occasions. About twenty-five years later, Teresa had frequent visions of Jesus Christ for over two years.

Despite these blissful states of fusion with the divine realm, Teresa advocated voluntary flagellation, on a weekly basis, during Mass. As for John of the Cross, he was imprisoned by his superiors because of his dedication to Teresa's reformation of the Carmelites order, and tortured with repeated public lashing and severe isolation, until he escaped about nine months later.

In contrast, along the millennia, the Eastern religious and philosophical traditions have kept accumulating knowledge about an array of techniques aimed at following one's inner path in order to attain the Oneness or nonduality state—the fusion of the ego with the Self and cosmic consciousness. They urge all individuals on a quest to harness one of the many yogas in order to achieve transcendent states of consciousness, namely Oneness states or *samadhis,* in which the little ego may become harmonized with the higher Self or soul, itself naturally bathing in the divine cosmic consciousness.

I'm now experienced enough to bear witness to the fact that, with a high-spirited intent, we can keep on improving both our spiritual and psi capacities, developing new ones, and even experiencing leaps in consciousness up to an advanced age. The only reason why it should stop would be if we believe we are "not gifted" or "too old" for such self-development and improvement.

This is seemingly the same for the souls of the deceased dwelling in the syg-dimension, who follow a continuous learning path, such as through their work and service to humanity, as they themselves have told me. In fact, if you remember, during my dialogue with Wolfgang Pauli—the quantum physicist who collaborated with Carl Jung on synchronicity—he told me that he was still in permanent contact with Jung, that they kept working together.

As I mentioned, telepathy is the most widespread of all psi phenomena, on the rise everywhere, and especially in the West. This is why it has been quite an enigma for me that people gifted with telepathy would generally not be able to tune in to the syg-hyperdimension and communicate with the deceased. In contrast, in Sub-Sahel Africa, the communication with deceased parents and kin is so frequent and well accepted that it is recounted to the rest of the family without hindrance and the information thus received is held in great esteem. However, it seems it is more generally the spirits of the deceased who appear of their own volition rather than the living initiating the contact. They mostly do that in order to give a piece of advice, and their silhouette is seen, and their voice heard clearly, either in or around the family property, or in unambiguous dreams. Also, in traditional West Africa, all decisions concerning the village and problems arising within the community are discussed and worked out with the chief of the village and the elders, while the people are assembled under the Palabre Tree (*l'arbre à palabres*). This tree is a century-old tree standing just in front of the village entrance, and in which the spirits of the ancestors are said to reside. It means that these ancestors are welcome to preside over and have a say in the global decisions and even in the solving of family problems (often they are consulted using a divination procedure such as *cauris,* or shells).

With regard to telepathy, I've been somewhat of a bad test subject. I've shied and shielded myself from it from my very first experiences in an Orthodox Christian monastery in Brittany when I was nineteen years old—something I recount in detail in *The Sacred Network,* because it was also my first experience of a telepathic field, a shared mind state. A poet and writer since my midteens, I felt the monks' telepathic voices as a sheer intrusion in my mind, a disruption of my state of consciousness and of my inner connection with my deep Self. And the fact that I was introverted and extremely shy at the time of course didn't help. I reveled in solitude and felt very awkward in social circles in France until well after I started being a published author. (In contrast, I was very open to people while traveling—and had to be in order to survive.) This connection to my inner Self has been the source of my spiritual life and of my creativity all along, and at that early time, I couldn't reconcile it with telepathy, which felt like a chatter interfering and putting me off balance, that is, until I reached India and had a similar shared-mind experience with ascetics and inward-prone meditators in a sacred town. That's when I understood that telepathic chatter was not of the essence—but a harmonic field of shared consciousness was; and I began to call them *harmonic fields;* then still later, when I understood the whole gamut of these collective shared-mind states, I coined the term *Telhar fields,* meaning "telepathic-harmonic fields."

While blocking out telepathy whenever it was on the social, extraverted side, I turned my attention to a whole other array of psychic capacities that fascinated me so much that I eagerly sought to explore and increase them. These included healing and precognition, as well as OBEs with full-fledged daily travels to otherworldly realms (for a few months during my first travel to India). Through meditation, I acquired a skill for tuning in to higher spiritual frequencies. And this could well be the reason why I became able to hear the deceased and connect with them in the hyperdimension. And yet, despite the fact I could feel and perceive immaterial bodies—whether of the deceased or of living friends in etheric or dream body, as in OBEs—my hearing or exchange of thoughts with the deceased remained at a primitive and basic stage for more than two decades.

Here are some examples of this kind of basic exchange . . .

I had quite a few interactions with Carl Jung, an otherworldly friend and mentor, that were always initiated by him in the early phases.

A first instance happened when I was at last able to buy a writing house, on the Cher River, where I could write and meditate far from Paris' frenzy. I chose the first floor of the square tower to be my summer writing room. This room was an ancient tile oven, a square about four yards by four yards, with raw, uncarved stones grossly striped from the antique black carbon. That's where they would pile up the tiles, using an outside staircase made of large stones and still visible, while just underneath on the ground floor (now a kitchen), was, I believe, where they would light up a sustained fire to cook the tiles. The renovated room also featured a brand-new roof looking like a mandala in beams and an open chimney in one corner. The room was stunning because the uncarved stones, whitish with deep black veins and spaces between them, were penetrating inside at various lengths, some long and flat enough on the top that I could set a flower vase there. The whole room was a sculpture by itself! After I had found a flat place where I could have my back to the wall, facing the tiny window and with a diagonal view of the fireplace, I installed my low writing table on a large carpet. Then, the only decoration I felt like adding to the room was a small sand-color carpet with a bronze candle holder, a unique sacred object, and a vase of fresh flowers. That same day . . .

In the evening, at my table I sat, contemplating this unbelievable writing place, its sheer beauty, its inspiring symbolism, thinking to myself with amusement: *Now I am in the alchemical oven—there to slowly bake!*

I was astonished to suddenly hear Jung's voice, coming with his face, and saying to me: "I found and prepared this place for you!"

I thanked him profusely.

It's true that only somebody well versed in alchemy and mandalas could have thought about making such a room from an old and blackened room-size tile oven, scraping the carbon-dirty stones just enough to make the white appear, yet not trying to equalize or square them, and as a result, the ancient oven fragrance was welcoming me each time I entered the room. (These stones were the white and soft *pierres de Bourré,* the stones used for the Cher and Touraine castles.) I knew that the preceding owners—a refined middle-aged couple—had been the ones to do all the restoration, and yet they had kept this countryside place only five years. I kept reflecting on what it signified that Jung had "prepared" this place for me, creating the absolute ideal writing place in a square tower overlooking the river. It meant, on the part of Jung, no less than a subtle influence on the previous owners while they chose how to renovate the building.

And Jung, beyond his depth psychology work, was a scholar and writer who had constructed his own writing tower, slowly along the years and in constant sync with the deep symbolism of his life's work (see plate 20). As he describes it in his memoirs, he had added at different epochs a round tower and a square tower to the main building set on the shore of Zürich Lake.

As for me, as soon as I was in this house on the Cher River, in a matter of days I focused on two major new works. One was my Semantic Fields theory (SFT) on nonlocal consciousness—on which I had written a first chapter in a creative trance when I prospected the region three months earlier at Easter, and indeed found *the* house of my visualizations (affordable to me only because it was on flood-prone land). The other was a literary biographic book, in poetic prose, called *Saya*. The theory one, I was writing during the winter in front of a large fireplace downstairs, and the literary one each summer in *la Tour* (the Tower). (The writing of both works lasted several years.)

Another instance happened a few years later. I was at the time finalizing the first draft of my SFT (a book in French called at that time "Wisdom of the Unconscious") in order to propose it to my publisher. I was in the Tower, sitting cross-legged on the ground mattress next to my desk and mulling over the table of contents, when I heard Jung telling me:

"This long chapter on your archetypal dreams [to which I had given a Jungian interpretation], it doesn't really belong to this book. You should take it out. It will find its place in another book later."

As I checked again the table of contents, I realized he was right and crossed it off, thanking him for his advice. This manuscript, judged too complex, was not accepted for publishing. It was only in 1998, exactly nine years (plus or minus a week) after the first chapter emerged spontaneously at Easter, that I published the book—now called *Networks of Meaning*—in the States with Praeger. And in the process, the work became a full-fledged cognitive theory, based on a systems and chaos theory framework—thus making the Jungian dreams chapter even more irrelevant. And indeed, despite the fact that I had lost the original chapter, my most striking symbolic and Jungian dreams were included in a whole book focused on Jungian thinking and my theory, *La Prédiction de Jung* (Jung's Prediction), where they did fit perfectly well—a book that I wrote in less than a year, in 2010–11. Thus Jung's hyperdimensional spirit had demonstrated a very precise precognition about fourteen years in advance (to the start of my writing *La Prédiction de Jung*), just as Pauli's spirit, as we will see in a moment, was right in his 1996 prediction of my cosmological theory that I started, this one also in a visionary trance, at the end of October 2012 (thus sixteen years later).

The most remarkable instance of communication and of forecasting given to me by Jung happened when I was finishing the book I just mentioned, *La Prédiction de Jung*.

I was already running late on the deadline—just a few days away—to submit my manuscript to my publisher via my collection director (we were in mid-2011). The whole book was ready and reviewed twice, references and notes in due order, and I was now rereading the last part, the "Theoretical Crown," which was a formal exposition of my whole Semantic Fields theory and its Jungian perspective. But then suddenly, an emergence of a totally new level of my theory, in a quantum physics framework, unfolded at blinding speed in the course of two or three days. The concepts were so novel, so astonishing, that I was immersed day and night in them, thus adding thirteen book pages to the last chapter before the already written conclusion. Strangely, this new stuff began to pour in just after the paragraphs that dealt with Pauli and Jung's revolutionary concept of a level of reality being both energy and psyche, and specifically with the former's dream about this "deep reality" being separate and independent from quantum mechanics (398–401). And I came up with three extra dimensions beyond the 4D of physical spacetime, and applied the concepts immediately to tackle the entanglement of particles from this radically novel perspective (presented in Hardy 2020).

After a full night of inspired writing and hardly four hours of sleep, I was in the kitchen in Provence preparing myself some food. I felt so awed and stunned by the stuff that had emerged during the previous night that I was in a state of shock. When, abruptly, I remembered that the deadline to give my manuscript to my publisher was the next day. I was pacing the kitchen, oppressed, toasting some bread yet totally focused on my thoughts:

With the quality and importance of what's springing up right now, maybe I should give the process a chance to further develop. Maybe I should just call (my publisher) and tell him that I need one or two more weeks?

I suddenly heard a voice and a mind addressing me from three feet away, and became aware of an energy field—that I recognized as Jung's—who said telepathically:

"No, don't do that. It's extremely important that you submit your book to your publisher at the preset date. Don't worry, all these novel concepts will all come together perfectly in a new book you'll write at a later time."

"Really? Then, if that's so, I'll wrap up the manuscript tonight and send it by email tomorrow."

Thereafter I was engulfed in some new projects, particularly in researching the Sumerian tablets and writing a work on the subject* that stressed the numerous analogies and the no-less-disturbing discrepancies between these and the biblical book of Genesis.

It's only in late 2012 that I started to develop the whole new level of my theory, this time modeling consciousness as a hyperdimension at the origin of the universe, as well as pervading the whole matter dimension (the 4D reality of space and time). Needless to say, the three entwined extra dimensions I had envisioned about a year and a half earlier— hyperspace, hypertime, and cosmic consciousness—were the foundation stones of this new cosmology.

It was again in an amazing visionary state that I came up, in only eighteen days (from October 28 to November 14, 2012), with this complete cosmological theory rooted in quantum physics but diverging from it (even if writing the book took me a year, these core chapters remained quasi-intact). It is remarkable that this creative state was, just as the previous year, triggered by the prior analysis of Pauli's highly symbolic dreams. Yet, despite the lengthy conversation we had sixteen years earlier, no real dialogue with him happened during this intense process. The only bewildering expression of our deep-reality connection, during my eighteen-day creative and visionary state, was the sudden

---

*The core of this work on Sumer was written in two sojourns of five weeks each, in India, in December–January and March of 2012, and published in two books in 2014 and 2016. I'm sorry for the chronology of this yet uncompleted decade being a bit confusing, even for myself, as I've been on a writing and publishing spree, with nine books published to date in seven years starting with *The Sacred Network* in 2011, and we are in November 2017 as I make (what'll be the first) review of this book.

appearance, as a whole complex wax structure in my large candle holder, of part of his "World Clock" dream.

This dream features two interlocked round clocks with thirty-two partitions (4 x 8)—one blue vertical and one four-colored and horizontal—sharing a unique (but void) center and first carried as a gold ring by a black eagle. The world clock has three rhythms: when the hand on the vertical clock has advanced thirty-two times (short rhythm), it moves the horizontal clock's hand 1/32 degree (middle rhythm). The completion of the 32 degrees on the horizontal clock, circled by the gold ring, is the great rhythm. This vision gave Pauli "an impression of the most sublime harmony" because the three rhythms express themselves in a base-4 spacetime (the two orthogonal clocks).* Moreover, my wax sculpture evolved dynamically (with the wax melting) to show the vertical clock's hand move down slowly during twenty or so minutes' time.

Furthermore, as I'll recount it now, Pauli had also forecast to me that I would one day add a whole new level to my Semantic Fields theory.

Let's keep in mind, though, that prior to this 1996 dialogue with Pauli, I hadn't experienced any lengthy conversation with souls inhabiting the hyperdimension, only short exchanges such as the ones in the early 1990s with Jung. (The two conversations with my father happened in 2001—the first while driving toward Provence, when he had received the visit from departed relatives in the hospital, and the second just after his death when he shared his discovery of the reality of the afterlife.)

DIALOGUE WITH PAULI

That day, a beautiful sunny afternoon in my writing house on the Cher River, I had decided to read an article on Wolfgang Pauli, one

---

*Carl Jung describes and analyzes the dream in *Psychology and Alchemy,* 194. See also the letter from Pauli to Jung relating to the dream in Wolfgang Pauli, *Atom and Archetype,* 20–21.

of the fathers of quantum physics and a university friend of Werner Heisenberg, who both became Nobel Prize winners. At Munich University in Germany where they prepared their doctoral thesis, Pauli and Heisenberg used to discuss and work together, exchanging ideas during long strolls. In the year 1925, the two brilliant friends must have experienced an extraordinary state of creative breakthrough since both had a stroke of genius: Heisenberg posed the bases of quantum mechanics a few months before Pauli came up with the exclusion principle for which he received the Nobel Prize in 1945. But what made the destiny of Pauli so singular was that he had, beyond his sharp scientific intellect, an extremely developed intuition that allowed him to comprehend the depth psychology of Carl Jung and get involved in research of his own.

Between 1928 and 1958, Pauli was physics professor at the Technology Institute of Zurich, the city in Switzerland where Jung had the chair of psychiatry at the university and had his psychoanalysis practice as well. However, Pauli left Zurich from 1940 to 1946 to become professor of theoretical physics at the Institute for Advanced Studies in Princeton, New Jersey. At twenty-eight years old, following his divorce, problems in his emotional life brought him to seek the help of Carl Jung; but very wisely Jung referred him to one of his assistants for his psychoanalysis, in order to continue a friendly and collegial relationship with him. This nearly thirty-year friendship between the two scholars was to give rise to the fascinating correspondence between them published in 2014 as *Atom and Archetype*.

Just in the first few months of his analysis, Pauli produced about a thousand dreams of exceptional quality that were a gold mine for Jung because they showed clearly a spiritual transmutation guided by the Self—a spontaneous spiritual awakening that he called *individuation*. According to Jung (and all Eastern religions), this spiritual development is a natural process in a healthy psyche, because the ultimate goal of the soul or Self of the person is the harmonization of the ego with the Self. Until this harmonization happens, the Self remains mostly hidden in the personal unconscious, but still able to guide the spiritual development of the person, notably through symbolic dreams.

Pauli's dreams were putting into play the very symbols of this transmutation and alchemical process, and they were a delight for Jung to interpret in his books (the Pauli dream material is Jung's main source for the dreams he analyzes). Pauli was a fantastic dreamer and obviously he was at the time in a dazzling awakening process, partly triggered and nourished by his discovery of depth psychology. It's fortunate for us that Jung and Pauli mostly used letters to communicate, whereas they would meet and converse in Zurich rather rarely. At the peak of their correspondence in 1952, Jung was working on two books simultaneously—one on the biblical book of Job (published as *Answer to Job*), and the other on *synchronicity*, the term he coined to refer to meaningful coincidences. Both men were also highly gifted with psi, Jung more on the visionary and precognitive side, while Pauli was more on the PK side (psychokinesis or mind-over-matter). In the course of their exchanges, they came to envision a layer of reality that would be both matter (energy) and psyche (consciousness), for which Pauli (through a dream) came up with the term *deep reality*. This specific deep reality dream presented an energy of consciousness existing below quantum fields and distinct from them. (Years later, I understood it was nothing less than the dimension of all the Selfs or souls—which I then called the syg-hyperdimension.)

The result of these fascinating written discussions (beyond their publication) was a co-authored book in 1955 called *The Interpretation of Nature and Psyche*. Jung's part—his essay on synchronicity—met an immense success when it was published separately as *Synchronicity*. As for Pauli's part, it was focused on the symbolism and the archetypes found in the cosmological theory of Johannes Kepler—the eminent astronomer and mathematician of the early seventeenth century. Pauli was thus showing that even hard science and the creation of new scientific concepts make use of the fecund soil of the psyche and its opening on the soul dimension.

All in all, when, in 1996, I saw an article (by H. Atmanspacher and H. Primas) called "The Hidden Side of Wolfgang Pauli" in the *Journal of Consciousness Studies,* I was extremely curious because I was expecting to learn *at last* what Pauli had to say on synchronicity. Whereas I had studied in depth Jung's book *Synchronicity,* I had not bought or read their co-authored book, and their correspondence would be published only in the year 2000 in France and in 2014 in English (as *Atom and Archetype*). Of Pauli, I knew only his major physics discoveries and the fact he had collaborated with Jung.

Now, allow me another digression that will illuminate the scientific background of this conversation.

When I had worked at the parapsychology lab in Princeton in the mid-1980s, preparing my doctoral thesis, the whole field of research was engrossed with QM, and our state-of-the-art theories explained psi by the entanglement of particles. The entanglement (called at that time nonlocal correlations) showed an interaction at great distances between particles that could be a medium for distant communication or exchange of information, such as in telepathy or in remote viewing. Most advanced and praised were the theories of Evan H. Walker and Walter von Lucadou, as well as Robert Jahn and Brenda Dunne's larger framework. The exaltation for quantum physics in our field reflected what was happening in all domains of science: all the forefront scientists as well as the public, were seduced by QM paradoxes and weirdness, especially now that Alain Aspect had just brought a resounding proof of both the entanglement and the QM indeterminacy. And in contrast Einstein's concept of fields and causality ("hidden variables" driving quantum processes) seemed rather outdated, despite a noted yet inconsistent enthusiasm for David Bohm's Pilot Waves theory.

Yet, as far as I was concerned (and a bit awkwardly for a foreign doctoral student with a basic assistant researcher's position), I held on to a field theory of psi, albeit quietly. In fact, the whole array of psi and spiritual experiences I had lived during the ten years of my quester's travels could make sense only if an unknown type of *energy of conscious-ness,* and *fields* created by this consciousness-energy, were involved. Whether telepathic-harmonic fields (Telhar fields of shared conscious-ness), the meaningful energy imprinted in any place and especially in sacred sites, auras, or rays around sacred objects or temples . . . all were implying fields of consciousness. And since my first travel to the East, I had given the name semantic fields (*semantic* equals "meaningful" in Greek) to these fields in order to make sense of my experiences. So, for example, I knew I was seeing and sensing the semantic energy and the semantic fields (or in short syg-energy, syg-fields) of trees and temples, or the specific Telhar field of a sacred town.

Curious about the unknown reaches of the mind, and eager to explore them, I would often give myself some challenge, on the spur of the moment, just to see if such and such feat was indeed possible. Here is a telling example that tested the specific print of a syg-field that, according to my worldview (and theory), had to exist in any building; in other words, because a building is a social space, it is charged with meaningful or syg-energy by the people using this social space, and by its sheer purpose when being built. And then the history of its use (and its semantic environment) adds to its semantic field, making it very spe-cial and distinct from any other building, even one having the same function. In that sense, St. John Cathedral in New York will have a syg-field different from that of Glastonbury Abbey, and different also from the syg-field of Paris Cathedral, despite being all contained within the larger semantic field of the Catholic religion. However, the syg-field, being mostly consciousness and mental energy, does not necessarily have a body or structure in space and time; thus, a scientific domain, or a faith, are collective syg-fields.

On with my example; here is the challenge I gave to myself when I visited Hong Kong for the first time in my life.

I had a discussion right at the end of the long flight from Europe with an English man living in HK, an expat; we had agreed to meet at a bar in HK island that same night, a bar he knew, called The Fringe

Club. When we parted at the airport, he was suddenly in a hurry to leave; I produced a map of the larger continental and island HK metropolis, about six inches wide, that I had gotten at the travel agency, and he drew hastily a circle about half an inch wide on the western side of the island, while telling me that anyway, I just had to ask anybody about the bar. In the late afternoon, I found an affordable guesthouse on the mainland side of HK. Later in the evening I left well ahead of our appointment because I knew there was a ferry to take and wanted to enjoy my first vision of the city. Indeed, the sunset view from the harbor, waiting for the ferry, was breathtaking! I immediately fell in love with this stunning city. When we reached the island, I was in high spirits and I had the impromptu idea to try to find the bar solely by stalking its semantic field. Would it be possible to find a place just by knowing its name? Could a mind connect with the syg-field of a bar (or any building) through its name alone—and be able to sense and track its location at a distance? That was an exciting challenge, and I started walking eagerly (grossly toward the left, as the drawn circle had indicated), keeping the name in my mind and trying to feel the surroundings and which streets to take. But generally I don't like walking, and so, after a while I got bored and reconsidered:

What if I'm going in the wrong direction, and then I'll have to cross the city the other way around to the place? Suddenly, there was a little voice in my head that replied, with a grain of humor:

And what if you're going in the right direction and stupidly stop the experiment and ask your way? You would never know if it's possible to find a bar just going by its name!

That was a point. I kept walking. But another few streets farther, again I got bored and wanted to stop this "stupid game"; the voice gave me the same counter-argument. And I walked intuitively again, climbing a peak through tiny alleys and staircases. Another fifteen minutes and I was not only bored but tired. Now I was going to stop and ask for the bar. The voice said nothing. I saw a man in a uniform guarding some kind of official or commercial building and asked him for The

Fringe Club. "Oh," said he, "it's just right there, next door!" And guess what: when I checked my minimal map the next day for the name of the street that I had finally written down, it was not even within the large circle drawn by my friend!

I knew now for certain that it was indeed possible to stalk a semantic field just by its semantic print tagged by its name. It showed that the syg-energy print of a place or building existed in the first place and was very distinguishable from other prints. But it proved something more: Some unknown and unexploited sense could make out that syg-print and trace it in space! Amazing! As far as I can sense it, the syg-field of an object (or system) is like a bundle of frequencies having a range of significations, and yet expressing a global meaning. Yet, the frequencies of syg-energy are not in the EM or even quantum spectrum. According to my cosmological theory—the Infinite Spiral Staircase theory—these are sub-quantum frequencies of the hypertime dimension, deeply enmeshed with the energy of consciousness (in the syg-hyperdimension).

It is through numerous experiences of this type that I had become utterly convinced of the existence of consciousness-energy and of syg-fields, while I knew all along they consisted of an unknown type of energy—nothing like EM fields whatsoever!

Yet, back at "the Lab," each time I would try to make my point about a field theory of consciousness and psi, I was kind of looked down upon as if I was a bit retarded. Fields were definitely not trendy at the time. Indeterminacy was. And if quantum events were indeterminate and random, they excluded fields at that scale—because a field is by definition an organization (with some order) between elements, and thus the opposite of randomness (which is an absolute absence of order).

And yet the entanglement—the correlation or communication between particles at great distances—if it was a proven fact, was still far from being understood. Just imagine a scholar in the Middle Ages able to demonstrate and prove that an iron bar is attracting scraps of iron, but without any knowledge of electromagnetism and electrons. I'm convinced that it is precisely the situation we are in right now with the entanglement: not only are we missing a specific type of energy—with a whole spectrum just as the EM one—but this energy is the one tied to consciousness, the one that supports our thinking process. It is also the syg-energy of the spirits of the deceased, of the dreamtime bodies (such as in OBEs), and that of our Self or soul. As the energy of the hyper-dimension, syg-energy is also what allows any system to interact with any coupled or resonant system through the hyperdimension, that is, beyond space and time—as expressed in the entanglement of particles and in psi as well.

The entanglement, in the mid-1980s, was no better understood than it is today. Thus, given our total ignorance of both the nature of the entanglement and the nature of psi, it was a leap of faith to assume that telepathy and other psi capacities were working "just like the entanglement" and to further assume that both had to rule out fields and any type of order. For one, the entanglement is obviously not a random process; to the contrary, it's a specific bonding derived from Pauli's law of spin, which poses that, in paired particles, if one is turning clockwise, the other one must turn anticlockwise. And second, theories such as David Bohm's Pilot Waves propose an underlying order or hidden variables that would guide or pilot the quantum processes, and there's nothing to preclude a hyperdimension acting as such.*

By saying that, I'm not putting into question the indeterminacy (randomness) at the quantum scale—a fact well established and proven. I'm rather suggesting that the entanglement doesn't belong to this quantum layer of reality, but to a sub-quantum layer: that of the hyperdimension itself operating with a specific energy linked to consciousness and not bound by either spacetime laws or quantum indeterminacy. And if it is so, then we must meet the inescapable consequence: since, in ISST's definition of the hyperdimension, consciousness is interwoven with hyperspace and hypertime, if the entanglement stems from a HD process, *then* it is endowed with consciousness (and the insights of

---

*See Bohm, *Wholeness and the Implicate Order.*

Jean Charon, that particles somehow had a form of consciousness, were just right on the mark!).

Now, the second assumption of mine back at PRL was that consciousness was an energy of an unknown type and operating beyond space and time. This one concept was even worse for the evaluation of my intelligence by my peers, because "everybody knew" that psi was *information* (as opposed to matter, energy, particles)—period. That was the demarcation line between being considered a sophisticated mind as opposed to a soft brain. Yet, a good proportion of these psi researchers—most of them Ph.D.s—had no problem accepting the reality of PK or mind-over-matter. For example, psychic healing or bio-PK experiments were consistently getting high positive results through the work of the most rigorous and highly regarded researchers, such as William Braud, Marilyn Schlitz, and later Elisabeth Targ. Nevertheless, for most of my colleagues, it had to be information only doing the trick, even if information is the opposite of randomness (and thus of QM indeterminacy).

Let's now get back to Jung and Pauli, the topics we just covered being crucial to understanding my dialogue with Pauli.

Jung had explained psi as a synchronicity, that is, coincidences that were not random but, to the contrary, highly meaningful. Thus psi was a synchronicity between a mind and (1) a distant place in case of clairvoyance; or (2) a future time in case of precognition. In fact, Jung knew the work of Joseph Banks Rhine, the pioneer who started the field of experimental parapsychology in his laboratory in Durham.

As for Pauli, he was himself an outstanding psi subject in the domain of PK, despite the fact that the large effects he produced on matter systems were involuntary. For example, when he was attached to the Institute for Advanced Studies in Princeton, each time he was on site at the lab, all the computers would crash simultaneously. It was to such an extent and so precise an effect that the researchers gave it a name: the Pauli Effect. One day, all computers crashed, and they expected Pauli to enter the lab any moment, but they were left perplexed when he didn't show up. However, they soon learnt that, at that very time, Pauli had been commuting at the nearby train station.

Jung had been a primary witness of Pauli's nonintentional PK. When Pauli entered a high-profile ceremony organized by Jung for the opening of his institute in Zurich, a large decorative vase broke in pieces all by itself, one that had a very important symbolic meaning.

Jung was himself prone to such "exteriorization of psychic energy," that is, to manifestations of the PK-type, with or without a medium-istic setting. Thus, as we saw, loud bangs resonated in Freud's library shelves during an exacerbated discussion they had on psi. Despite the fact that Freud had designated Jung as his successor in the psychoana-lytic movement, this event led to the split between the two scholars and Jung starting his own depth psychology research and school. Jung was also gifted with other types of psi—precognitive dreams, dialogues with the deceased, and visions (as recounted in his autobiography).

Let me recount what I knew about Pauli at the time I read the article:

- I knew that Jung and Pauli had worked together on synchronicity, sorting out its basic principles—meaningful coincidences, non-random and noncausal, not abiding by space, time, and EM laws (such as the decrease of EM signal with distance).
- Both of them had personal experiences of psi, including PK.
- Jung had, early on, stated that consciousness (the psyche) was a psychic energy.
- Jung held that there was a dimension of the Self (or the Archetype) beyond matter, space, and time, in which mind (consciousness) and matter (energy) were merged.

This is why, when I discovered the article promising to shed the light on the "hidden side of Pauli" I thought I was going to get—at last—some great revelations about Pauli's physics work on synchronicity. (I'll ask you, my readers, to visualize the scene and to be keen to notice all details, because this event provided me with a major break-through on the workings of our unconscious Self—who seems to go on *hiser** own life in the hyperdimension without our conscious mind being aware of it most of the time. In the event recounted below, there was an intriguing blend of awareness and unawareness about my Self being in contact with the soul of Pauli—especially in the utterly weird way it started—and this is precisely the anomaly that's tearing the veil on the workings of our hyperdimensional Self.)

That day, the time was just right for a good read in my library, and I was eager to discover Atmanspacher and Primas' article on Pauli: It's sunny and hot, and I've a table there just in front of the large window. I open it wide, and, now sitting, I've a view of the garden—four rows of vineyards, and to the right, I'm able to see three-quarters of an old apple tree whose branches extend to within about two yards of my window. (No sunrays hitting the plastic table or my eyes, the tabletop void of anything but what I brought with me.) And I go on reading the article. Suddenly, to my utter disappointment, I realize something.

Raising my head from the journal and turning my head to the right and up—thus looking to the tree's branches without seeing them—I exclaim telepathically to Pauli: "But why, *why* didn't you invent the physics of synchronicity?"

And I hear a booming male voice, definitely on the defensive: "You always make the same mistake: you keep telling people 'we took a century to understand quantum physics.' But this is not at all what happened! The concepts you're thinking I could have used [to build such theory] didn't emerge before 1976."

I was, in my conscious mind, totally bewildered to hear a reply—so clear and so loud it could have been that of somebody in the room; let alone a voice charged with a reproachful tone that cried for authenticity. To top it all, I couldn't not remember a sentence I had uttered at least

---

*The Self being beyond gender, and able to reincarnate as a woman, a man, or a hermaphrodite, it's only for our own convenience that the Self appears in the features we associate with their latest incarnation; hence my use of *hiser* or *himer* to keep this in mind.

once in a public lecture, and other times in smaller circles—the very sentence he had just cited.

So I had been wrong all along; it had not been the birth of QM all at once like that of the goddess Venus, in an adult body, out of a scallop shell on the sea (see plate 21). It seemed suddenly evident: it had been a gradual process that, by adding more meaning and by elaborating on various interpretations and schools, had made physics evolve up to where it was now. For example, it wasn't the first inventor of QM, Heisenberg, who produced the main equation of QM, it was Schrödinger; and it was only much later that Von Neumann came up with QM's mathematical proof. I readily believed him about the date 1976 for the emergence of the concept of nonlocal correlations—later morphed into the entanglement. (Let's note here that, since Pauli died in 1958, he obviously had watched in earnest, from the hyperdimension, the development of quantum physics on the earth plane!)

It was only in 1964 that John Bell produced the arguments that were to lead to the successful experimental protocol and first inescapable results found by Alain Aspect in 1982–84, that proved the entanglement. I checked Pauli's date later, and it was sound indeed as marking the first significant experiments on the EPR (Einstein-Podolsky-Rosen) paradox by J. F. Clauser, strongly suggestive of the entanglement, but not a solid proof yet.

What Pauli was suggesting was of crucial importance: the invention of a global scientific theory or domain was much more of a collaborative build-up—by all forefront researchers *and* the larger intelligent audience—than the slow unfolding of a packed and complete original work! A fascinating perspective in itself, because it implies that the collective consciousness is part of the process!

This conversation with Pauli lasted more than an hour, during which I would continually look at, and dialogue with, a sort of blob or round energy field, situated in the branches of the tree some two and a half yards from the ground (higher than my head and slightly to my right).

But let's get back to the stupendous event at its very start. Here is the mind-blowing anomaly (and not so much my telepathic dialogue with a deceased scientist):

1. In my conscious mind (my flow of consciousness) I'm not aware of anything apart from being anxious to read this article and discover Pauli's part in the work with Jung on synchronicity. Then, I'm disappointed, it's not what I was expecting.
2. Yet, my body gestures and my mind start to address Pauli—in the tree, higher than my head and to the right—and to reproach him for not having done enough. He instantly answers and counterattacks.

So, we have to assume that

- a supraconscious part of my mind—my Self—*knew all along that Pauli was there,* seemingly interested in the way I was going to react to the article;
- and also knew that his immortal Self in the hyperdimension (his syg-field) was standing (or rather intruding) in the apple tree;
- and it means that *my own Self was having an exchange with the Self of Pauli* (appearing in the tree) even *prior* to my addressing him as an individual mind;
- *my ego consciousness then merged with my Self consciousness* and, at the very moment I posed the question, I became *half aware* of talking to him. Then, on hearing his sonorous answer, I abruptly became fully aware of holding a telepathic conversation with a real independent and powerful mind, that of Pauli.

Of course, we have to presume that wherever and whenever I would have chosen to read the article, he would have appeared somewhere in front of me; but, interestingly, the fact that he was slightly on my side and that I had turned my head to the right and upward to address him, obliges us to admit that I wasn't just looking ahead to the infinite as somebody in deep thought (and just having a telepathic exchange with him). In other words, the hyperdimensional Self can choose any space-time coordinates to manifest *himer*-self in our social space in order to communicate with us.

Let's make a short digression here to ponder the stupendous way in which our Self consciousness is enmeshed and interacting with our ego consciousness (often called the conscious, as distinct from the unconscious).

In the example above, the discussion with Pauli is at first going on between our two Selfs, in the hyperdimension; and then my Self consciousness suddenly merges with my conscious, makes me look at a specific spot and I start directing the dialogue. This totally seamless and smooth taking over of my body (gestures, utterances, posture) by my higher Self is something I've experienced quite often while hitch-hiking on the roads of India, Southeast Asia, and Africa, generally in situations of great danger. Of course, I experienced it also in my own country (such as in the car accident on an icy road I recounted earlier) and these cases more easily make my point. In these instances, my Self's higher consciousness merges with my ego consciousness in such a swift, easy, and flowing way that I experience no modification of my sense of self. In other words, it's still *me* (meaning the usual "I") being in charge, speaking, and acting, such that,

- I act with my usual intention, will, and style, having full control of my body and identity (for instance, saying "I")
- and yet my actions and paroles express and imply the greater knowledge of my supraconscious Self (knowledge that my conscious doesn't possess)—a Self who knows the right actions to protect me, including a precognitive and/or a PK one, and who has the means and power for implementing them.

So let's go back to the lengthy dialogue of about an hour I had with Wolfgang Pauli, full of detailed information, notably on quantum physics, while reading an article on his work.

After his thundering statement as to my mistaken opinion about the development of QM, and some exchanges about quantum physics, I fully realized that Pauli was not only addressing me with a direct and friendly tone but talking as if he knew me and my work inside out. That's when it occurred to me that I could ask his expert advice on a particularly intricate problem I was confronted with at the time. Despite my Semantic Fields theory being at a quite advanced stage, near completion, and a publisher in view, my scientist husband had, on perusing my manuscript, raised a question about my use of *semantic field* irrespectively of whether it referred to a human consciousness, or to a matter system (a tree, a building). His Greek philosophical roots found this stand abhorrent. In my view, of course, even if I hadn't developed the concept of a HD yet, each and every system must have had a semantic field pertaining to the semantic dimension beyond space and time. The whole point of my theory was to get beyond the classical mind-body split—and I held and expounded in the book that the (Cartesian) duality framework was itself creating the famous mind-body problem! But I nevertheless agreed with him that the way I had modeled it posed a philosophical and ontological question. (This conversation with him had happened only a couple of days beforehand in Paris, and I was a bit stressed about the issue, indecisive as to what to do.)

So, I asked Pauli how, in my SFT, I could draw the difference between the semantic fields of people (meaning their consciousness) and the semantic fields in natural systems.

"Shall I qualify the first ones as active and the second ones as passive?"

"You saw the sea—didn't you?" came the cryptic and slightly amused voice of Pauli.

On hearing this, after an instant of absolute bewilderment, wondering what he was talking about, my mind suddenly jumped back to a spiritual experience I had had so long ago that it belonged to another cycle of my life.

During my crossing of the Sahara Desert, a truck driver, driving alone with his young son, had given me a lift in the far south of Morocco. Crossing that stretch of desert happened to be an unforgettable experience. The driver drove all night outside of any track, guiding himself with the stars and through an amazing hyperlucid state the three of us shared for twelve hours straight and in perfect silence, as if we were one single mind. The driver and his son had taken me into a magnificent Telhar field with a direct connection to his Self, which allowed him to drive intuitively, guided by the knowledge of his Self.

We reached at dawn a totally deserted beach where the desert met the Atlantic Ocean, at the south end of Morocco. While the driver and his son were preparing a fire with desert scrubs to cook some camel meat for breakfast, I climbed down the cliff toward an immaculate sand beach. This beach was just one place along a thousand-mile stretch of deserted land bordering the coast. It was immaculate, as if devoid of any human trace. In this perfectly wild state of nature, the ocean had played with me with convincing humor and intelligence. I had experienced the living consciousness of the ocean, eternally young, joyful, and free.

I then realized I had to make room for an actively sentient and autonomous consciousness in complex natural systems (and not just a passive one). There was a concept I could use . . . So after a moment of pondering, I said to Pauli: "Self-organizing natural systems, then?"

To which he replied, with more than a tint of humor: "If that's the forefront concept, why not?"

While the questions I asked Pauli were mostly intellectual, he was prodding me to cross the gap in my life between a scientific cycle and a previous cycle in which I had mostly been experiencing with consciousness. And in that period, I had recurrently communicated with the consciousnesses of not only the wild sea, but also trees, rivers, and sacred mountains. We are talking here about a type of experience widely acknowledged in many civilizations—in Eastern cultures, in shamanic ones all over the world, and in Western Hermetic thought and esoterica as well. In our epoch that sees the awakening of a gamut of spiritual and psi talents, it has also been the stuff of real-life experiences for many sensitive individuals, whatever their culture. So much so indeed that it's only in the narrow mindset of the materialistic science of the past two centuries that natural systems have been deemed "inert" and without consciousness. Not only do meditators and shamans see the sentient energy field around sacred trees and rocks, but they can communicate with these beings: they definitely know they are endowed with consciousness!

Then Pauli resumed a serious tone to tell me: "As far as your actual theory is concerned, know that you'll develop in the future a whole new level of this theory. The only thing you have to be careful of is not to limit or close any of the main concepts, in order for you to make them evolve at this later time."

Pauli was thus prodding me to adopt a strategic perspective in view of this later development. As it happened, within the next two days I finally solved the problem by calling the human semantic fields "noo-semantic fields" and those of complex systems "eco-semantic fields" (*noo-fields* and *eco-fields* in short).

Interestingly, when I elaborated the Infinite Spiral Staircase theory (ISST) in November 2012 (thus sixteen years later), the problem, in this new framework of hyperdimensional physics, had wholly disappeared. As far as physics goes, any hyperdimension (such as hyperspace, hyper-time) has to be a layer of reality superposed to, or underlying, any point in spacetime (thus any particle or any system). Therefore the question of differentiating between a self-reflective human consciousness and matter and natural systems does not even arise. If a theorist posits consciousness in the cosmos as an attribute of this hyperdimension (as I do in ISST), then consciousness pervades the whole pluriverse, being thus a continuum over all systems, whether a human mind, a cell, or even a planet. The question then becomes how do you model the organization of specific systems in this global framework, that is, their inherent structure, complexity, hierarchy, specificity? The hyperdimension cannot be a uniform field; it has to fit and manage the individual information of each and every system in an alive, dynamic, and creative way; it has to set the difference between them in terms of complexity, organization, knowledge, and information processes.

As it turned out, the sole concept that was absolutely necessary to bridge and connect our 4D reality (as specific matter systems) with the reality of the hyperdimension was that of semantic fields—namely an (individual) semantic layer of organization on all systems (their syg-fields). Now, the new concept of hyperdimensional syg-fields was also, as I pointed out, solving the "hard problem" in cognitive sciences, by annulling the famous mind-matter split. A mind existing in 4D reality was *also* a *hyperdimensional Self, pervading all the particles and cells of its own body and brain.* In other words, the huge split and abyss between matter and mind that had plagued cognitive sciences had now become an infinity of micro-links between 4D particles and HD *sygons* (the sub-quantum waves and frequencies constituting the syg-energy of the HD). We had now, at the sub-quantum scale, an infinity of micro-links between our body-brain, our world-centered ego mind, and our HD-Self.

As we see, in this dialogue with the hyperdimensional spirit of Pauli, he not only gave me a highly pertinent novel perspective on a theoretical problem I had at the time, but he also went as far as predicting I would at some later time elaborate a whole new level of this theory—which is exactly what happened with ISST.

Now, the ending of our conversation gave me another bit of information about their own syg-HD. If you remember, Pauli had appeared to me as a blob of energy in the apple tree during our hour-long discussion.

When I feel our conversation is nearing its end, I ask Pauli, "And Jung, are you still in contact with him?" And then, suddenly, on introducing his long-term friend Carl Jung, Pauli takes now the appearance of a full silhouette within the same energy globule, yet now elongated, and extending his arm to slightly behind himself, with a light ray extending from it, he points to Jung who has suddenly appeared (with the gesture it seems) at a distance, as a tiny silhouette in another oval globule, and who waves hello at me. And simultaneously Pauli says: "Of course! We're always connected. In fact we're working together!"

Now, this ending scene gives us a lot of information as to the nature of this HD and as to the souls' life in the HD. As to the first: the fact that both scientists appear within some enclosure, an oval bubble, could be interpreted as the hyperdimension being like a hole in our 4D reality. The intrusion from one dimension into the other, in physics terms, is like a bubble or vortex of a much higher frequency-domain, piercing into a lower energy domain, and needing to be hermetically surrounded by an energetic boundary (of the sort postulated to separate the quantum dimension from the sub-quantum one, for example, by Jack Sarfatti; see my book *Cosmic DNA at the Origin*). Hence the oval bubble of energy surrounding both scholars.

As to the second, this is a rare glimpse into the fact that the transcendent souls keep on researching, learning, in their preferred domain of interest. First, it appears that often (at least for these evolved minds), what has been the focus of their last incarnation remains their path of knowledge in the soul dimension. Second, they are organized, in the HD, as groups working with a shared focus and common aims. Third, they keep track of what's happening on Earth in this domain. And furthermore, I think I may surmise from the fact that Pauli appeared just as I was going to read an article about him, and at the moment I was looking desperately for a solution about some terms in my theory, that they also keep a keen eye on researchers on Earth who are working along the same lines of research and with a similar worldview. Something that was also evidenced by the numerous (around fifteen) scientists who appeared to me during the structuring of general data about the ISST cosmology (the second phase of research).

The picture we get from these glimpses in the HD is indeed as remote as possible from a boring endless angels' concert in paradise! And I must say that to me it's both funny and a relief—like setting some accounts straight with religious authorities that, all too often, have been dead set on enforcing their narrow-minded dogma on us and, too many times in history, by using very violent means.

COMMUNICATING WITH HYPERDIMENSIONAL MINDS

First, let me stress how fitting it was that I had this dialogue with Pauli at the very moment I was struggling with a nagging dilemma concerning my theory, and the fact Pauli oriented me toward a solution. Indeed, this fortunate timing can be considered a synchronicity! As we will see shortly, a similar synchronicity happened when a spontaneous dialogue with the physician Paracelsus led to my being healed from an acute illness.

Now, let's ponder the style of my dialogue with Pauli, as well as the short communications I had with Jung and other scholars and questers, to throw some light on how great minds in the HD position themselves and interact with us living on Earth.

The main point I want to stress is that, despite their past eminence and what we can assume to be a pivotal role in the HD, they nevertheless mostly initiate a friendly and equal-to-equal relationship. I'm tempted to say peer-to-peer and collegial, but that would be too limiting, as it refers too much to science. Furthermore, I witnessed the same type of friendly interaction from deceased artists and questers on a path, and I'm sure it's the same style they use with any sensitive (as long as the latter are open to it).

This congenial communication stands in stark contrast with any would-be teacher or guru intending to impose their views and values on someone, full of themselves and believing they know it all. The HD spirits I talked to never imposed their viewpoint, nor indulged in a grand teaching, preaching, or prophetizing stance. (I wouldn't have allowed it anyway in my own workspace; I've been adverse to these types of personalities, getting clear of them, or worse, countering them whenever I encountered them.) They were more eager to meet the demand of a questioning mind, to offer their help and support to another quester. Exchanges were from the start focused on an important point and remained so for the duration of the interaction—nothing trivial, shallow, or just mundane.

Let's zoom in on how Pauli answers my irksome theoretical problem. In fact, he doesn't answer it! He just prods a totally different way for me to look at the problem, a way that's not even remotely rational! He suggests that I should extract the spiritual elixir from my real-life experiences, and thus reconnect with the living knowledge I gained through them. And only then would I find the best way to express this living knowledge via some concepts.

He is not handing me a ready-made solution of his own, which I would have been tempted to debate and possibly deconstruct. No, he is triggering a different mode of thinking, linked to and rooted in my own hard-won knowledge. He opens a path for me to find *my own* answer to my question—a solution I would readily own and feel deeply in sync with.

PARACELSUS HEALS ME FROM THE HD

Experiencing a spontaneous connection with the author of a book is not a rare event in my life, but on this specific occurrence, I felt a deep mental link to Paracelsus while I read *about him* in a book by Jung—his *Alchemical Studies*. Paracelsus was a renowned Swiss physician and alchemist who, at the beginning of the sixteenth century, traveled and practiced medicine everywhere in Europe, treating the poor with a dedication equal to how he treated those who were royal or imperial. The *magus monstruosus,* as he was called by his enemies (as numerous as his followers), transformed the field of medicine, which was still stuck in the decrepit precepts of Galen and Avicenna. He was also the herald of a new current of liberty and spiritual renewal with the Rosicrucian movement.*

---

*See Waite, *Hermetic and Alchemical Writings of Paracelsus.*

Paracelsus held that quaternary structures were particularly sacred. Already in the Pythagorean tradition of ancient Greece, some geometrical structures were held sacred, for example, the circle that passed the four vertices (or corners) of a square, thus enclosing it; or the inner circle instantiating the *squaring of the circle*—that is, whose circumference was equal to the perimeter of a square that had the same center.

A square within or outside of a circle is the fundamental structure of the *mandalas* used by Tibetans to enhance concentration and meditation. Each mandala is drawn around a central Buddha or enlightened being, and shows the symbolic attributes of this cosmic Being. There can be larger circles or arcs of Buddhas, Mahasiddhas, and gurus surrounding the central being (see plate 22).

We have also to mention the magnificent geometrical quaternary structures created in stone: the crossing of four (or eight) arcs at the keystone to support the global architecture of sacred buildings in the Gothic and Roman styles, as well as in Muslim architecture. The geodesic domes and the cathedrals' rosaces are complex mandalas, many of which have a base-4 numeral system, meaning that they are constructed on multiples of the number—squares and octagons set in a circle (see fig. 9.2 on the following page and plates 23 and 24).

In my study of Paris' network of ley lines, *The Sacred Network,* I've unraveled magnificent geo-architectures—composed of several churches and buildings precisely set on straight ley lines—forming huge geometrical figures based on the golden number, such as pentagrams, six-pointed stars, and golden rectangles (see fig. 9.3 on page 235).

According to the tradition, the knowledge about sacred geometry and architecture, and the golden number* expressed so superbly by the cathedrals' builders, was handed down from Pythagoras in ancient Greece. Further back it was part of a knowledge transmission from Egypt, where the main Greek philosophers (and geometricians) were initiated in philosophy, science, architecture, and medicine, starting

---

*See Matila Ghyka, *The Golden Number.*

Fig. 9.2. Clermont Cathedral's south rosacea, central France: (a) exterior view;
(b) interior view with the sun lighting the stained-glass colors. The mandala starts at
the center with 1 into 4 petals, then 16 into 32, then 2 rows of 16 crosses, and finally
the outside circle ring combines 1 into 3 x 16. This circle being embedded into a square
with, at the 4 corners, a cross on a round rose.

Photos by Stockholm, CC BY-SA 4.0

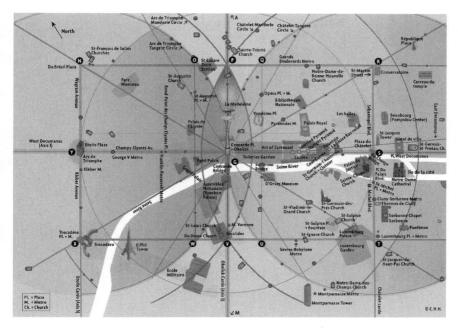

Fig. 9.3. Golden rectangles delineated by sacred lines in Paris,
and setting geo-architectural ensembles, based on the golden proportion phi
From **The Sacred Network,** *219; artwork and concept © Chris H. Hardy*

with the first one Thales (ca. 624–548 BCE), and where Pythagoras (ca. 570–495 BCE) studied for over twenty years. This knowledge about sacred numbers linked to letters and sacred sounds or syllables (such as mantras) is also found in the Judaic Kabbalah and in diverse tantric traditions in India, China, and Tibet.

Still further back, this integral knowledge is said to have been revealed by the Egyptian god Thoth—known as Hermes in Greece and as the Sumerian Ningishzidda, son of Enki. Hermes is reputed to have written numerous books spanning all domains of science and philosophy, of which a few are known to us as the *Corpus Hermeticum* or *Hermetica.* The current view is to attribute them to different authors along the centuries, especially (as some texts show a deep intertwining of Hermetic and Gnostic knowledge) to the first centuries of the common era in the cosmopolitan city of Alexandria. Yet Ahmed Osman,

Fig. 9.4. The four elements in alchemy—earth, water, air and fire—as a basic quaternary. Copper engraving on paper by Stephan Michelspacher, 1654.

in his challenging book *The Egyptian Origins of King David,* notes, "According to the third-century church father Clement of Alexandria, the Hermetica represents Egyptian religion, and identifying the history of Hermeticism means describing how the knowledge of this wise old Egyptian, Hermes, was passed down through the centuries" (176).

It was only in 1460 that Cosimo de' Medici, the ruler of Florence (and patron of Renaissance artists) acquired a set of seventeen short books and two major texts, the *Asclepius* and the *Virgin of the World,* written in Greek.* In the latter, Isis discusses the four natural elements fire, water, air, and earth. The four elements will be a staple of alchemy's work on symbols as well as metals (as seen on fig. 9.4). This is despite the basic duality of mercury (feminine) and sulfur (masculine) that are the elements to be worked on by the action of the salt.

These two Hermetic texts were translated into Latin by Marsilio Ficino in 1463, the translator of Plato and founder of the Platonic Academy in Florence, under Cosimo de' Medici's patronage. Cosimo's grandson Lorenzo the Magnificent (ruler of Florence from 1469 to 1492) would become a patron of Leonardo da Vinci, Michelangelo, and Botticelli (among many others), which suggests that Italian Renaissance artists had access to the *Corpus Hermeticum*. Then of course we discovered the treasure trove of many unknown Gnostic and Hermetic texts in Nag Hammadi in 1945.

Let me now recount my interaction with Paracelsus.

I was reading Jung's account about Paracelsus and how he thought quaternaries were highly sacred. Suddenly, I felt my mind was connected to that of Paracelsus. For two or three days, I had been very sick. The illness had been getting worse for a few months, and it culminated that day in an acute crisis. It was Sunday, so I was unable to find a physician. To try to take my mind out of my distressing situation and get into a higher state of consciousness (which I thought was the best path toward self-healing), I had searched for a thought-provoking book in my library. Taking out Jung's main work on alchemy (knowing there was a wealth of inspiring symbolic drawings in it) I opened it at random to a section describing Paracelsus's work and how he used quaternaries in his medical and magical practice. Yet, there was no mention, in what I read, about specific quaternaries—that of plants or magical mandalas related to both planets and angels.

---

*Find the *Corpus Hermeticum* texts at sacred-texts.com/eso/vow/index.htm and gnosis .org/library/hermet.htm

Suddenly and unexpectedly, I experienced a deep connection to Paracelsus's consciousness and felt it was strong enough to allow for an exchange. I spontaneously had the idea to plead for his help regarding my illness, and I asked him for a cure, which he gave me with explicit details. He spelled out the importance of using four different herbs (that was a quaternary), three of which were not only rare, but also extremely unusual in the context of herbal therapy. I had no idea, for example, that ivy, and hop from which beer is made, could be used as medicines and I doubted that I could even find them in a chemist's shop specializing in herbal drugs. Paracelsus then went on to explain their dosages and the technique of preparation, which included something as exotic as leaving the concoction under the light of the moon for a few hours.

After thanking him, I decided to try to find these rare plants right away. Because it was a Sunday, pharmacies, apart from some rare ones, were closed, and to top it all, I was in the countryside.

I intuitively decided to take a road I didn't know well. After ten miles or so, not only did I find a pharmacy that was open, but to my great surprise, it specialized in herbal therapy. As I handed her the list of plants, I told the pharmacist that a physician of alternative therapy had given me the list over the phone. Astonishingly, she had all four herbs but she was so surprised by the list that she told me she wanted to check them in her handbook. I answered that I myself would be very interested in knowing more about these herbs. So we both read the entries. I couldn't believe it. My illness was linked to the matrix: two of the herbs were natural hormones, the third was specifically for gynecological illnesses, and the fourth was a general tonic.

The moon was quite large that night, and I left the open, nonmetallic container of the mixture outside on a table, feeling a bit nonsensical (yes, even me!) but I was determined to follow the instructions to the letter. Late in the night, I started drinking the potion. After twenty-four hours the symptoms started to decrease, and I felt much better in a matter of days.

EMPIRICAL PROOFS

The dialogue with Paracelsus, which had given me detailed information about a cure for my illness, led to several empirical proofs.

First, all four plants were classified as curative, and three of them were specifically treating gynecological disorders. Second, the cure worked beyond my wildest expectations. Third, except for one of them (the tonic), I had never heard about these plants being used as medicines. Last, a series of synchronicities happened that were clearly linked to the communication: driving intuitively, I stumbled on a pharmacist who carried those uncommon plants and who prodded me to check them in a handbook, thus providing a sound proof of their relevance. But, as I emphasized earlier, the greatest synchronicity was indeed to open a book randomly on a section presenting Paracelsus and to experience a sudden connection to his hyperdimensional mind!

The dialogue with Pauli similarly carried empirical proofs. First, I later checked on the time information he gave me about quantum physics developments (he had stressed I was wrong on that point), and it turned out that the date he gave me was correct. Second, for days prior to this conversation I had been pondering the problem with my theory, unable to find a better solution than the active-passive description; and yet I didn't feel satisfied with it. Third, Pauli took my mind back to a real-life experience that I would never have imagined was linked to the subject at hand, and yet it perfectly answered my question. In doing so, he helped me to better merge intellect and spiritual experience. Fourth, his biting humor was refreshing and was not the kind of self-gratifying nonsense that a deluded person would create out of pure imagination.

And there was also the prediction about elaborating a new theory, as a prolongation of the first one, SFT. And he was right on two counts: on the one hand because ISST was, as he had forecast it "a whole new level of this theory"—a leap from cognitive sciences to cosmology and quantum physics. And on the other hand, he was also right because this cosmological theory remained indeed so rooted in the previous Semantic Fields theory, that I kept its core concepts and terms and was able to do so because they were fecund and open concepts (as he had urged me to see to that).

A Sumerian Priest Helps Decipher an Ancient Text

I have found only one example in the survival literature of a deceased scholar (here a Sumerian priest) giving crucial scientific information to a living researcher. The case of Dr. Hilprecht and the Nippur cylinder was reported by Myers (1903, 365; 2012, 158, app. 4B), who wrote the account. J. C. Hilprecht was professor of Assyrian at the University of Pennsylvania.

According to Professor Hilprecht, "One Saturday evening, about the middle of March, 1893, I had been wearying myself, as I had done so often in the weeks preceding, in the vain attempt to decipher two small fragments of agate which were supposed to belong to the finger-rings of some Babylonian." However, "dozens of similar small fragments had been found in the ruins of the temple of Bel at Nippur with which nothing could be done." Furthermore he had "only a hasty sketch" of them, showing the same stone but of a different color. He put the two fragments in two different categories in a book he had to approve by that night, despite not feeling satisfied, and went to bed. In the night he had a dream.

> A tall, thin priest of the old pre-Christian Nippur, about forty years of age and clad in a simple abba, led me to the treasure chamber of the temple, on its south-east side. . . . Here he addressed me as follows: "The two fragments which you have published separately upon pages 22 and 26, belong together, are not finger-rings, and their history is as follows. King Kurigalzu (*circa* 1300 B.C.) once sent to the temple of Bel, among other articles of agate and lapis lazuli, an inscribed votive cylinder of agate. Then we priests suddenly received the command to make for the statue of the god Ninib a pair of earrings of agate. We were in great dismay, since there was

no agate as raw material at hand. In order to execute the command there was nothing for us to do but cut the votive cylinder into three parts, thus making three rings, each of which contained a portion of the original inscription. The first two rings served as earrings for the statue of the god; the two fragments which have given you so much trouble are portions of them. If you will put the two together you will have confirmation of my words. But the third ring you have not yet found in the course of your excavations, and you never will find it." With this, the priest disappeared. I awoke at once and immediately told my wife the dream that I might not forget it. Next morning—Sunday—I examined the fragments once more in the light of these disclosures, and to my astonishment found all the details of the dream precisely verified in so far as the means of verification were in my hands. The original inscription on the votive cylinder read: "To the god Ninib, son of Bel, his lord, has Kurigalzu, pontifex of Bel, presented this."

Then, that same year, in August, he was able to go to the Constantinople Imperial Museum and see the fragments first hand. He discovered that the original stone had a whitish vein, thus explaining the fragments' different colors.

Myers classified the case in his Sleep chapter; he concluded that five items of information, scientifically accurate, were given by the dream, notably: the fragments belonged together; they were fragments of a votive cylinder; the cylinder was presented by King Kurigalzu; it was dedicated to Ninib; it had been made into a pair of earrings; and the "treasure chamber" was located upon the southeast side of the temple.

As I see it, this case is a remarkable example of a conversation happening in the hyperdimension, between the transcendent Self of a deceased Nippur priest, aware of a kindred researcher toiling with matters pertaining to his past work, and initiating the contact with the latter's Self during the dream state. We all have this capacity to connect through the HD, and we do use it often, yet the problem is to be able to remember such communications. This case shows us also how the transcendent spirits keep track of what's happening on Earth in matters that are of primary importance to them, here the classification of sacred objects that this priest himself made, excavated from the very temple where it happened.

What the Dialogues with Transcendent Selfs Tell Us

As we can see from my own discussions with past geniuses, it is possible to move beyond symbolic dreams conveying a message from our Self, into a full-fledged conversation with inspiring minds of the past (not just a reception of vague ideas from them).

Drawing on these two occurrences of mine, let's sort out what they suggest about the capacities of human consciousness.

Accessing the semantic dimension (or syg-HD) consciously is done in a high state of consciousness in which the individual is in the consciousness of his or her Self. It presupposes much more than a telepathic ability. Unless we are talking about extraordinary occurrences, it is based on a stable connection with one's own Self and the capacity to fuse with it—at first during transcendental states (meditation, creativity, peak states, and the like) and then on a regular basis.

All paths of inner knowledge in all cultures lead to this identification and eventually to the fusion with our Self. When, on this path, we start getting connected with our Self, we also start accessing the hyperdimension of consciousness. When the harmony and fusion are reached, many possibilities open in front of us, including the co-creation of Telhar fields (shared collective consciousness) and accessing the so-called Akashic Records—which are no more or no less than the meaningful information contained in (or rather pervading) the whole hyperdimension. Any further path of knowledge, based on our own responsible quest, can be explored. This is why the best guidance for our spiritual quest, from the start, is to develop our own access gate to our Self (in inner silence, in meditative and altered states), which will lead us without fail into accessing the semantic dimension.

10
TRANSDIMENSIONAL BEINGS

In the two occurrences of substantial dialogues with Pauli and Paracelsus that I just recounted, the hyperdimensional Selves with whom I interacted inserted themselves in our 4D material dimension quite differently. Pauli, most of the time, was just a blob of syg-energy in the apple tree. Then both he and Jung were in sort of enclosed elongated energy bubbles, as full standing but small human silhouettes, with a ray of energy shooting from Pauli's arm straight to Jung's bubble. Moreover, his voice had been so resounding and clear, it could have been mistaken for that of somebody nearby. Whereas in Paracelsus's case, only his voice was heard, however without any sonority, resonance, or substantiality to it. Maybe I should rather say that only his thoughts were audible, yet with a definite psychological and frequency print: that of a male, with the great alchemist's mind syg-print to it, thus easily recognizable—as in all telepathic conversations lacking the coupled apparition of a head or body form.

The funny part is, while I'm trying to pinpoint and sort out the minute detail and differences in the quality of the exchanges, I'm putting myself back in time, hearing Paracelsus, in front of the fireplace, the nose still bent on the page in Jung's book (while not seeing it anymore), with all my mind and attention focused on the thoughts I was hearing; then grabbing a pad and pen and writing down the strange list of medicinal herbs and the advices as to the preparation. And while I immerse myself back in the dialogue, I "see" or sense more detail about what happened: the syg-print of the conversation is there, for me to open it as a bubble, or an inner video in 5D or rather 7D (if we count hyperspace, hypertime, and cosmic consciousness), which I can observe at length, and even more attentively. All this reminds me of the dream-time sequence in which my own Self and Paul's Self were analyzing his subconscious drives in the scene at the restaurant, which (I believe) had been an event in his past: replaying a full 4D plus inner psychic scene— as a sort of 7D video.

Let's see now a communication with a transdimensional being, a case of high strangeness.

A TRANSDIMENSIONAL BEING

This anomalous event happened in my house in Igny, before my two journeys to the East. My study on the second floor had, on a small side, a large window facing the forest to the east, set quite low to fit under the pointed beamed roof. The wooden floor was covered with a large wool carpet—a quite old and worn village one bought in a street market in Turkey, on which I had set my mattress along this window. Across the room was the low table I used for writing, my back to the wall, and an altar in the middle of the room, facing my desk.

One morning that I had been sleeping as usual on my back, I awoke with my head, and that was unusual, turned at an angle toward a specific spot next to my bed; moreover, when I became conscious, I had already opened my eyelids just a tiny bit in that direction, as if I was trying to observe something yet avoid being seen doing it.

And what I was seeing was a thin young man, immaterial and luminous, sitting cross-legged at the side of my mattress, and looking at me; and I could see clearly the detail of his face and shoulder-length blond hair, as well as his rather normal white clothing. He was very peaceful and poised, in a yogic posture, and silently looking at me when I awoke; he appeared to be in his late twenties or early thirties.

I felt like I was given a peek into another dimension, seeing a friendly angel or guide visiting me. I was awed and didn't move, hoping to keep observing through the tiny slit of my eyelids. My impression was that of a well-known and friendly soul, yet in an immaterial and luminous form, a yogi with a very high-frequency consciousness and syg-field. He was somebody I must have known well in the syg-hyperdimension and with whom I (or rather my Self) obviously had been in a profound conversation while my conscious was asleep. He looked Nordic yet with a thin and delicate body frame. Despite the fact my eyelids were nearly closed and I hadn't moved my head at all, this being sensed I had now awakened and, in one smooth movement, began getting up. At which point I fully opened my eyes and started to raise myself on an elbow, while I swiftly sent him telepathically:

"Please stay! I'm perfectly able to withstand the view of an immaterial entity," (meaning: in a conscious state).

But the being kept on getting up and then turned on his heels (he was barefoot) and walked toward the door, which was opposite the window. And while he crossed the room, I heard distinctly the wooden floor crack with each of his footsteps. And then, as I was fully sitting by that time, I saw him pass right through the still closed wooden door, and while I observed his thin translucent silhouette slowly traversing the wood, it made the door crack in a louder and more explosive way than the floor had.

Needless to say, this human-looking entity was a total unknown to my conscious ego; yet I knew he was a free and living entity, whatever his plane of existence, and that we obviously were close friends and allies in the hyperdimension.

So, here again, we have a near-immaterial entity—a human being not in the flesh but in a syg-energy body. And this syg-energy body is able, when willing it, to pass through matter (at least wood), and yet it has enough substance/energy to make some noise when walking on a wooden floor (moreover, without passing through it). And when interacting with matter—such as traversing a door—it makes creaking noises, as if its energy field was disturbing the cellular fabric of the wood.

In these aspects, the yogic entity shows the same type of immaterial body as the spirit of the deceased Ledos. And, as concerns the philosophical question of the will and self-determination of these hyperdimensional entities, it is evidenced in many instances—such as the house genie climbing up the staircase behind my too curious friend—by their displaying conative capacities, that is, intentional, directed, and controlled actions and behaviors.

Yet, the Nordic entity was of a much higher order. He was a higher-dimensional human-type being, hyperconscious, with a beautiful and high-frequency syg-field; he was connecting with me willingly, most probably on a regular basis in the hyperdimension (he felt like a close friend to me, albeit dignified and respected).

Another interesting point is the fact that the Nordic entity, in the dreamtime or hyperdimension, seemed to follow a preset decision of his or else a prearranged agreement between our Selfs, when he sprang to his feet as soon as he sensed that I was awake. Yet, I did have a glance at him in his immaterial state, whether he planned it that way with me or not. It seems evident that I myself managed (within the hyperdimension) to instruct my body consciousness to get my head turned toward precisely the right direction and to open my eyelids ever so slightly as to have a glimpse at him before he saw or sensed that I awoke. And given that our interaction was telepathic and empathic, he couldn't ignore that intention of mine and its enaction.

So, all in all, the greatest probability is that we planned together this short and swift peek at a higher dimension of my own and his own being, so that I could grasp more of it in my conscious.

At first in my life it seemed that these kinds of peak states or anomalous events were like transient windows opening on the semantic dimension (as I called it at the time), or the hyperdimension, enabling us to peek into its reality. The logic was that our higher Self (the consciousness with whom we merge during peak and meditation states) was grounded on Earth via the ego, yet able to "visit" the higher dimension. But my view on that point has evolved.

Along the years, with many more such peeks into the hyperdimension, I've become convinced that we live a kind of double or, more precisely, a multidimensional, existence. One part of our consciousness, the conscious ego, is grounded on the physical plane and our life here. And another part, our hyperdimensional Self, is rooted in heaven—the HD layer of the universe—and has as much of a full-time life there as we have on Earth. The Self enjoys loads of friends and connections in the HD, and pursues all kinds of works and studies, and makes great accomplishments aimed precisely at the higher realization of our whole being and that of humanity as a collective consciousness (see fig. 10.1).

This double or rather multidimensional life is possible precisely

Fig. 10.1. *The Resurrection of the Dead*, by Blake (alternative drawing for the title page of Robert Blair's *The Grave*), 1806

because the HD is beyond our material world, the 4D spacetime. And therefore, apart from the sleep state, there is no disruption in the duration of our life here; and meanwhile our Self in the HD has a similar full life and sense of undisrupted duration; and moreover, it is endowed with a flawless perception of our 4D-ego life.

The entity didn't feel to me like the Self of a deceased person, and if he was connected to an actually living human, then the visitor would have been the Self taking the appearance of a body—a dreamtime body, in an out-of-body state or astral journey. However, the visitor's style and the context of the visit doesn't fit any other encounter I ever had with the spirits of deceased friends or parents, even of the highest order. It doesn't fit the interactions I had with the etheric bodies of friends in OBE state either, none of which ever showed such a mastery of their etheric body, whether in terms of posture and insertion in 4D space and time, their unwavering focus, or the light and high frequency of their syg-fields (which I have only rarely witnessed).

First, here is an entity sitting in a perfect yogi posture, peaceful and poised; second, he obviously visited me to have a focused dialogue with my Self consciousness while I was sleeping (as part of a long-term relationship with me); yet, it seems like he wanted me to become aware of my connection with him, and managed to have me get a glimpse of this higher reality—something that, in my twenties, was of a crucial importance to me, as I relied on many such peak experiences and cracks in the usual reality for understanding the complex semantic dimension.

Another highly unusual feature was the astonishing nearness of our souls during the silent but visual part of our encounter (when I became conscious of peeking at him through my slightly opened eyelids). It was an empathic communion of the highest order. This entity was definitely a soul brother, part of my soul family. With a lot more experiences and encounters with deceased persons, having seen high souls and masters enter by the door, sit in my living space or at a garden table, and having had discussions with them, I still think there was something highly singular with this specific encounter. It was in his syg-field and in the nearness of our souls, in the empathic communion.

That's why I'm inclined to think he was a transdimensional being, either from a higher dimension, or from another world or time altogether, yet part of our human-type species. And nevertheless an entity extremely close to my own Self, as a twin soul brother. And, in this respect, let me share that our HD Selfs are deeply connected to a much wider corner of spacetime than our little planet, and as far as ancient souls are concerned, they have been and are simultaneously incarnated on various worlds and of course at various times. But developing this point is beyond the scope of this book . . . Indeed, it would take another book to recount visions and communications I had with spiritual entities and transcendent beings, for the most part while in high meditative states; as well as encounters with alien machines, crafts, and beings, including a space-suited alien who visited me in Princeton.

A GLIMPSE INTO THE TRANSDIMENSIONAL WORK DONE BY ASCENDED SOULS

I'll now describe an interaction in which the ascended soul, behaving as the friend he had been, explained the work they were doing in the syg-hyperdimension.

Michel Bercot was a skilled heart surgeon who, at one point, renounced his medical career and focused mainly on his and his wife's spiritual quest. They were, if I understood correctly, connected to some esoteric-spiritual group, namely the Alice Bailey (new theosophy) school of thought. He and his wife organized two famed conferences in Paris (in the early 1990s) on the energy body (*Corps énergétique*). He died of cancer. I had been a collegial friend of both of them, yet never in close relationship, even before they organized the conferences.

This contact happened after I had separated from my husband, Mario, and (I believe) a few months or a year at most after Michel's death (despite the fact I had had no substantial contact with his soul just after he died).

I was in the kitchen of my aunt and uncle's house (where I had lived more than a decade). This kitchen was a narrow rectangle, about ten feet long, with on one long wall a kind of bar-shaped table with two chairs, the one that had been used by Mario farther toward the window, and the one I had used nearer to the door. There was only a small space, if one person was sitting, for another one to stand in front of the cooking plate or the sink, all aligned along the other long wall. I was busy on the gas stove, making some Greek coffee, when, turning my head, I see Michel with a broad smile on his face standing at the open kitchen door; I'm both astonished and extremely pleased.

"Oh! Michel! How great! I'm so happy to see you! How nice! Look, come on in and sit down, let me finish preparing the coffee, and then we'll share a coffee together." (Now I must confess that I'm so used to meeting friends from the other side, that I'm thrilled at having a chat over a coffee or, as would happen repeatedly with the Yaqui Indian Don Juan for a whole summer in the Cher River house, while enjoying a drink at the garden table.) But I've the impression that was the first time ever sharing a coffee, because I went as far as serving him a cup— just for the smell of it and the welcoming gesture of course! Something I'm not usually doing. But I do often offer them a chair, or even arrange it (or a few of them) so that I may see them easily while we talk. (But they *do* love the thought and the affable, friendly gesture, as any symbolic offering.)

So I turn my back to him to watch my *briki,* the coffee is soon bubbling and rising and, grabbing two cups and the briki, I turn around to face the table and bring it. That's when I see that Michel, instead of sitting on Mario's chair, has sat on mine. *Of course,* I reflect to myself, *I didn't specify any chair for him to sit on.*

"Sorry, Michel, could you just sit on the other chair, please?" And now he gets up and kind of slides there, and I put down the briki and serve the coffee; and then we chat for a while.

I didn't, despite all his moving in this reduced space, feel any substance moving, nor hear anything, nor have to let him pass. Apart from his thoughts reaching me, his etheric presence was totally noiseless and immaterial. (Another case showing that spirit manifestations are quite varied, as we have seen.)

I was eager to ask him a question that had bothered me since I got the shocking and unexpected news of his death.

"But tell me, how is it that you decided to die so young?" (His two daughters at the time were still in their late teens.)

"Look, with all these great changes and transformations coming for humanity, I realized that I would be of much more help to assist them from the other dimension. There was only so much I could do as an alive person."

As we kept talking, he explained that all of them, in the soul dimension, were closely watching the events unfolding on Earth, in all the domains of life and thinking related to this great leap; how they (these ascended souls) were acting, in these different domains, in a coordinated way (as specific group-minds), sending positive, spiritual energy to us, accompanying the transformative process in any way they could.

I think it was the first time that I had a real grasp on the tremendous work they were doing, conjointly with us, to steer this transformative process, this leap in consciousness that humanity *had* to accomplish, at great speed; otherwise consequences would be too gruesome.

I understood, as he explained all that and more, that we had to start thinking about the syg-dimension of the souls as being not so much a realm "beyond" material earth, but rather an integral part of the *same* planetary syg-field, and evolving conjointly with those of us still on the earth plane. When we would complete the already happening leap, it would be a leap for all of us, whether existing in pure syg-fields or rooted on the earth plane.

And again, let me stress that I'm deeply convinced that the two dimensions are progressively coming closer together, with greater intrusion of one into the other, back and forth, and a transdimensional access becoming more and more open. This is part of the key to the great transformation of our planet.

DIFFERENT APPEARANCES OF THE DECEASED

It seems to me more and more evident that the deceased appearing as a face and body we have known—yet more luminous, and much younger or energetic—is just a projection they send us so that we may recognize them. Or maybe they also use this sort of projection among themselves to maintain their network of relationships. I'm sure our 4D-space is something unreal in the semantic dimension of the souls and they can play and tinker with it fairly easily. Of note is a nightly lucid dream I had in Igny in my late teens. I was hovering above the body of my mother (as a small blob I guess) while she had gotten up in the middle of the night and was walking around her Paris flat. She could sense me and talk to me; she was in her fifties at that time, and as I wondered and asked her telepathically how she could do such a feat, she answered, "Oh, but I know much more about these matters than you think!"

Let me list the varied ways in which the spirits and ascended souls have appeared to me, mostly while interacting with me (apart from the "flying phantom" category, with whom I didn't interact). Let me say that I've had a great many contacts with ascended souls, on the order of three or four dozen.

- *As phantoms* with head features and arms, but no feet, flying (or rather sliding) at a height of about thirty to forty feet in the sky, their body being a loose white sheet, along the traditional representation. (There were two of these, in the field flanking the monastery in Brittany, who however didn't pay any attention to me.)
- *As just a face or just a voice with a mind print* (1) popping up in my workroom about one or two yards from my desk, or from wherever I was sitting or standing, generally at my head level or slightly above, and starting to talk; (2) appearing in the three-edged angle of the ceiling and two walls (my father in the Provence kitchen); and (3) in the three-edged angle of the car roof, the windshield

and the side window (my father). I've noted that souls who are not well acquainted with the syg-hyperdimension (or to crisscrossing dimensions) tend to appear at the level of the ceiling; for example, when they have just passed away, many are still unable to fathom how to move their energy body into our 4D physical space, in order to appear as walking, or going to sit on a chair. This seems to have been somewhat the case with the deceased parents who appeared to my father on his hospital bed—and who descended from across the ceiling, but yet were seen by him sliding down all the way to the left side of his body lying in bed.

- *As a faceless high-energy syg-field* within a luminous blob of energy, stable in the foliage of an apple tree (Pauli); yet with a booming and clear voice;

- *As a whole body* with a human body shape and clothing, able to make noise while walking or climbing the stairs, breathing quasi air, able to tap on the shoulder, or touch somebody living; such as Ledos settled in his old home as a house genie (which doesn't mean he was not simultaneously living in the HD);

- *As a whole body in a mandorle,* with a recognizable face, small and fully contained in an ovoid volume with a luminous energy, seemingly far away, themselves rooted in another dimension (Carl Jung) and connected with a ray to the person I was primarily talking to (Pauli); this was also the case with Pauli at the end of our exchange;

- *As a whole body behaving as a friend or guest,* with a recognizable face and precise body shape and clothing, apparently taking the normal space of a body and walking on the ground, entering the place or room I'm in, and when greeted, sitting on a chair and conversing. I've had a great many contacts with very evolved souls, such as Don Juan, Michel Bercot, and the Rosicrucian Guy Corneau just earlier today (July 4, 2017).

11

OUR SELF IN THE HYPERDIMENSION

So let's now focus on our higher Self—our soul anchored to the hyperdimension, and simultaneously rooted in our body and brain for the duration of our life. This hyperdimension of consciousness—the syg-HD—is the cosmic consciousness spread in our universe and pervading all its parts, yet immensely wider than the matter dimension, since it resides beyond space and time. As individual minds on Earth, we are of course bathing in this syg-HD and interacting with it. Indeed, the core of our consciousness, our Self or soul, is permanently living in this soul dimension, despite being in part connected to our mind and brain anchored to the matter level of reality. And this, despite our being most of the time unable to register consciously what reality our hyperdimensional Selfs are immerged in. Only brief glimpses befall us, through peak states, or visions, or dreams. Yet, a focused practice will open "the doors of perception" (to use Aldous Huxley's term). When a quester enters into deep meditation, or undertakes a solitary journey in the desert, or a vision quest—as do the Native Americans retiring in the wilderness, the yogis in Tibet and India, and the saints of old as well, they open the gates of this heightened consciousness that reaches up to the spirit dimension and receive visions and understanding. We have magnificent artwork expressing these states, for example the great

Fig. 11.1. The ecstatic regard of *St. Jerome in the Wilderness*, painting by Dürer, detail of the face

yogi Sankaracharya in meditation (plate 27), or the ecstatic regard of *St. Jerome in the Wilderness,* by Albrecht Dürer (see plate 25 and a detail of the face in fig. 11.1).

Our Self consciousness, our syg-field, is dwelling there in the HD, and yet our Self's palette of hyperfrequencies is also interwoven in the most intimate manner with each of our thoughts, feelings, states of consciousness, creative acts, and great ideas; or else, in our visionary purpose, momentum for action, and aspirations. In the same way, the HD is pervading each of our bodily systems, including our brain—each tissue, cell, and atom and particle composing them, since each of these is opened on the HD via innumerable sinks at the sub-quantum scale.

So let's see how Jung and Pauli had the visionary intuition of a "deep reality" as a whole other dimension of the universe, allowing underlying connections between all our psyches within the collective unconscious; then we'll explore how we can get in greater harmony with our own individual Self, and more aware of our interconnection with it, more receptive to the constant exchange of syg-energy we entertain with the syg-hyperdimension. Finally, in the next chapter, we'll dive into what is the hyperdimension, both as a global field pervading the universe and in terms of a soul dimension.

JUNG, PAULI, AND THE DEEP REALITY

The hyperdimension of consciousness would fit what psychologist Carl Jung and quantum physicist and Nobel laureate Wolfgang Pauli had conceived as a level of reality that would be both matter (as energy) and psyche (consciousness)—a *deep reality* underlying both spacetime and the quantum void. Toward the end of their two and a half decades of correspondence (and especially from 1952 to 1955), Pauli and Jung were sorting out the properties of this deep reality.* Jung was working at the time on his revolutionary concept of synchronicity (as a force in the universe as strong as, but totally different from, causality) and, as we saw earlier, they completed a book together in 1955, *The Interpretation of Nature and the Psyche,* that included Jung's *Synchronicity* and Pauli's study of Kepler's symbolism.

For Jung, the idea of a deep reality follows his earlier discovery of a *collective unconscious,* a sort of psychic ocean within which we are all communicating and exchanging, via our personal unconscious. Already Frederic Myers and William James had said that we were all connected at an unconscious level. It was the major opus of Carl Jung to demonstrate that our unconscious is far more sophisticated and organized than these previous researchers had seen it, and way more elevated and significant than Freud's notion of the *id* as a coarse produce of repressed impulses. For Jung, the personal unconscious has a subject—the Self—just like our ego is the subject of our conscious mind. And the Self is supraconscious and endowed with a spiritual aim (a true concept of soul in a psychological framework); the Self, reaching beyond space and time, is able to roam through the collective unconscious and to draw information from it. The deep reality, the hyperdimension beyond spacetime, is thus the dimension in which dwell the Selfs (or souls) of all beings.

And now we get a totally different landscape: the soul dimension is

---

*See Pauli and Jung 2014.

no more the sole dwelling of divine and ascended masters—it is accessible to, and continually accessed by, the Selfs of all individuals, whether living or deceased! But there is a catch: an individual must be attuned to one's own Self in order to partake of its knowledge and be aware of its communications. And along that path of attunement, actively working on oneself, through meditation and self-development techniques, is the key.

OUR HD SELF AND OUR 4D EGO-BRAIN-BODY

Our Self is the part of our consciousness/mind who is living in the hyperdimension, and it is able, from this HD, to operate and act upon the material plane. The Self can arrange meaningful coincidences (synchronicities) and make meaningful encounters happen for us. We may picture our whole consciousness as a huge tree: its roots are in the physical plane—our body and brain as a 4D system (biomatter in space and time), as well as our ego, intellect, and psyche (emotions, subconscious drives). The tree's branches extending into the air are the higher dimension of our being—our personal and highly original hyperdimensional Self, the part of our consciousness reaching out in the collective unconscious and living in the hyperdimension.

The operations of our Self in the HD are for the most part unconscious and inaccessible to our daily consciousness, unless we have worked on ourselves to peek into its mysterious realm, through meditation or self-development techniques. This is why Carl Jung has called it "the unconscious" or the psyche, and why he called its immense network of links to other Selfs "the collective unconscious."

Indeed, our Self is the HD part of our consciousness connected to other people's Selfs, via HD waves and links, creating meaningful and faster-than-light interconnections. It is through these HD connections that our Selfs are operating and are able to change things in the physical reality—such as stirring up events and synchronicities.

All physical systems—such as animals, plants, and complex natural

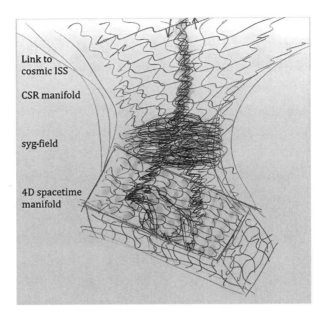

Fig. 11.2. The hyperdimension interlacing with the 4D spacetime:
the HD (Center-Syg-Rhythm, or CSR, manifold) connected to
spacetime via the bird's semantic field (the dense cloud)
Concept and artwork by Chris H. Hardy

systems—have, just like us humans, both physical 4D bodies and a HD
consciousness (their syg-field). For example, a bird will have an individual syg-field, and a forest a collective one, that extends in the HD and
connects with other beings in their environment, see fig. 11.2. (This is
the keystone of the ISS theory.)

It is through the HD that our personal Self gains a knowledge of
other people's mindset (as in telepathy), or of events far away in space
(as in clairvoyance), or else of events in the future (precognition). In
brief, the hyperdimension of souls and Selfs is what allows all psi capacities, and even the ability to modify matter systems, as in psychic healing
or in PK.

Our Self's knowledge extends to what's in store for us in the near
future, and to *lines of probabilities* in the far future. Let me explain.
Our future personal destiny may have a HD blueprint showing some

inevitable key events that will surely befall us (and these node-events can thus be foreseen); but the way they will happen and the precise time of their occurrence is not predefined and fixed, because it's our choices and intention that will be the decisive factors regarding what will really happen in our lives. Let's see for example Pauli's predictions to me: *from the standpoint of his HD soul* (having a sweeping gaze over future *probabilities*), I'll very certainly develop in the future a new level of my theory along certain predictable lines; yet, the actual realization—the finished theory book—will remain fuzzy in its details *until* I actually work it out. That's what I mean by *lines of probability* in regard to any future event.

The other part of our consciousness (the one that's not the Self) is what we call our *conscious mind* or ego—the ordinary waking state of consciousness driving our social and physical life, as well as its shallow subconscious layer.

If we have developed an awareness of our soul dimension, we may get a lot of information and spiritual momentum from the HD. But even if we haven't, our individual Self, being constantly connected to a vast syg-HD network and the collective unconscious, is constantly buzzing its information back to us, via our unconscious, and especially through the dreaming state and all creative and imaginative states. Among the many kindred spirits with whom our Self is constantly or regularly connected through the syg-HD, some can be actually living anywhere on the planet, while others are ascended, such as our cosmic guides and the spirits of our deceased friends and parents.

Thus, due to the existence of the syg-HD in the universe, we have to consider the ability to talk with ascended souls, but also directly to the souls of living individuals, as one more capacity in our human heritage, just like the psi capacities of clairvoyance and precognition. Everybody can develop this capacity, once the materialistic and moralistic blinkers are examined and discarded. Materialist scientists *believe* that psi capacities are impossible (thus a fraud or just random coincidences), *because* psi infringes on spacetime physics, and also because, in their views, the soul dimension doesn't exist at all (only matter exists). And some religious fundamentalists may consider psi capacities as immoral and dangerous—and will then try to put a sinful and diabolic stigma on them—only because these "miracles" are supposed to be the restricted dominion of prophets and saints. In their perspective, if these psi capacities were to be extensively developed in the society at large (beyond the faithful and the saints), say, as a grassroots emergence, laypeople and nonbelievers would encroach on this divine dominion.

WHAT IS THE HYPERDIMENSION LIKE?

At the scale of the universe, the hyperdimension lies beyond spacetime, that is, beyond our 4D material world. The term *beyond* could be misleading, yet it is a correct one in terms of physics. In fact, the HD starts at any point in spacetime, in any particle (in the infinitely small), as a sink plunging even below, into another realm of reality altogether—that of the sub-quantum, sub-Planckian layer. So that is a *beyond* as far as this whole HD layer of reality is a giant consciousness field surrounding our 4D universe; and at the same time, it is also a *below* (a sub-) in the sense that it literally pervades any being and system in the universe (at all scales, from stars to particles), given that each particle opens unto it at its own sub-quantum scale. And yet, the HD is *also* a cosmic field that, far from being one monolithic, amorphous, or uniform stuff, is composed of all individualized Selfs or souls of all beings, at all levels. In that sense, the Oneness divine field is the ensemble of all the Selfs in the universe, and we are, each one, part of it. Yet it is also a giant consciousness field, the whole being more than the sum of its parts. But in no way can it be represented as a human-type personality.

In brief, your own Self is individualized and sort of immortal in the HD, and you may access it by visualizing a resplendent sun high above your body and raising your consciousness to it (as in traditional Indian meditation); or you can access it by "going deep" inside yourself to reach the state of "inner silence" that the Yaqui Indian Don Juan spoke about; and, similarly, you can quiet your body and thoughts, as do the Buddhists and Taoists who aspire to reaching the "void state," that is, the state devoid of any particular thought, and filled instead with the pure cosmic consciousness—a state of fusion with the Tao, the brahman, aka the HD.

The Hyperdimension as a Sub-quantum Cosmic Field

In terms of physics, the hyperdimension exists at a sub-quantum level, below Planck scale, below the quantum particles and waves, thus both below and beyond both matter and the quantum domain. This sub-quantum level is beyond space and beyond time because spacetime starts only at and upward of the Planck scale, which is the lower boundary of the quantum domain. Thus the hyperdimension that lies below Planck scale is not constrained by spacetime and electromagnetic laws. The HD is the realm of syg-energy, the energy of consciousness, which operates at immensely faster-than-light speed and also via a dimension of resonance and rhythmic waves (the hypertime, or Rhythm HD). Syg-energy is wavelike, rhythmic, and endowed with meaning. In the ISST, as I mentioned earlier, the hyperdimension is triune, with a hypertime, a hyperspace, and a syg-HD—the latter being a dimension of meaning (syg- being short for semantic), of cosmic consciousness, in which all souls and Selfs dwell.*

On the global, cosmic side, the hyperdimension is like a sea of distinct vibrations, a sea of negative energy (Dirac sea), in which these supraluminous waves are themselves the meaningful entities interacting with each other through an infinite gamut of rhythms and vibrational forms (or topology, the hyperspace or Center HD). Each of these clusters of frequencies/waves/form is a HD *being* in itself, a meaningful entity endowed with consciousness.

---

*For more detail, see my scientific articles "ISS Theory: Cosmic Consciousness, Self, and Life Beyond Death in a Hyperdimensional Physics" and "Nonlocal Consciousness in the Universe: Panpsychism, Psi & Mind over Matter in a Hyperdimensional Physics."

In this sea, *hypertime* is the global field of rhythms and frequencies (as if extended in quasi space). These wave clusters respond to secret harmonies as they vibrate in sync with other specific clusters of frequencies, irrespective of distance and quasi-instantaneously.

As for *hyperspace,* it marks the center and boundary of each syg-energy wave cluster, creating its individuality as a meaningful entity (or system) within a specific geometry, a distinct being in itself. The global hypergeometry is based on the golden spiral with the golden ratio *phi* that gives us a form (the spiral) whose dynamic growth (the spiral extension) is steered by both phi and the center-radius-circle link *pi*. In the matter realm, both the golden spiral and the center-circle matrix are creating innumerable biological beings and dynamics, especially in

Fig. 11.3. Living beings based on the phi ratio: sunflower florets arranged in crisscrossing golden spirals, a special type of logarithmic spiral

Photo by L. Shyamal, CC BY-SA 2.5

plants and also in the galaxies (see fig. 11.3). They are also basic archetypes and modes of organization.

Thus, hyperspace is the edge line of a myriad of quasi-infinite spirals made of quarters of circles—each one a specific set of hyperfrequencies, boundlessly alive and highly meaningful. These myriads of Infinite Spiral Staircases (ISS) are innumerable variations on the archetype of the first cosmic ISS that sprang out of the original white hole at the origin of our universe, itself birthed from the terminal black hole of a previous such universe-bubble, thus creating a whole double system in the form of an X, at the X-point of origin (see fig. 11.4).

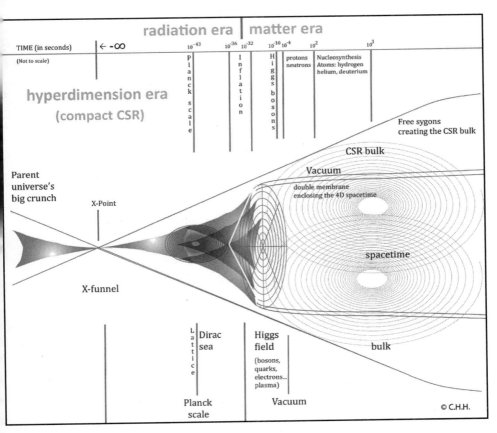

Fig. 11.4. The cosmic spiral (ISS) at the origin of our universe that sprang out of the original black hole–white hole X-point

Concept and artwork by Chris H. Hardy

COMMUNICATING WITH SOULS
VIA THE HYPERDIMENSION

As for the third component of the cosmic hyperdimension, the *syg-hyperdimension* (or syg-HD), it is the global field of collective consciousness weaving together all these highly conscious, self-driven, dynamic, learning, and evolving entities. It is the medium of interconnection of all the Selfs and souls of all beings in the universe. And the HD operates via syg-energy—the HD energy of consciousness, subquantum and supraluminous—to create clusters of frequencies/waves, that are alive and vibrating systems, autonomous, and self-organized. Your own Self/soul, in the HD, is a supraconscious entity, an incredibly complex semantic field endowed with an astounding energy power, in sync (via rhythm and resonance) with a network of kindred minds and loved ones, comprising both friends in the HD and friends in the material world. The Selfs/souls in the HD also keep in constant contact with their own avatars, or incarnated individualities, on Earth and elsewhere in our spacetime universe.

The syg-hyperdimension is thus the dimension of souls, just as Earth is the dimension of incarnated life (with a center of consciousness, the ego, anchored to the body). Given that syg-energy allows communication and interconnection with other Selfs quasi-instantaneously—without space, time, or matter being a barrier—a deceased soul, now fully dwelling in the HD, has access to any possible information pertaining to any being or system in the universe. At least in principle. Now, in the HD, the criteria for such exchange of information with the syg-field (the consciousness field) of any being or system, is going to be the quality of the syg-energy involved; this means that our Selfs (permanently dwelling in the HD, while we are living on Earth) can access only the range of soul and thought frequencies they are attuned to. Thus, it is theoretically possible for any Self to communicate with the highly evolved consciousness of a transdimensional being or immortal liberated master—such as the immortal Christ (called in India Babaji), or the immortal spirit of Maitreya (the Buddha of the future), or the Great Grandfather, or the Nagual Eagle, or the Dogons' Nommo dwelling on Sirius; however, in terms of syg-frequencies, it won't be feasible in reality unless we are attuned to these extremely high-intensity and high-quality soul energies.

And in the same way, it's possible to communicate by telepathy with the consciousness of a sacred tree, with a wild animal or our pet, or to perform a healing (a laying of hands) on a specific organ, or to try to tame some disrupted or amped up natural systems—some talents greatly on the rise and that, no doubt, will be increasingly welcomed by the inhabitants of Earth. But in order to do that, in each case we have to be able to tune in to the consciousness level of the being or alive system (its syg-field), in such a way that we get in sync with the very syg-energy and hyperfrequencies of this entity. Only then, being in deep empathy and harmony, or rather reaching a resonant state between one's own syg-field and the system's syg-field, can we have a meaningful exchange, and even an influence, on the other system (to perform a healing for example).

What's really happening, then, is the creation of a larger harmonic syg-field of shared consciousness comprising the two fields now in sync—a telepathic-harmonic field, or Telhar field. In *The Sacred Network* I have recounted only the occurrences of Telhar fields created among human beings—this in a wide gamut of situations and cultural/religious contexts in which I willingly immersed myself during my worldwide travels. And I have thus sorted out and analyzed the dynamic laws of syg-energy, because its properties and modus operandi are very tangible and easily deciphered in these peak Telhar states. But it's becoming evident to me that it is indeed the exact same attunement of syg-frequencies and fusion of syg-fields that allow both the conscious communication with the HD and deceased souls, and the kind of psychic influence on matter at play in healing and in macro-PK (PK on bio-systems and on matter systems).

I cannot stress enough the fact that our own Self is permanently dwelling in the HD and thus entertains lots of contacts with other kin-dred spirits on a regular basis, which remain mostly unconscious for the ego; but sometimes, we pick up on them and get some informa-tion via dreams, intuitions, or heightened states of consciousness. So, how does that type of hyperdimensional communication work? As far as I've experienced it, it is through *spontaneous connections* with minds sharing our worldview, values, and interests (beyond the relationships with our loved ones). Let me stress here the *spontaneous* aspect of these interconnections—a trait largely unacknowledged by spiritual teach-ings and practices, apart, in some way, from the Zen enlightenment and shamanism. Spontaneous links *is* the way our HD souls live, and the way syg-energy operates. These links are triggered like electric arcs between resonant syg-frequencies—the key point here is resonant: there must be a deep sympathy or resonance between the two souls, and then they connect spontaneously, getting in perfect sync and creating an ad hoc Telhar field. (Contrary to electricity in which the spontaneous arc is triggered by sign opposition (negative and positive), in the HD and in syg-energy, it's the similarities and resonance that trigger the connection.)

This is why, in the HD, we connect—as souls conversing with souls—with many friends, great minds, eminent artists and thinkers, guides, in fact all those whose genius realizations or works of art are a source of inspiration and creativity for us. Extraordinary encounters in dreams with the person who is going to become, at a later date on Earth, our life companion or great friend are not uncommon (it is of course their Self that we meet in the HD while in the dream state). And this is why, on meeting them for real for the first time, we may get the very strong and vivid impression we already know them.

What Do Spirits Do and Know in the Hyperdimension?

It is in this hyperdimension of consciousness that our own Selfs (despite our being alive on Earth) and the Selfs of the deceased permanently reside, giving these Selfs access to information about any being or event in any space or time. The fact that this syg-HD exists can explain a lot in terms of psi and spiritual states. Namely, as the Self is hyperdimensional, it is endowed with a natural psi, able to see and connect at a distance in space or in time—and that means the Self is gifted with clairvoyance, remote viewing, and precognition. The deceased can therefore zoom in and follow as in a movie what's happening on Earth, or they can project their consciousness in the location of their choosing on Earth, where dwells a loved one or a kindred spirit (as we saw Pauli do in the garden tree). Indeed, as we have seen, spontaneous cases show that the deceased keep contact with their loved ones on Earth, and can give them advice and even protect them, as we saw with the Lucy Dodson case in chapter 3, with the late mother of the percipient asking her to take care of the two children of the just-deceased sister-in-law.

The syg-HD explains also why, in my early rare and brief telepathic exchanges with Carl Jung, and in the specific lengthy conversation with Pauli, both of them seemed to know everything about me, my work, and my past, something that really baffled me at the time (for example, when Pauli started by saying, "You always make the same mistake"). But it's something you grow accustomed to! You have to take it for granted that, as far as highly evolved spirits are concerned—such as past scholars or spiritual guides—*whoever* you're communicating with in the HD, will know you inside out and will have a perception of ancient events as well as future ones in your life. I've recounted in this book several instances of long-term predictive statements that were afterward corroborated by real events—sixteen years later in Pauli's prediction of my ISS theory. However, this does not mean, as I've stressed it, that our whole future is already written or predetermined, but only that some core events have such a high probability of befalling us that they will indeed happen, despite their detail being still fuzzy.

Claude Lecouteux, while presenting the Scandinavian mythology from the *Gesta Danorum*—the Danes' sacred book—recounts that a giant genie meets humans in the Beyond and greets them by their names; in his *Mondes parallèles,* he notes: "Supernatural beings always know everything about humans and always address them by their names" (88, n. 21, my translation).

In numerous instances, the apparitions display a knowledge of the actual state of things on Earth, meaning they have clairvoyance—such as the state of their tomb or where they have hidden money or their will (as in Palladia's case, chapter 7); or else a knowledge of things to come; for example, in the brewer Karl D. case, he mentions the exact date and time at which he will be buried (chapter 4). In the outstanding case of Sisir Kumar (chapter 5), the deceased father displays a knowledge of the past incarnation of his young son (retrocognition) and of plants and metals warding off angry spirits (knowledge of integral medicine).

You can count on the fact that even a person of moderate spiritual achievement, with whom you've had problems during their earthly life, will now have a much clearer, less egocentric and less biased, perspective on what happened between you. They will also have some degree of knowledge of your actual life situation, and what's in store for you. But here is a salient piece of advice: you have to expect that their degree of clarity, knowledge, and wisdom reflects the degree of advancement of their soul—meaning the spiritual awakening they have achieved so far, not only in their life but also in the afterlife. The majority of souls will be more advanced and wise in the afterlife than in their past earthly life, yet they may still be encumbered and hampered by psychological problems that could bias or cloud their understanding. Others will still be limited and blocked by their past passions and hatred. Thus, keep in mind that while still living on Earth, you may, in some cases, have a much higher spiritual understanding and sense of your future destiny, than they do in the afterlife.

All in all, I would not recommend that you ask your past relatives for any life-altering advice or forecast about your future. But you may ask them to try their best to help solve some of the problems they contributed, by their past actions, to creating in the first place. As for exact predictions and sensible advices, they are not to be expected from deceased spirits apart from those who are your dedicated allies (such as my aunt and my father turned out to be) or else those who have achieved a high spiritual state.

What Do the Ascended Scholars Aim for in the HD?

The highly spiritual entities dwelling in the hyperdimension act as guides for humanity in their specific domain of excellence, while they themselves keep on learning and evolving in all respects. In the years from 2012 to 2015 during which I was elaborating the ISS cosmology positing the hyperdimension of consciousness, and while working at my desk (and immersed in my work), I would suddenly see a great scientist visiting me, engaging the conversation on one aspect of my work and their own past work, and I would ask them questions and keep the dialogue going. All those who visited me knew everything about what was happening in actuality in the field of physics and, as I explained earlier, everything about me and my work. References to a future work of mine were interspersed in sentences focused on a specific topic. In the communications with spirits, especially Jung and Pauli—who are like my soul family— humorous comments on my life and on my current emotional or material situation were not rare. I also got from them lots of very pointed and precise information, whose veracity I could easily check. For example, one of them with whom I conversed several times, Nicola Tesla, dropped by while I was busy writing (as every night) my *Cosmic DNA* book; during our discussion, he mentioned that I had just made an error in terms of physics in a statement I wrote "two pages earlier." It took me some time to sort it out later from the dense text, but sure enough, I found the mistake (which I may not have detected, were it not for the advice given). (Now, to be clear, these contacts—mostly initiated by the HD scientists themselves, or quite spontaneously on my part—give me reasons to believe my ISS theory is moving in the right direction. But it doesn't mean it's the only possible theory implying a hyperdimension of consciousness. Also, its mathematical-physics side has yet to be elaborated upon.)

When we consider these scientists' all-encompassing perspective from the HD, and the fact that they keep on working and evolving themselves, this state of affairs is quite sensible. They are just as eager to see physics and science at large evolve as they were while living. I gather that they would readily speak with any promising and dedicated researcher touching on their favorite field(s), if only he or she could just be able to "hear" them. It is quite possible, in fact, that Koestler's famous angel of libraries—making researchers stumble on their next piece of needed information, thus creating fantastic synchronicities—could be these mentors or spiritual guides helping us from the hyperdimension. But, to be fair, our own Self could do just the same for us, and let's remember that our Self is our primary guardian angel and maker of synchronicities.

All in all, I'm grateful to have developed and constantly improved that talent of being in sync and communicating with kindred HD spirits. One thing that was crystal clear with all scientists with whom I conversed, was that they expected physics and psychology, all sciences in fact, to move out of the materialist paradigm and make inroads into a more spiritual, or at least multidimensional, paradigm. As several expressed it clearly to me, that's precisely the work they are pursuing for themselves and for humanity in the hyperdimension, and also the reason why they have achieved such preeminence in the spirit dimension, due to their previous earthly research in that direction.

12

A HYPERDIMENSION PERVADING THE UNIVERSE

Where our grasp of the soul dimension gets truly exciting, and a whole other story, is when we tackle the concept of a hyperdimension as an extra-dimension to our spacetime and quantum universe—a dimension of consciousness that would be at the same time spread over the whole cosmos, and pervading all of its cells and particles. One hyperdimension that would exist before the Big Bang and after the Big Crunch in our universe—in a chain of such universe-bubbles—retaining the memory of all things past and future because it exists beyond time and beyond matter.

THE ONE, THE WORLD SOUL

This concept of a global consciousness field extending to the universe, called the One, or World Soul (*Anima Mundi*) has been a cornerstone of many ancient philosophical and religious schools of thought, beyond shamanism. We find it notably in nonreligious, yet spiritual, philosophies, that is, philosophies exploring the nature of reality beyond the matter dimension, without reference to a personalized god or to deities; in these, the cosmic soul is a global entity of the same divine nature as the individual immaterial soul, yet nonpersonalized.

Among these philosophies of Oneness are the Advaita Vedanta, the ancient philosophy of nonduality in India (*advaita* means "nonduality," and *vedanta* means "philosophy" in Sanskrit) and Taoism in China, as best expressed in Lao-Tzu's *Tao Te Ching* or *Book of the Way* (see plate 26). We find the concept of a dimension of souls, called the monads, in Gottfried Leibniz's philosophy that is quite similar to the concept of syg-fields in a hyperdimension, in that not only all beings but also all things in the universe have an individual monad, and these monads exist on their own elevated level of reality. The concept was best expounded in his 1714 essay *Monadology*.

The soul in Christian lore is believed to be "near" to God, and the saints themselves to be in a specific semantic space, the communion of the saints, that is, in constant conversation and divine energy sharing (in the ISS theory, they are interconnected in the syg-HD via their resonant syg-fields).

Advaita Vedanta and the Akasha

The philosophy of nonduality (Advaita Vedanta) was first expounded by Sri Sankaracharya (or Sankaracarya), an eighth-century Indian philosopher, and had its roots in the early Upanishads (see plate 27).* It reveals the Oneness of cosmic consciousness. As the last and most comprehensive part of the Vedas, the Upanishads are of unknown but very ancient age.

In the Upanishads, an individual (as ego, or jiva) may, by reaching samadhi states in meditation, rise to connect and get harmonized with his or her atman (or Self, soul); in that state of fusion, the atman-ego gets spontaneously in communion with the cosmic consciousness, the beyond-duality purusha (or brahman).

As for the concept of *Akasha* (found in Vedic, Hindu, and Tibetan Mahayana Buddhist religions), it poses that all events that ever happened in the universe are memorized in a sort of central databank called the

---

*See Sri Sankaracarya, *Pancikaranam*.

Akashic Record, or Library. The fascinating 1998 movie *What Dreams May Come,* by Vincent Ward in which Robin Williams was the main character, shows the souls of the deceased, in the Bardo, consulting such Akashic Records. Some ancient texts attribute this spontaneous imprinting process to the *prana* energy. Prana is cosmic consciousness as a subtle (nonmaterial) energy or force, and as such it pervades the universe and is also replete in the atmosphere. The Hindu prana yoga is a set of techniques for inhaling this spiritual and healing force through breathing. The Akasha (just as the prana) has several levels; at the most basic one, it is the world's memory field. At its global level, the Akasha is a highly spiritual ether defined in somewhat identical terms with the brahman or cosmic consciousness. Both lay beyond the matter universe, preexisting it, and lasting after the current universe has ended, in an eternal chain of such universes—referred to as Brahma's breathing, the god Brahma breathing universes in and out of existence.

Brahman, Tao, and prana could be the concepts the nearest to our actual scientific term of *hyperdimension.* This is the meaning retained by Ervin Laszlo, who proposes a theory of the void (the vacuum) as being such Akashic field in the universe. In his book *The Self-Actualizing Cosmos,* Laszlo quotes Swami Vivekananda's statement in *Raja Yoga* that at the beginning of creation as well as at the end of "a creation" there's only the Akasha, and all matter has disappeared. In this latent state of the universe, all forces are called prana; and all things will again emerge from the Akasha for the next creation. The very ancient text, the *Rig Veda,* says also: "First Hiranyagarbha (Prana) came to existence."

Plotinus

Another way to understand the One as a giant cosmic field of consciousness, is to view the universe as a complex hologram: any part of the universe-hologram will contain the information on the whole, whether in space or time.

Astonishingly, the Greek philosopher Plotinus, who lived in Alexandria in the third century CE, expressed clearly in his *Enneads*

Fig. 12.1. Plotinus
*Ostiense Museum, Ostia Antica,
Rome, Italy, CC BY-SA 3.0*

this conception of the universe as a hologram, moreover organized by a central cosmic soul (*psyche* in Greek, *anima* in Latin) who pervades all its parts: "A unique Soul [universal, the One] pervades all things without dividing itself in them and indwells as a whole at every point throughout the world."* (See fig. 12.1.)

For Plotinus, the universe is a conscious and alive hologram, in which the One is existing in any "part"—that is, as we would say now: in any particle, being, or system. He explains in Ennead 2 that the universe in its wholeness, just like the body, constitutes a vast organism; all planets and beings are parts of this Whole, and the *sympathy* they share, which unites them together, creates a unique harmony. In tractate 3, Plotinus states "All things must be enchained; and the sympathy and correspondence obtaining in any one closely knit organism must exist, first, and most intensely, in the All."†

Thus the harmony of the One is infusing and organizing the

---

*Plotinus, Ennead 6, tractate 4, section 12; my translation from Bouillet.
†Plotinus, Ennead 2, tractate 3, section 7; MacKenna translation.

universe. Such concepts are astonishingly resonant with the basic tenets of holographic universe models and systems theory!

Given that, for Plotinus, intelligence is a specific force, if this force is at work somewhere in the universe's hologram, then it is "known" by all the facets in all times; thus, at the minimum a sort of primeval or "proto-consciousness" has to be at work everywhere (this was proposed by philosopher David Chalmers in the mid-1990s). The bottom line is, the universe can't disregard and ignore sentience, intelligence, and consciousness as powerful triggers of evolution, if it knows about it. And in a holographic universe, it does know about it!

This was the perspective developed in the early 1980s by physicist David Bohm, in his *Wholeness and the Implicate Order* book, and the most important force he posited in this holographic universe was "active information," an organizing force based on meaning. This holographic or holonomic framework was further developed by brain scientist Karl Pribram in the early 1990s, in the field of brain sciences.

Hermes

With Hermes Trismegistus (or Thrice Great), we have, just as with the Eastern philosophies of Oneness, both a theory of the One, and a practice of meditation and contemplation of this transcendent realm.

In "The Cup or Monad," Hermes explains the One to his son Tat:

The Oneness being Source and Root of all, is in all things as Root and Source. Without [this] Source is naught.

In the astounding *Discourse on the Eighth and Ninth,* Hermes guides his son Tat to experience the state of Oneness while contemplating it in a heightened and visionary state. Their meditation includes also a chanting of sacred sounds or words. This is a later stage in their meditative practice, the aim of which is to raise their consciousness from the high sphere of the Eighth to the sphere of the Ninth—the cosmic dimension of the One. The sphere of the Ninth is

Fig. 12.2. The dimension of the One as a nine-pointed star.
Front page (Antiporta) in A. Kircher, *Arithmologia*, 1665.

symbolized by a nine-pointed star in an alchemical drawing from the *Tractatus Aureus* (see fig. 12.2).

At the end of their meditation, they both receive an illumination from the Ninth, and Hermes, in an enraptured state, reaches the light and wisdom of Mind.

> Rejoice over this! For already from them the power, which is light, is coming to us. For I see! I see indescribable depths. How shall I tell I see another Mind, the one that moves the soul!
>
> I see the one that moves me from pure non-thought, non-ego (forgetfulness). You give me power! I see myself! I want to speak!
>
> Fear restrains me. I have found the beginning of the power that is above all powers, the one that has no beginning. I see a fountain bubbling with life. I have said, my son, that I am Mind. I have seen!
>
> Language is not able to reveal this.

Indeed, in the most ancient philosophies of Oneness, the meditative practice is the very tool that enables these yogis and philosophers (or Lovers of Sophia/wisdom, in the Greek roots of the term) to know the One by experiencing it. This is of course far remote from our Western concept of an intellectual-only way of knowing. The intellect, as stated by Plotinus, is wholly unable to access the subtlety of the dimension of the cosmic soul, unless it "contemplates" the realm above itself, which is intuitive intelligence, itself at its highest when contemplating the One.

This is why the Eastern masters have devised techniques of meditation to lead us to experience higher states of consciousness, namely the states of oneness or fusion states. In the highest states of meditation, called samadhi, we become harmonized within our inner being, harmonized with nature, and One with the whole—connected to cosmic consciousness (brahman, the Tao). These heightened states of deep harmony are reaching beyond duality, and allow us to live within ourselves the dimension of the Self and that of the cosmic soul, and thus to know about the deep reality.

World Soul and Cosmic Consciousness

The syg-hyperdimension is the global field of consciousness-energy in the cosmos. It sets the universe as one system, conscious, filled with meaning, self-organizing. This syg-field at the cosmic scale is also the ensemble of all the Selfs and syg-fields of individual beings and systems in the universe, and as such it transforms itself continuously through all its parts.

Here is how it operates (as I've been able to fathom it up to now).

- The syg-hyperdimension, that of consciousness-as-energy, pervades the whole universe—all living beings, and all matter systems, from particles to galaxies. It is of the same nature and dynamics (triune, hyperspace, hypertime, and cosmic consciousness) as our individual syg-field, and comprises all syg-fields in the universe.

- The syg-hyperdimension acts as a creative and negentropic force, prodding all innovation, creation, intention, feeling, and action.

- It also contains all the memory of the universe (the Akasha). It includes what was and what will be. However, it is not deterministic, thus not bound or constrained by its past states as a whole.

- The syg-hyperdimension is at the same time a whole (the One), and an infinite plurality. As a whole, it is the cosmic consciousness of our universe bubble—the collective unconscious of Jung, the Sphere of the One of Plotinus and Hermes, the brahman and Tao of Eastern religions. It has similarities with the world of ideas of Plato, the noosphere of Teilhard de Chardin, and the implicate order of David Bohm. As a plurality, it is made of all the syg-fields of biosystems and ecosystems in the universe—whether as intelligent entities, as sentient beings, or as the proto-consciousness of complex systems.

- The syg-hyperdimension of our universe includes all planet-scale syg-fields, and thus all intelligent self-reflexive civilizations in the universe, as well as all complex star systems and cosmic systems. Whether housing an intelligent civilization or not, each planet will have a syg-field. Similarly, all complex systems on Earth, however tiny, have their own syg-fields in the hyperdimension.

As for Earth's planetary syg-field (Gaia), we all co-create it. Our personal Self blends in with the cosmic consciousness, setting a synergy. Any Self may have an influence on the whole, just as, conversely, the whole will influence all its cells. As human beings, together we form the nodes of the giant network of our collective Self, Gaia. However, the whole, Gaia, is much more than the sum of all syg-fields it contains. Gaia's consciousness will be of a higher order than a human consciousness; and yet, since we are part of it, in synergy, we can also influence it.

QUANTUM PHYSICS, PSI, AND A HYPERDIMENSION OF CONSCIOUSNESS

Hyperdimensional physics is very much on the rise now, and it represents the forefront theories in physics. This is not by chance or a fad. On the one hand, the evidence is growing that physics cannot be integrated into the unified theory that Einstein pursued all his life, unless it posits some type of hyperdimension. The challenge here is to integrate the Relativity physics of 4D spacetime with quantum physics, yet this can be done (and is being done) only by postulating a hyperdimension, at the minimum a 4th dimension of space (to add to the 3D of space plus the 1D of time)—this means postulating a 5th dimension, or hyperspace.

On the other hand, the stated aim of physicists is to attain a complete "theory of everything" (or TOE), yet most of them leave out of the said "everything" their own consciousness and mind—that very part of reality that allows them to create theories in the first place!

Actual physics, both Relativity and Quantum Mechanics (still striving to get fully integrated), has not been able to account for consciousness. Another type of model altogether is needed to do so. And maybe physicists are still too restricted by their matter-only framework; maybe such theory will be fathomed by minds having a better grasp of consciousness and its dynamic processes. (Needless to say, I'm a candidate with my ISS theory!)

Most physicists postulate a hyperspace endowed solely with physics properties such as faster-than-light speed and, as a 4th dimension of space, a complex structuring such as the hypercube (tesseract). Astrophysicist and psi researcher Bernard Carr, author of *Universe or Multiverse*, is a rare theorist linking his modeling of hyperspace with specific spiritual and psi capacities. Of note also is Michael Talbot's model that he develops in *The Holographic Universe*. Both researchers have integrated psi capacities in their understanding of reality.*

The fact is, psi has been duly proven by hundreds of experiments, but we still can't explain it. Psi, in all its forms, shows a clear violation of Relativity physics based on EM fields. (The strength of the psi signal doesn't decrease as a function of the distance, and this signal is not evenly distributed in space—both laws and markers of EM fields.) And this is the reason why many scientists in the past have claimed that psi is impossible or just a fraud. Yet psi is a mental phenomenon, and mind is definitely the most crucial part of our lives, since without it we wouldn't even talk or know that we exist. So, in brief, we know that psi works, but we don't know why or its nature: something is lacking here, that's clear!

Consequently, several psi researchers have tried to explain psi by specific quantum processes, such as the entanglement of particles. When entangled, two paired particles do communicate and influence each other at such faster-than-light speed and such great distances

---

*For a detailed presentation and discussion of the diverse physics theories implying consciousness, psi, and a hyperdimension, see my book *Cosmic DNA at the Origin: A Hyperdimension before the Big Bang*, and my scientific papers on ISST at independent .academia.edu/ChrisHHardy/Papers

that it excludes a signal propagated through space. The problem is, the entanglement has been proven and we know how to make it work, but we don't know why. So first, there's a problem in trying to explain some mysterious yet proven psi phenomena by using some mysterious yet proven entanglement process. And second: sorry, but quantum waves are still bound by the speed of light limit, and cannot, by themselves, explain a faster-than-light communication. Something is lacking there too, that's clear!

So, could it be that what's lacking to understand psi is just the same thing that's lacking to understand the entanglement? Namely, the hyperdimensional layer of reality—existing in each particle, atom, cell, organism, any living or matter system, all the way to stars and galaxies, and yet existing also as a whole coherent layer of the universe or pluriverse itself?

This is where the research in psi and physics lends ground to envisioning a vast field of universal consciousness, as has been postulated by philosophies of oneness, by Hermetism and the Eastern religions, and what they refer to as the One, the Divine realm, the Tao, the brahman, the Great Spirit of Native Americans, the Eagle of Yaqui Indians, cosmic consciousness. This is the conclusion also reached by journalist Lynne McTaggart in her famed book *The Field*. The Great Spirit (Wakan Tanka, Gitche Manitou) is not only the sacred and universal spiritual force, but one with whom a medicine (wo)man or vision quester could communicate, and receive visions and healing powers from (see fig. 12.3, page 282).

As for me, given my background in ethno-psychology, psi research, and my life-long yogic and psi practice, a physics-only model of the universe is not, by any means, able to explain and represent the reality of our beings and of our lives filled with meaning, feelings, and thoughts. I agree fully with Bernard Carr who maintains that consciousness has to be integrated in any theory of the universe. This is why the ISS theory stands apart from the current hyperdimension theories in physics. In ISST, the hyperdimension is more than just a 5th dimension or

Fig. 12.3. *Appeal to the Great Spirit,* by Cyrus E. Dallin, 1909,
Museum of Fine Arts, Boston
Photo by Jim Heaphy, CC BY-SA 3.0

hyperspace that (because it's only a 4th dimension of space) would deal exclusively with space. In ISST, the HD is triune, with a hyperspace, a hypertime (time extended as a field), and moreover a hyperdimension of consciousness, our syg-HD, operating like a cosmic consciousness in which our minds and souls are bathing.

Remember the movie *Interstellar,* by Christopher Nolan, in which the hero, after passing through a black hole, finds himself in this

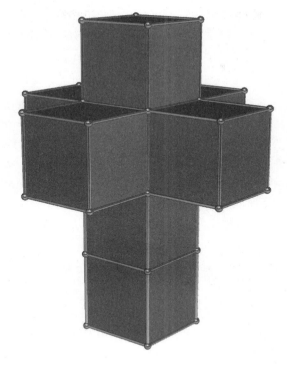

Fig. 12.4. The tesseract—a 4D-space cube—can be unfolded into eight cubes in 3D space (called a Dali Cross), just as the cube can be unfolded into six squares in 2D space
Created by Robert Webb with Stella software (www.software3d.com/Stella.php)

5th dimension, in the tesseract, and in an all-pervading dimension of consciousness that allows him to communicate with his daughter in her own bedroom (see fig. 12.4). The 5th dimensional tesseract (or hypercube), being beyond space and time, permits one to connect with any material space, and the father-daughter psychic bond creates the psychic convergence and junction of the two dimensions—that of Earth 4D spacetime, and that of the hyperspace—near a certain person and in a specific location. The movie was on target, but the purported theory behind it was not, as the crucial psychic bond can't be explained solely by hyperspace.

In ISST, at our planetary level, the syg-HD is the collective unconscious—a field indeed that connects all minds and penetrates all spaces and times. It is through this all-pervasive field that we are able to communicate with higher dimensional beings and with the Selfs of the deceased, and also telepathically with the living.

CONSCIOUSNESS PERVADING NATURE

Panpsychism is a philosophical worldview—a paradigm—that attributes to all natural and physical systems, and all beings, a level of sentience or consciousness. Of course there are various degrees of complexity. Most of us would readily agree that our pets show emotional intelligence and that a real bonding occurs with them; this expression of emotions goes beyond simple fondness for their masters, as for example with the fidelity and protectiveness of dogs (just think of dogs caring for the blind, the elderly, or the kids).

According to cognitive sciences, only humans have the capacity to use reason and abstract thought (as with math), symbolic thoughts and actions (such as offering flowers to express love), and to reflect on themselves (or self-reference). In a panpsychist worldview, in order to distinguish between the abstract thought and a level of sentience, when this consciousness is rather basic and undeveloped, it is called a "proto-consciousness," following philosopher David Chalmers's term.

Emotions, Symbolic Behaviors, Telepathy in Animals

Materialist scientists still adamantly deny any thinking or emotions in animals, and will attribute to them only instinctive, hormone-based behaviors, and the kind of conditioned learning they study with laboratory rats. Yet data keep accumulating in the field of animal behavior and learning to show the contrary. It's beyond the scope of this book, and I'll just cite a few cases.

We are now certain that apes are laughing and often indulge in social behaviors just to have a good laugh. (Several videos can be found on the internet.) Moreover, "Our primate ancestors have been laughing for 10m years," ran *The Guardian* on June 4, 2009.

Already in the late 1980s, French psychiatrist Boris Cyrulnik had documented symbolic behaviors in birds; birds offer presents to the courted partner that are definitely beyond simple food sharing and denote a symbolic gesture, such as offerings of inedible plants. Classical scientists claim that symbolic thinking and behavior are typically and solely human; just as would be a show of love without immediate mating expectation or mother-child bonding (see Cyrulnik 1989).

Recently, there was the stupendous case of a Humboldt penguin, called Grape-kun ("Mister Grape" in Japanese), falling in love with a cardboard cutout of an anthropomorphic female penguin called Hululu (from the Japanese anime series *Kemono Friends*). His emotional fixation happened after his decade-long mate Midori had left him for a younger male. Hululu's cutout had been set in the penguin enclosure of Tobu Zoo in Japan, together with sixty other ones, for a promotional event around the anime in April 2017. Grape would spend so many hours contemplating his loved one every day, forgetting to eat, that the zookeepers had to take him away regularly to feed him. Grape kept trying but was unable to get near his loved one, given that the cutout was set on a tall rock. He died a celebrity in October 2017, aged twenty-one—the equivalent of eighty years old for humans. Given that Grape could not approach his loved one, and never received any real-life response from it, his behavior was clearly symbolic and implied a quite sophisticated emotional behavior, neither instinctive nor conditioned.*

Furthermore, there is growing evidence that some species are clearly telepathic. The research findings not only include home pets in general, but also the famously friendly dolphins and the cetaceous species at large (even the shark and the scary orcas). Biologist Rupert Sheldrake shows a striking evidence of telepathy in pets, in his fascinating book *Dogs That Know When Their Owner Is Coming Home,* in which he described his various experiments. Needless to say, Sheldrake used a sophisticated protocol that set randomly selected times for the return home of the

---

*More detail on Grape-kun can be found in the online Wikipedia article "Grape-kun."

master and shunned any obvious signals in their home that the pets could perceive. Yet the dogs were going to wait for their owner near the door or the gate for a short time before their unexpected arrival from the airport or town.

Tuning In to the Spirits of Nature: Keys and Practice

It is interesting to note that, in such a panpsychist worldview, all complex natural systems such as a lake or a mountain, would thus possess some form of sentience, tangible enough for sensitives to perceive them and communicate with them as individual entities. Sometimes, genies or fairies of these natural systems are encountered and show an ability to talk, interact, and act willfully; we find accounts of such encounters in all cultures on Earth, and specifically in shamanism and among the First People.

It is evident that, in our Western societies, people during the Middle Ages were much more prone to see and interact with these entities than us, firstly because they were living in a much wilder nature and closer to it, and secondly because their rational left brain didn't have the oversized and overwhelming control it gained on us in the last three centuries. Lecouteux gives numerous examples in his various books.

Now let's figure that some of these genies are the consciousness level, the syg-HD level, of natural elements such as water (springs, lakes, rivers), fire (especially the hearth or house chimney, or the camp fires of the First People), land (the dreamtime places and paths of aborigines), mountains, rocks, or plants (the fairies of flowers, the high consciousness of sacred trees). Generally, elves and undines are genies of water; dwarfs, sylvains, and goblins those of forests and land; whereas fairies are mostly linked to flowers, crops, and springs. Most genies display a body-form reminiscent of a human body (with a head, arms, and legs and an upright walking posture, often of petite size); yet they are able to cross and pass through matter such as walls and doors. But Lecouteux stresses that these genies are nevertheless quite material in the way they make noise while walking or acting, such as the genies of old taking care of stables and horses. Genies have great strength, and of course they have their own individuality and are able to develop personal relationships with humans, as in the case of house genies or fairies.

The Irish poet William Butler Yeats has written down the oral knowledge and legends attached to fairies and elves in Ireland, namely in *Fairy and Folk Tales of the Irish Peasantry*. Jacques Vallee, in *Passport to Magonia,* has made an in-depth study of the behaviors attributed to fairies and compared them to accounts of alien abduction and sightings of aliens. Some comparisons are indeed striking—such as the fact that people abducted by fairies may suddenly reappear in their village and community after a long time has elapsed, evoking also the well-known "lost time" in alien abduction. It is quite possible that some of the so-called fairies had been aliens based on Earth; and inversely, that some would-be observations of aliens had been in reality that of earth-born dwarfs and genies. But that wouldn't account for all observations of either fairies or aliens (especially the great number of alien crafts observed by military radars and pursued by fighter planes). Jacques Vallee is in no way dismissing the alien problem, as we can see in his autobiography *Forbidden Science* or his novel *Fastwalker* in which he signals anomalous observations made by astronomers such as himself (his own were scratched from the official records of the Paris observatory).

Just think about many precious stones being 3 billion years old (the oldest object on Earth being a zircon fragment of 4.4 billion years—just 150 million years younger than our planet!); think about the Grand Canyon in Colorado now estimated to be about 70 million years old. Think about the giant sequoias and the redwood trees—whose oldest specimen, Muir Snag, now biologically dead, was estimated to be over 3,500 years old before it died, and is still standing in the Giant Sequoia National Monument in Sierra Nevada (Converse Basin) (see plate 28). Yet, Methuselah is a 4,850-year-old bristlecone pine (White Mountains, eastern California) and was the world's oldest known living single-stem tree until 2012, when a still unnamed one was discovered in the same grove topping 5,068 years (who thus sprouted in 3050 BCE!). Let's note that the syg-field of the tree, Muir Snag, is still existing and living, even if its biological system is dead. The spirit of the tree is there!

With such ancient natural systems, this layer of consciousness would have become much more complex and organized, endowed with an immense memory of events (natural or otherwise) that had happened in their environment.

As for myself and starting from my late teens, I can attest I had many sophisticated interactions and short dialogues with a variety of organic beings, including trees, flower plants, the wild ocean in the south of Morocco, the Ganges River, genies of mountains (as the genie of the Tamalpais, the Indian sacred mountain mentioned in chapter 6), sacred fire, the genies of stones (Fontenay Abbaye in Burgundy), and more—and of course numerous telepathic interactions with animals in the wild or tamed, so many that it would take a study in itself. Indeed, it has become a constant in my life that I tune in to the level of consciousness of these beings, wherever I am. And these beings respond spontaneously to such attunement. Let me express how I do that. It feels like a sub-layer of reality, a level underlying our own noosphere (or dimension of collective human intellect, as Teilhard de Chardin called it). And it makes sense that the diffuse consciousness field of the living, and of the Earth as Gaia—as a living entity endowed with the global consciousness of Earth—would be a layer in our collective unconscious.

The way to get tuned to it is to be in an open, listening, and welcoming mode—an empathy with the living that allows for a sort of deep resonance with it. And when one gets attuned to this layer, the communication can happen spontaneously with either vegetal entities or wild animals. In other words, it's the same layer of diffuse meaningful consciousness in which individual organic entities can express themselves and their specific memory and knowledge. Yes, I maintain that these beings have, as shamans know well, a particular knowledge that they can bestow on humans.

THE ONE FIELD, EARTH AS A SINGLE SYSTEM

The concept of the Earth as Gaia, seen as a whole ecological and synergic system, was developed in the late 1970s by James Lovelock in his book *Gaia: A New Look at Life on Earth*. It was itself rooted in a new paradigm brought forth by Ludwig von Bertalanffy in his revolutionary 1968 book *General System Theory*. The new perspective was to perceive reality as systems, and not individual mechanical objects anymore. Systems as in biology, where it would not make any sense to study the heart as an organ by itself, without understanding the whole blood circulation system. Then, with psychosomatic medicine, we came to understand that body and mind are a whole system, our body being interconnected to our emotions and our thoughts. Thus, emotions and beliefs may affect our organic health, just as a physical disease can affect and perturb our mental life. It has been proven experimentally and detailed in his book *Learned Optimism* by Professor Martin Seligman that optimistic people were less prone to catch infectious diseases, and that their immune system was stronger and functioning better; moreover, they tended to live longer.

In other words, we finally discarded a clock-mechanism universe—based solely on causal mechanisms, linear chains of causes-effects evolving in a past-future way (A causes B, which causes C, and in no way can C act on A or B).

And we started to explore an interactive and synergic vision, thus launching ecology and complex systems sciences (chaos theory); in this new world vision based on systems thinking, all parts of a system are interconnected; they co-evolve and influence each other. Thus we see a network of factors, all dynamically interacting with each other, and this ongoing interaction creates sudden changes in the system's global organization; this being called a change of attractor—either a leap to a higher or lower complexity, or a catastrophic collapse. As I've argued in one paper,* causality breaks down as an explanation when

---

*"Self-Organization, Self-Reference and Inter-influences in Multilevel Webs: Beyond Causality and Determinism"

we consider complex systems, that is, all natural systems (including our brains and bodies), and even more so, minds and societies; in other words, causality is unable to explain the dynamics within and among syg-fields, only a double and simultaneous influence, a synergy or synchronicity, can.

Then this systems perspective led us to understand how all natural systems are deeply interconnected; and this brings us to our actual planet woe. We can't remain blind to the fact that the extraction of coal and gas, and the burning of fossil fuels is leading to catastrophic global warming and climate crises; to do so would show a suicidal disdain and carelessness toward humanity at large and the future generations. Climate crises are obviously reaching a new level of violence and devastation with monster hurricanes in 2017 (hurricanes Harvey and Maria) and 2018 (hurricanes Florence, Mangkhut, and Michael); as well as an unprecedented destruction of flora and property due to massive wild fires, notably in California, Greece, Eastern Australia, and the Amazon forest in 2019; and also a massive red tide of algae bloom, that, by October 13, 2018, extended from the Gulf of Mexico to Fort Lauderdale, killing millions of fish, while massive deaths of birds, fish, sea mammals, and animals are happening worldwide.

A 2017 article in the *Proceedings of the National Academy of Sciences,* by Ceballos, Ehrlich, and Dirzo, titled "Biological Annihilation via the Ongoing Sixth Mass Extinction Signaled by Vertebrate Population Losses and Declines" sounded the alarm. The authors, using a sample of 27,600 vertebrate species surveyed between 1900 and 2015, stated "Our data indicate that beyond global species extinctions Earth is experiencing a huge episode of population declines and extirpations, which will have negative cascading consequences on ecosystem functioning and services vital to sustaining civilization. We describe this as a 'biological annihilation' to highlight the current magnitude of Earth's ongoing sixth major extinction event."

Since then, new scientific data have only shown the magnitude and extent of this extinction to be worse than feared. As an example, in a

November 13, 2019, article in *The Guardian,* Damian Carrington warns of an unfolding "insect apocalypse" and writes "A new report suggested half of all insects may have been lost since 1970 as a result of the destruction of nature and heavy use of pesticides." He reports that 40 percent of the 1 million known species of insect are facing extinction.

Are we going to just realize what's happening and move at light speed from now on? Or are we going to let a breakaway group among the 0.01 percent richest deny the human share and responsibility in the already unfolding catastrophe while they secretly build their little Elysium (as in Neill Blomkamp's 2013 movie, starring Matt Damon and Jodie Foster)?

Now, let's be clear. The fact is, we still let the greed of the richest few and of powerful multinationals determine and endanger the future of all people; we still allow the egotist madness of those hoping to amass more riches until the very dire ashen end—when water, air, food, and oxygen will replace all money (as the most precious resources) and they won't have any use for the latter anymore. Even more insulting, we still buy their lies and put them in power, while we still enjoy democratic systems . . . that's just hard to believe! Next thing we know, democracy is gone in America and the previously hopeful base rejoins the rest of society toiling for survival on a devastated planet, while the Elysium off-planet paradise satellite soars, seemingly unperturbed, in the sky.

And predictions are more distressing by the month, thus "The Global Group says the planet's temperature will reach critical disaster threshold by the year 2030" titles CNN with an interview of meteorologist Eric Holthaus by CNN's Ana Cabrera, in the dire wake of Hurricane Michael that erased, among other devastation, the whole town of Mexico Beach, Florida.*

The way it's going, it's either humanity and Earth alive, *or* the 0.01 percent of humanity enjoying a synthetic and fully artificial life in

---

*This interview, "Experts: Climate catastrophe could hit by 2030," October 14, 2018, is available on the CNN website.

an above-the-toxic-clouds Elysium! And if we want to choose humanity and Earth, then we need no less than a leap into a new world vision. We have to shed the materialistic outlook and profit-based, grab-all economy for a world vision intending to heal the planet and driving a new green economy.

We have to envision that we thrive, as an intelligent (so to speak) species precisely because the soul dimension is entwined with the matter dimension. The reason I add "so to speak" is that we cannot deem a species that is not able to manage its own survival and that of its planet as really intelligent. Some types of viruses kill their host, thus killing themselves—that's what we are now doing to our planet, which is no less than our host.

We need, more than ever, a new world vision to tackle the unfolding catastrophe of global warming already decimating our animal and vegetal life, and thus putting at risk our very survival both as Earth-humanity and as a planet.

And the foundation of this new vision is to realize that a soul dimension is entwined with the matter dimension, at all scales. This grounds the sacredness of Earth as a living entity, endowed with the collective consciousness of humanity and the living, itself part of the larger system of a universe endowed with a hyperdimension of consciousness.

ON ALIENS AND ASCENDING TO THE HYPERDIMENSION

Let's ponder the survival of souls in a higher dimension, endowed with the consciousness, personality, and memory of the person they had been while living, and this soul having even more understanding and wisdom in this higher realm. If these two realms of existence and consciousness co-exist and are the fundamental reality of the universe, then, in purely psychic and consciousness terms, there ought to be some interaction between dimensions and we ought to find some clear signs of this soul dimension in our lives. And indeed, in our earthly life, the NDEs and OBEs, together with the perception of ascended souls and our communicating with them, are a solid ground for the reality of the dimension of souls and they show us how to explore it. Most researchers (including myself) have used these data to build the case for a conscious afterlife.

Of course, things are much clearer when we use the physics concept of a hyperdimension (as an encompassing and more complex non-matter dimension, with a higher frequency-domain), and especially that of a hyperdimension of consciousness. Because, if our universe is multidimensional, then in purely physics terms there ought to be some interaction between dimensions. Call them portals, or vortexes,

Fig. C.1. Supermassive black hole at the center of a galaxy, emitting
two opposite jets of plasma orthogonal to the accretion disk
Artist impression, ESA/Hubble, L. Calçada (ESO), CC BY 4.0

or stargates, there must be sinks and openings out of our 4D matter
dimension into the higher dimension(s). The most evident of these
sinks is the black hole, in which all matter is crushed by colossal grav-
ity, while only energy is released, as X-rays and gamma rays (fig. C.1),
especially now that we know that there's such a huge black hole at the
very center of each galaxy. In 2002, astronomer R. Schödel and his asso-
ciates detected that our galaxy, the Milky Way, has at its center such a
supermassive black hole, with a mass about 4 million solar masses, near
the Sagittarius A* region of space. It was confirmed in 2008.

In the ISS theory, it's in the white hole at the origin of our universe that matter was generated out of the pure hyperdimension containing all information about previous universes (the prana or Akashic

field, the cosmic consciousness field). And the black hole at the end of our universe bubble is where all matter will be translated back into the hyperdimension, as syg-fields (information fields). This life of a universe in a chain of universes is somehow similar to the soul incarnated in a body at birth and ascending back to the hyperdimension at death. As we saw, it is a core concept in Hinduism, called Brahma's breathing—in which Brahma is breathing universes in and out.

DO ASCENDED SOULS SEE ALIEN SOULS, AND DOMAINS OF FREQUENCIES?

Now as I'm deciphering things, at the matter and biological level, a galactic federation of intelligent civilizations, mastering faster-than-light travels, must already exist, and we should get integrated into it any time soon, or at least get the information we're already in contact with it. This is the theme of a sci-fi I wrote, *Space Allies,* analyzing the situation in terms of exopolitics, that is, how are we going to deal with this Galactic Federation, and why are we still not included in it?

But as far as a hyperdimension in the universe is concerned, the Selfs (of the living and of the deceased as well) are not impeded by any space or time barrier, and therefore can communicate easily via the HD, whether in meditation, astral journeys, altered states, or during sleep. So, the same must happen to alien intelligent beings living on exoplanetary worlds. In consequence, while we roam in the HD (in any heightened state), we must have extensive interconnections with intelligent civilizations on various inhabited planets, especially from stellar systems surrounding us. Of course, this interconnection and communication with alien worlds and intelligences must be even more easily achieved by the ascended Selfs, fully conscious within the HD. But this is true not only about alien civilizations, but also about the true nature of the fabric of reality, and about the eternal creation and weaving of the hyperdimensional cosmos, and its layers of frequency-domains with their dwelling Selfs.

At this point, I must explain something about the eighteen days (or rather, nights) I spent elaborating and writing the ISS theory (in the autumn of 2012), and during which I modeled this hyperdimension of consciousness as an Infinite Spiral Staircase, or ISS, at the origin. I was not only in a creative spree, but also contemplating the constant vision of this spiral staircase of sub-quantum frequencies exiting out of the white hole at the origin. And this white hole itself generated from the terminal black hole of the preceding universe, forming a giant X shape out of which the spiral was enlarging. And that's how I was able not only to model it but also to make drawings of what I was seeing.

So let's consider what supraconscious Selfs, immersed in an extremely high frequency-domain, may be able to perceive. It's logical that they would be capable of seeing, in a sort of quasi space, the whole of the hyperdimension (the whole of the sub-quantum, sub-Planckian domain), including the ISS at the origin, shining as a Cosmic Self, as a sun. So that within the HD, because of the supraconscious capacities of the ascended Selfs, the Cosmic Self (the subject and origin of cosmic consciousness, the soul of the whole universe) must appear in their "sky" as the mandala of the origin: the Infinite Spiral Staircase of frequencies issued from the white hole at the origin. In a display of light and music, and resplendent, all the time visible just like our sun (a pale symbolic replica).

As far as our own matter world is concerned, I have perceived the existence of layers of frequencies, of which the lowest one is our matter and biological plane. Thus, I have seen several times the repercussion of sacred objects on a series of frequency-planes. (Could these be linked to superposed hyperdimensional layers or surfaces, called sheets?)

While meditating side by side with a quester friend on the beach in India, I was lifted (as very often) and began traveling in an OBE state. I encountered in the syg-hyperdimension my ninety-year-old Sufi master, with whom I had been residing a few months earlier in Iran. He appeared, a resplendent bearded sage, in an entrancing garden manifested by his mind, the immaterial and luminous features of which, such as flower bushes, a fountain, some statues, would keep transforming themselves into other ones, following his thoughts and intentional projections. He was standing and greeting me smiling, while I contemplated the sheer beauty of the place. He then manifested—with a simple hand gesture—a garden table and several chairs and invited me to sit there with him. (As this was happening while I was meditating, and he was still alive, what I was contemplating was definitely his Self's garden in the hyperdimension.) As an immaterial body myself, and following his inviting gesture, I went to sit on a garden chair, around the white wrought-iron garden table where he was now himself sitting, and we started conversing. Now, an incredibly funny thing happened. As I mentioned, when I had started meditating, I was not alone, but with a friend who, right next to me, was also meditating cross-legged, in front of the sun setting on the sea. And while both my master and I were eyes wide open and sitting properly on the HD chairs, this friend of mine suddenly appeared about thirty inches above a third chair next to me (yet perfectly above it), exactly as he was on the beach, in a rigid yogic posture, eyes closed and immersed in an inner state. So I asked my master, "Azra Darvichi, why is my friend not sitting on his chair?" To which he replied, "He is not accustomed to this dimension, he doesn't know how to move around within it."

This happened during my first eighteen-month journey to the East, as I had traveled and reached India after a couple of months spent with my Sufi master, during which I had started to experience astral journeys at will during meditation, exiting voluntarily via the crown chakra. In India at that time, I would spend one or two hours every day in astral journeys, mostly exploring this semantic dimension, visiting higher-dimensional, paradisiacal, and very spiritual worlds.

As I ponder this now, this experience contains a strong proof not only of the reality of the HD, but also of a sort of matter-effect within it. To the Selfs or souls living within a higher frequency-domain, the projected environment and objects, being of the same frequency band, are quite tangible, and solid enough that one may sit on a chair, and rest one's hands on the table, as I was just doing. Yet, some other properties of the HD allow for this projected environment to be changed at will, or just with the flow of peaceful and deep thoughts.

ASCENSION TO AND COMMUNION WITH THE HYPERDIMENSION

Let me now address the bridging of the material world and the syg-dimension in our time. It seems to me that the endeavor of the SPR mediums and researchers was definitely the beginning of a long-term task and that, as live human beings on Earth, we have indeed to become more and more sensitive to the syg-dimension—not solely as the Beyond of the deceased, but also as a cosmic consciousness and the dwelling of our Selfs. By being more and more in contact and harmonized with our inner Self, each one of us, we will indubitably get more attuned to the dimension in which our Self is living. In brief, we will become multidimensional in our daily consciousness, and will be in secret connection and deep attunement with all sensitives worldwide already functioning in a multidimensional mode.

We'll be actors in the great leap in consciousness implying the whole of humanity as it is moving to a multidimensional mode: the increasing unconscious interconnections between people appearing as synchronicities; the blossoming of psi talents and their constant evolution and refinement over the years; the progressive merging and self-reinforcing loop between the analytical left-brain and the intuitive right-brain capacities; the attunement and fusion with our own Self in high or peak states of consciousness; the harmonization of minds in the collective unconscious slowly becoming conscious with the experience of Telhar fields—collective harmonization and shared consciousness states; and finally the progressive building of the Earth's collective consciousness field—the planetary Telhar field.

The global effect of the grassroots leap in consciousness happening within all sensitive individuals from all countries at once, will accelerate the change of paradigm at the societal and scientific levels—and this will happen despite major setbacks and a few steps backward.

All of these changes, started in small groups in the late 1960s, are now reaching a full-blown collective process.

It is my understanding and experience that the two dimensions of our planetary wholeness—the 4D matter world and the syg-hyperdimension—are progressively becoming nearer and more attuned to each other, allowing more frequent communications and intrusions of one frequency-domain into the other. We are endowed with this gift of vision and ascension, as our human heritage, and we are with certainty on our way to co-creating a telepathic-harmonic field at the planetary level, and to becoming, as many traditions have predicted it, a Sacred Planet.

GLOSSARY

collective unconscious: A concept proposed by Carl Jung that posits that we are all interconnected on Earth through our psyche—and notably our unconscious—and this is why a European can dream of a remote tribe's myth. Spiritual growth, setting a harmonization with the higher Self, brings part of the unconscious knowledge (such as **psi**) into awareness.

consciousness: The process by which a mind or a sentient being operates and becomes aware of the world—of its interactions with the world and other beings/things, of its thoughts and of itself (for self-conscious human beings). In **ISST**, our mind, or consciousness, is our personal **syg-field**.

cosmic consciousness: Postulated by Eastern philosophies and religions, and called brahman, or Tao; this is a layer of supraconsciousness in the universe, in which dwell all Selfs, or souls, including immortal beings and guides. In **ISST**, it is the **syg-HD**, the **hyperdimension** of consciousness.

cross-correspondences: A specific study of mediumship conducted for several years between New York and London at the end of the nineteenth century. The mediums, forbidden to have contact with each other, were receiving regular messages from the deceased as pieces of a puzzle, which, when patched together by the researchers, pointed to a coherent overall theme (such as a poem). The complexity of the various puzzles was such that it excluded telepathy between the mediums and was considered solid proof of the survival of self-driven souls.

CSR (Center-Syg-Rhythm) manifold: The triune **hyperdimension (HD)** postulated in **ISST**, a braid of hyperspace (*Center, C*), hypertime (*Rhythm*, R), and consciousness (*Syg*, S), organized as a double phi-based golden spiral (or **ISS**), both at the origin of the universe and at the core of particles. The HD also has a *bulk*—a quasi-spatial extension—that surrounds the matter universe. The ensemble of all **syg-fields** (of all beings and systems in the universe) form the cosmic CSR HD as a gigantic hologram, self-conscious and evolving (see fig. 11.2, page 258).

deep reality: A level in the universe postulated by Wolfgang Pauli and Carl Jung, which is both mind and matter (energy), and in which dwell the Selfs (or souls) of all people.

entanglement: In Quantum Mechanics (QM), the process by which paired particles (i.e., particles issued and propelled simultaneously from the same source) keep retaining nonlocal correlations between them, irrespective of the growing distance between them. Entanglement has been proven since 1982.

group-soul (or group-Self): A level of spirituality and frequency higher than an individual Self. The Selfs of two people who don't even know each other and live in distinct cultures can be part of the same group-soul, together with a hundred more people. (To be distinguished from a *soul-group*, denoting a family of souls having strong links and affinities.)

hyperdimension (HD): A dimension that is above and beyond the four dimensions of spacetime (3D of space plus 1D of time). The 5th dimension (as a 4th D of space), or hyperspace, was first posited by Theodor Kaluza in 1919, and is necessary to unify the four forces in physics (meaning to unify Relativity theory with Quantum Mechanics), thus leading physicists to postulate any number of dimensions (10D or 11D). In **ISST** the HD is triune, see **syg-HD**.

ISS (Infinite Spiral Staircase): A double phi-based golden spiral at a sub-Planckian scale, topologically organized both (1) at the origin of the universe (issued from the white hole at the origin), and (2) as an individual HD spiral that remains at the core of all particles, atoms, and molecules.

ISST (Infinite Spiral Staircase theory): A cosmology theory that features consciousness in the universe as a cosmic consciousness (yet complex and infinitely plural) belonging to a hyperdimension. ISST posits a triune hyperdimension (HD) preexisting and pervading the spacetime region (our 4D matter realm) because it dwells at a sub-Planckian scale—both at the origin (before the inflation phase or Big Bang) and at any spacetime coordinates in all systems (at the core of any particle or system).

nonlocal/ity: A property of a system that presents clear beyond-space and beyond-time processes that are not limited or bound by spacetime and electromagnetic laws.

panpsychism: A philosophy framework that posits a level of consciousness or sentience in all beings, ranging from a self-aware human mind to a proto-consciousness (or basic sentience) in animals and plants (*proto* in Greek means "primary").

psi: A set of mind capacities that are anomalous in terms of both classical (Relativity) physics and cognitive sciences; it includes the well-proven precognition, clairvoyance (remote-viewing), telepathy, and healing (bio-PK). Proven to operate beyond the brain and beyond spacetime—that is, in a **nonlocal** manner.

semantic field (syg-field): In Semantic Fields theory (SFT), a global dynamic network of semantic (meaningful) mental and emotional processes that, as a whole, is the self-organized system we call a mind or an individual consciousness. It is operated by **syg-energy** in a beyond space and beyond time manner, and is composed of smaller networks (or semantic constellations). All beings and systems have a syg-field (a level of sentience or consciousness). In ISST, the syg-field is part of the **syg-HD**.

Semantic Fields theory (SFT): A cognitive sciences theory that models a consciousness or semantic layer of organization in all systems—their syg-fields (**semantic fields**) ranging from proto-consciousness to self-consciousness. As human beings, our mind or consciousness is our global syg-field, organized in dynamic networks and steered by **syg-energy**.

syg-energy, sygons: Sub-quantum strings or waves belonging to the **hyperdimension (HD)**, operating at sub-Planckian frequencies. The *free sygons*, with very high frequencies, are creating and operating in the HD bulk; the lower frequency sygons are the compact HD within particles, atoms, and molecules. The sygons create instant nonlocal connections between resonant minds, or **syg-fields**, thus explaining telepathy and psi at large.

syg-HD: One of the three dimensions of the **hyperdimension** in ISST, the one linked to consciousness and made of the syg-fields (the consciousnesses) of all beings and systems, all self-organized, similarly to the syg-HD itself. It is the cosmic consciousness postulated by Eastern philosophies. See also **CSR**.

synchronicity: Jung's concept of meaningful (nonrandom) coincidences happening between a person's mind state and an event occurring to them in reality at this moment. In his book *Synchronicity*, Jung includes precognition, clairvoyance, and telepathy as examples of synchronicities.

BIBLIOGRAPHY

In addition to the bibliographic references listed below, I recommend the following two online sources for ancient and sacred texts:

Sacred Texts (all religions) online at Internet Sacred Text Archive website (sacred-texts.com) (Notably, Plotinus's Enneads, translated by S. MacKenna)

The *Corpus Hermeticum* texts, available online at the Gnostic Society Library (gnosis.org/library/hermet.htm)

Barrett, William F. *Deathbed Visions*. London: Methuen, 1926.

Bender, Hans. "New Developments in Poltergeist Research." *Proceedings of the Parapsychological Association* 6 (1969): 81–102.

Benor, Daniel. *Spiritual Healing: Scientific Validation of a Healing Revolution*. Bellmawr, N.J.: Wholistic Healing, 2001.

Bohm, David. *Wholeness and the Implicate Order*. London: Routledge & Kegan Paul, 1980.

Bohm, David, and Basil J. Hiley. *The Undivided Universe: An Ontological Interpretation of Quantum Theory*. London: Routledge, 1993.

Bozzano, Ernest. *Les phénomènes de hantise au moment de la mort*. Paris: Ed de la B.P.S., 1923.

Braude, Stephen E. *Immortal Remains: The Evidence for Life After Death*. Lanham, Md.: Rowman & Littlefield, 2003.

Broughton, Richard. *The Controversial Science*. New York: Ballantine, 1991.

Brune, Francois. *Les morts nous parlent*. 2 vols. Paris: Poche, 2009.

Brune, Francois, and Rémy Chauvin. *A l'écoute de l'au-delà*. Escalquens, France: Okxus/Piktos, 2003.

Bruno, Giordano. *On the Infinite, the Universe and the Worlds: Five Cosmological Dialogues.* Translated by Scott Gosnell. N.p.: CreateSpace, 2014.

Carr, Bernard. "Seeking a New Paradigm of Matter, Mind and Spirit." *Network Review,* Spring/Summer 2010, 3–8.

———. *Universe or Multiverse.* Cambridge, UK: Cambridge University Press, 2009.

Carrington, Damian. "'Insect Apocalypse' Poses Risk to All Life on Earth, Conservationists Warn." *The Guardian,* November 13, 2019.

Castaneda, Carlos. *The Fire from Within.* New York: Pocket Books, 1991.

———. *The Power of Silence.* New York: Pocket Books, 1991.

Ceballos, Gerardo, Paul R. Ehrlich, and Rodolfo Dirzo. "Biological Annihilation via the Ongoing Sixth Mass Extinction Signaled by Vertebrate Population Losses and Declines." *Proceedings of the National Academy of Sciences of the United States of America* 114, no. 30 (July 25, 2017).

Chalmers, David J. *The Conscious Mind.* New York: Oxford University Press, 1996.

Charcot, Jean-Martin. *Lectures on the Diseases of the Nervous System: Delivered at La Salpêtrière.* N.p.: Andesite Press / Creative Media Partners, 2015.

Charon, Jean E. *The Unknown Spirit.* London: Coventure, 1983.

Combs, Allan, and Mark Holland. *Synchronicity: Science, Myth, and the Trickster.* New York: Marlowe, 1995.

Corbin, Henri. *Jung, Buddhism, and the Incarnation of Sophia.* Rochester, Vt.: Inner Traditions, 2019.

———. *Temple and Contemplation.* London: Routledge, 1986.

Cremo, Michael A. *Human Devolution. A Vedic Alternative to Darwin's Theory.* Badger, Calif.: Torchlight, 2003.

Cyrulnik, Boris. *Sous le signe du lien.* Paris: Hachette, 1989.

———. *The Whispering of Ghosts: Trauma and Resilience.* New York: Other Press, 2005.

De Maupassant, Guy. "Lui?" In *Les Sœurs Rondoli.* Vol. 9 of *Oeuvres Complètes.* Paris: Louis Conard, 1902.

Devereux, Georges. *Psychoanalysis and the Occult.* New York: International University Press, 1953.

Dossey, Larry. *Recovering the Soul: A Scientific and Spiritual Approach.* New York: Bantam New Age Books, 1989.

Duval, P., and E. Montredon. "ESP Experiments with Mice." *Journal of Parapsychology* 32: 153–66.

Dyer, Wayne, and Dee Garnes. *Memories of Heaven: Children's Astounding Recollections of the Time Before They Came to Earth.* Carlsbad, Calif.: Hay House, 2015.

Evans-Wentz, Walter Y., ed. *The Tibetan Book of the Dead; or, The After-Death Experiences on the Bardo Plane. According to Lama Kazi Dawa-Samdup's English Rendering.* 3rd ed. Oxford: Oxford University Press, 2000. First published in 1927.

———, ed. *Tibetan Yoga and Secret Doctrines: Seven Books of Wisdom of the Great Path; According to the Late Lama Kazi Dawa-Samdup's English Rendering.* 3rd ed. New York: Oxford University Press, 2000. First published in 1935.

———. *Tibet's Great Yogi Milarepa.* New York: New Age Books, 2004.

Ghyka, Matila. *The Golden Number.* Rochester, Vt.: Inner Traditions, 2016.

Greeley, Andrew M. *Sociology of the Paranormal: A Reconnaissance.* Beverly Hills, Calif.: Sage, 1975.

Gurney, Edmund, Frederic W. H. Myers, and Frank Podmore. *Phantasms of the Living.* 2 vols. London: Trubner, 1886.

Hardy, Chris H. *Cosmic DNA at the Origin: A Hyperdimension before the Big Bang; The Infinite Spiral Staircase Theory.* N.p.: CreateSpace, 2015.

———. *DNA of the Gods: The Anunnaki Creation of Eve and the Alien Battle for Humanity.* Rochester, Vt.: Bear and Co., 2014.

———. "Faster-Than-Light Anomalies in Pre-Spacetime and Interstellar Translocation via ISST's Hyperdimension." Preprint, 2020. Available at independent.academia.edu/ChrisHHardy.

———. "ISS Theory: Cosmic Consciousness, Self, and Life Beyond Death in a Hyperdimensional Physics." *Journal of Consciousness Exploration & Research* 7, no. 11 (2016): 1012–35.

———. "Nonlocal Consciousness in the Universe: Panpsychism, Psi & Mind over Matter in a Hyperdimensional Physics." In "The Other Singularity: Psi and the Nonlocal Mind," edited by Ben Goertzel. Special issue, *Journal of Nonlocality* 5, no. 1 (2017).

———. *The Sacred Network.* Rochester, Vt.: Inner Traditions, 2011.

———. *Space Allies.* N.p.: CreateSpace, 2017.

Hardy, Christine. *La Prédiction de Jung: la métamorphose de la Terre.* Paris: Dervy/Trédaniel, 2012.

———. *Networks of Meaning: A Bridge between Mind and Matter.* Westport, Conn.: Praeger, 1998.

————. "Self-Organization, Self-Reference and Inter-influences in Multilevel Webs: Beyond Causality and Determinism." *Journal of Cybernetics and Human Knowing* 8, no. 3 (2001): 35–59.

————. "Synchronicity: Interconnection through a Semantic Dimension." Presentation at Second Psi Meeting, Curitiba, Brazil, April 21–26, 2004.

Heim, Albert. "Remarks on Fatal Fall." 1892. Translated by Russell Noyes and Roy Kletti. In "The Experience of Dying from Falls." *Omega* 3, no. 1 (1972): 45–52.

Hermes Trismegistus. *Corpus Hermeticum*. Gnostic Society Library website.

————. "The Cup or Monad: Of Hermes to Tat." (*Corpus Hermeticum* IV). Translated by George Mead. Available on Gnostic Society Library website.

————. *The Discourse on the Eighth and Ninth*. Translated by James Brashler, Peter A. Dirkse, and Douglas M. Parrott for the Gnostic Society Library and available on their website.

Huxley, Aldous. *The Doors of Perception, and Heaven and Hell*. 1954. Reprint, New York: Harper Perennial Modern Classics, 2009.

Hyslop, James H. *Contact with the Other World*. New York: Century, 1919.

————. *Psychical Research and the Resurrection*. New York: Small-Meynard, 1908.

————. "Visions of the Dying." *Journal of the American Society for Psychical Research* 1 (1907): 45–55.

Jahn, Robert G., and Brenda Dunne. *Margins of Reality: The Role of Consciousness in the Physical World*. Princeton, N.J.: ICRL Press, 2009.

Joines, William. "A Wave Theory of Psi Energy." In *Research in Parapsychology 1974*, edited by J. D. Morris, W. G. Roll, and R. L. Morris, 147–49. Metuchen, N.J.: Scarecrow Press, 1975.

Jung, Carl Gustav. *Alchemical Studies*. Vol. 13 of *The Collected Works of C.G. Jung*. Edited by G. Adler and R. F. Hull. 20 vols. Bollingen Series. Princeton, N.J.: Princeton University Press, 1968.

————. *Answer to Job*. New York: Routledge and Kegan Paul, 1954.

————. Foreword to *An Introduction to Zen Buddhism,* by D. T. Suzuki. New York: Grove Press, 1964.

————. Introduction to *The Secret of the Golden Flower: A Chinese Book of Life,* by Richard Wilhelm. Wilmington, Mass.: Mariner Books, 1962.

————. *Memories, Dreams, Reflections*. Translated by Richard and Clara Winston. New York: Vintage, 1965.

————. "Psychological Commentary on The Tibetan Book of the Great

Liberation." In *Psychology and Religion: West and East*. Vol. 11 of *The Collected Works of C. G. Jung*. Edited by G. Adler and R. F. Hull. 20 vols. Bollingen Series. Princeton, N.J.: Princeton University Press, 1970.

———. *Psychology and Alchemy*. In *The Collected Works of C. G. Jung*, Bollingen Series, vol. 12. Adler, G., & R.F. Hull (Eds.) Princeton, N.J.: Princeton University Press, 1968.

———. *The Psychology of Kundalini Yoga*. Edited by Sonu Shamdasani. Bollingen XCIX. Princeton, N.J.: Princeton University Press, 1999.

———. *The Red Book*. Edited by Sonu Shamdasani. Philemon Series. New York: W.W. Norton, 2009.

———. *The Seven Sermons to the Dead* [*Septem Sermones ad Mortuos*]. 1916. Included as appendix to *Memories, Dreams, Reflections*, by Carl Jung, 190–91. New York: Vintage, 1965. Online text (translated by Stephan A. Hoeller) is available on the Gnostic Society Library website.

———. *Synchronicity: An Acausal Connecting Principle*. Vol. 8 of *The Collected Works of C. G. Jung*. Edited by G. Adler and R. F. Hull. 20 vols. Bollingen Series. Princeton, N.J.: Princeton University Press, 1960.

Jung, Carl Gustav, and Wolfgang Pauli. *The Interpretation of Nature and the Psyche*. New York: Pantheon Books, 1955.

Kardec, Allan. *The Genesis, Miracles and Premonition According to Spiritism*. 1868. Reprint Orlando, Fla.: Edicei of America, 2011.

Koestler, Arthur. *The Act of Creation*. New York: Penguin, 1989.

Krippner, Stanley, and Patrick Welch. *Spiritual Dimensions of Healing*. New York: Irvington, 1992.

Kübler-Ross, Elisabeth. *On Death and Dying: What the Dying Have to Teach Doctors, Nurses, Clergy and Their Own Families*. New York: Scribner, (reprint) 2014.

LaBerge, Stephen, and Howard Rheingold. *Exploring the World of Lucid Dreaming*. New York: Ballantine Books, 1990.

Lao-tzu. *Tao Te Ching*. Reprint, n.p.: Amazon Digital Services, 2015.

Laszlo, Ervin. *The Akashic Experience: Science and the Cosmic Memory Field*. Rochester, Vt.: Inner Traditions, 2009.

———. *The Self-Actualizing Cosmos*. Rochester, Vt.: Inner Traditions, 2014.

Lecouteux, Claude. *Mondes parallèles. L'univers des croyances au Moyen âge*. Paris: Honoré Champion, 2007.

———. *The Return of the Dead. Ghosts, Ancestors, and the Transparent Veil of the Pagan Mind*. Rochester, Vt.: Inner Traditions, 2009.

———. *The Tradition of Household Spirits.* Rochester, Vt.: Inner Traditions, 2013. Originally published in French as *La maison et ses génies.* Paris: Imago, 2000.

Ledos, Gabriel E. *Lacordaire.* Paris: Lib. des Saints-Pères, 1902. Reprint, n.p.: BiblioBazaar, 2009.

———. *Sainte Gertrude.* Paris: Lib. V. Lecoffre, 1901. Reprint, n.p.: Nabu Press, 2012.

Leibniz, Gottfried W. *Discourse on Metaphysics and the Monadology.* 1714. Reprint, New York: Prometheus Books, 1992.

Le Scouëzec, Gwen, and Philippe Court-Payen. "Géosophie des hauts-lieux: Lignes de force terrestres ou instrument d'un pouvoir?" *Bulletin du Corps à vivre* 19 (March 1979).

Lovelock, James. *The Ages of Gaia.* New York: Bantam Books, 1990.

———. *Gaia: A New Look at Life on Earth.* Oxford, UK: Oxford University Press, 1979.

Markale, Jean. *Cathedral of the Black Madonna: The Druids and the Mysteries of Chartres.* Rochester, Vt.: Inner Traditions, 2004.

———. *The Druids: Celtic Priests of Nature.* Rochester, Vt.: Inner Traditions, 1999.

McMoneagle, Joseph, and Charles Tart. *Mind Trek: Exploring Consciousness, Time, Space Through Remote Viewing.* Charlottesville, Va.: Hampton Roads, 1993.

McRae, Ronald. *Mind Wars: The True Story of Government Research into the Military Potential of Psychic Weapons.* New York: St. Martin's, 1984.

McTaggart, Lynne. *The Field: The Quest for the Secret Force of the Universe.* New York: Harper Perennial, 2012.

Mishlove, Jeffrey. *The Roots of Consciousness.* New York: Marlowe, 1997.

Mitchell, Edgar R. *The Way of the Explorer.* New York: Putnam, 1996.

Moody, Raymond. *Donner du sens au non-sens: Comment concevoir la vie après la vie.* Paris: Guy Trédaniel, 2016.

———. *Glimpses of Eternity: Sharing a Loved One's Passage from This Life to the Next.* Paradise Valley, Ariz.: Sakkara Productions, 2016.

———. *Life after Life.* San Francisco: HarperOne, 2015.

Moreau, C. *Freud et l'occultisme.* Paris: Editions Privat, 1976.

Morse, Melvin. *Parting Visions.* New York: Villard Books, 1994.

Myers, Frederic W. H. *Human Personality and Its Survival of Bodily Death.* 1903. Reprint, Memphis, Tenn.: General Books, 2012. Available online at Project Gutenberg website.

———. "On Recognised Apparitions Occurring More Than a Year after Death." In *SPR Proceedings of the Society for Psychical Research* 6:13–65. London: Kegan, Paul, Trench, Trübner, 1890.

Nelson, R. D., G. J. Bradish, Y. H. Dobyns, B. J. Dunne, and R. G. Jahn. "FieldREG Anomalies in Group Situations." *Journal of Scientific Exploration* 10, no. 1 (1996): 111–41.

Osis, Karlis. *Deathbed Observations by Physicians and Nurses.* New York: Parapsychological Foundation, 1961.

Osis, Karlis, and Erlendur Haraldson. *At the Hour of Death.* New York: Avon, 1977.

Osman, Ahmed. *The Egyptian Origins of King David and the Temple of Solomon.* Rochester, Vt.: Inner Traditions, 2019.

Pauli, Wolfgang. "The Influence of Archetypical Ideas on the Scientific Theories of Kepler." In *The Interpretation of Nature and Psyche* by C. G. Jung and W. Pauli. 1955. Reprint, New York: Ishi Press, 2012.

Pauli, Wolfgang, and Carl G. Jung. *Atom and Archetype: The Pauli/Jung letters, 1932–1958.* Edited by C. A. Meier. Princeton, N.J.: Princeton University Press, 2014.

Peat, F. David. *Synchronicity: The Bridge between Matter and Mind.* New York: Bantam Books, 1987.

Penick, Douglas J. *The Brilliance of Naked Mind: Secret Visions of Gesar, King of Ling.* Boulder, Colo.: Mountain Treasury Press, 2011.

Pigani, Erik. *Psi, enquête sur les phénomènes paranormaux.* Paris: Presses du Châtelet, 1999.

Plato. *The Dialogues of Plato.* New York: Theommes Press, 1977.

Plotinus. *The Enneads.* Translated by Stephan MacKenna. LP Classic Reprint Series. Burdett, N.Y.: Larson Publications, 1992.

Plotin. *Les Ennéades.* Trans. from the Greek original by M.N. Bouillet. Paris: Hachette, 1857.

Poincaré, Henri. *Science and Method.* 1908. Reprint, New York: Dover Publications, 1952.

Pribram, Karl H. *Brain and Perception: Holonomy and Structure in Figural Processing.* Hillsdale, N.J.: Lawrence Erlbaum, 1991.

Radin, Dean. *The Conscious Universe.* New York: Ballantine, 1997.

———. *Entangled Minds.* New York: Paraview Pocket Books, 2006.

Radin, Dean, and Roger Nelson. "Evidence for Consciousness-related Anomalies in Random Physical Systems." *Foundations of Physics* 19, no. 12 (1989): 1499–514.

Rees, W. Dewi. "The Hallucinations of Widowhood." *British Medical Journal* 4 (1971): 37–41.

Reynolds, John M., ed. *Self-Liberation through Seeing with Naked Awareness*. Barrytown, N.Y.: Station Hill Press, 1989.

Rhine, Louisa. *The Invisible Picture: A Study of Psychic Experiences*. Jefferson, N.C.: McFarland, 1981.

———. *Mind over Matter*. New York: Macmillan, 1972.

Richet, Charles. *Thirty Years of Psychical Research*. Translated from the 2nd French edition. New York: Macmillan, 1923.

Rogo, Scott. "Apparitions, Hauntings, Poltergeists." In *Psychic Exploration*, by Edgar Mitchell, 375–95. New York: G.P. Putnam's Sons, 1974.

Roll, William. "Survival Research; Problems and Possibilities." In *Psychic Exploration*, by Edgar Mitchell, 397–424. New York: G.P. Putnam's Sons, 1974.

———. "Toward a Theory of the Poltergeist." *European Journal of Parapsychology* 2, no. 2 (1978): 167–200.

Sabom, Michael, and Sarah Kreutziger. "Physicians Evaluate the Near-death Experience." *Theta* 6, no. 4 (1978): 1–6.

Schlitz, Marilyn. *Death Makes Life Possible: Revolutionary Insights on Living, Dying, and the Continuation of Consciousness*. Louisville, Colo.: Sounds True, 2015.

Schwartz, Stephan. *Opening to the Infinite*. Langley, Wash.: Nemoseen Media, 2007.

Schwartz, Stephan, and Larry Dossey. "Nonlocality, Intention, and Observer Effects in Healing Studies: Laying a Foundation for the Future." *Explore* 6, no. 5 (2010): 295–307.

Seligman, Martin. *Learned Optimism: How to Change Your Mind and Your Life*. 1991. Reprint, New York: Vintage, 2006.

Sheldrake, Rupert. *Dogs That Know When Their Owner Is Coming Home*. Rev. ed. New York: Broadway Books, 2011.

———. *Morphic Resonance. The Nature of Formative Causation*. Rochester, Vt.: Park Street Press, 2009.

———. *Science Set Free*. New York: Deepak Chopra Books, 2012.

Sidgwick, H., E. Sidgwick, A. T. Myers, F. Podmore, A. Johnson, and F. W. H. Myers. "Report on the Census of Hallucinations." *Proceedings of the Society for Psychical Research* 10 (1894): 25–422.

Simmer-Brown, Judith. *Dakini's Warm Breath: The Feminine Principle in Tibetan Buddhism*. New York: Shambhala, 2002.

Sri Sankaracarya. *Pancikaranam*. Reprint, Calcutta: Advaita Ashrama, 1997.

Stevenson, Ian. "Are Poltergeists Living or Are They Dead?" *Journal of the American Society for Psychical Research* 66, no. 3 (1972): 233–52.

———. *Cases of the Reincarnation Type*. Vol. 1, *Ten cases in India*. Vol. 2, *Ten cases in Sri Lanka*. Vol. 3, *Twelve cases in Lebanon and Turkey*. Charlottesville: University Press of Virginia, 1977–80.

Swedenborg, Emanuel. *Heaven and Hell*. 1758 (in Latin) [Heaven and its Wonders and Hell: From Things Heard and Seen]. Reprint, n.p.: CreateSpace, 2014. More information available at the Swedenborg Digital Library website.

———. *Swedenborg's Journals of Dreams*. 1859. Reprint, West Chester, Penn.: Swedenborg Foundation, 1986.

Talbot, Michael. *The Holographic Universe: The Revolutionary Theory of Reality*. New York: Harper Perennial, 2011.

Targ, Russell, and Harold Puthoff. *Mind-Reach: Scientists Look at Psychic Abilities*. Charlottesville, Va.: Hampton Roads, 2005.

Tart, Charles, ed. *Altered States of Consciousness*. New York: John Wiley & Sons, 1969.

———. *States of Consciousness*. New York: Dutton, 1975.

Tart, Charles, Harold Puthoff, and Russell Targ, eds. *Mind at Large*. New York: Praeger, 1979.

Teilhard de Chardin, Pierre. *Phenomenon of Man*. New York: Harper Torch Book, 1965.

Ullman, Montague, Stanley Krippner, and Alan Vaughan. *Dream Telepathy*. New York: Macmillan, 1973.

Vallee, Jacques. *Fastwalker: A Novel*. Berkeley, Calif.: North Atlantic Books, 1996.

———. *Forbidden Science: Journals 1957–1969*. Berkeley, Calif.: North Atlantic Books, 1992.

———. *Passport to Magonia*. Washington, D.C.: H. Regnery, 1969.

Vivekananda, Swami. *Raja Yoga*. Calcutta: Advaita Ashrama, 1982.

von Bertalanffy, Ludwig. *General System Theory*. New York: G. Braziller, 1968.

Waite, Arthur Edward, ed. *Hermetic and Alchemical Writings of Paracelsus*. Boston: Shambhala, 1976.

Yates, Frances A. *Giordano Bruno and the Hermetic Tradition*. Chicago: University of Chicago Press, 1991.

Yeats, William B. *Fairy and Folk Tales of the Irish Peasantry*. New York: Walter Scott, 1888. Reprint, n.p.: CreateSpace, 2014. Full text available online at Project Gutenberg website and Internet Sacred Text Archive.

———. *The Celtic Twilight*. London: A. H. Bullen, 1902. Reprint, n.p.: CreateSpace, 2018. Full text available online at Internet Sacred Text Archive website.

Yogananda, Paramahansa. *Autobiography of a Yogi*. 1946. Reprint, Los Angeles: Self-Realization Fellowship, 2014.

Yogi Ramacharaka. *The Science of Psychic Healing*. Mumbai: D. B. Taraporevala Sons, 1965.

INDEX

Page numbers in *italics* indicate illustrations.

About the Author

Systems scientist, Ph.D. in ethno-psychology, and former researcher at Princeton's Psychophysical Research Laboratories, Chris H. Hardy is both a seer and a scientist. After her bachelor's degree, she traveled extensively to the East, Middle East, and Africa to study the ancient paths of wisdom, developing further an array of spiritual and psi talents that had blossomed at eighteen with her meditative practice. She then explored thought-provoking psi and mind potentials through systems and chaos theory and Jungian psychology; on the way, she developed her own cognitive and cosmology theories accounting for psi and transcendent states of consciousness, thus laying the foundation of a hyperdimension of consciousness in the universe (*Cosmic DNA at the Origin,* 2015). Author of more than seventy papers and eighteen books tackling nonlocal consciousness, she is an authority in scientific terms and as an author and workshop facilitator.

Recently, she has also made an in-depth study of the Sumerian tablets, and their comparison with biblical and gnostic texts led to two books: *DNA of the Gods* (2014) and *Wars of the Anunnaki* (2016); and she has authored two sci-fi books.

For more information (such as new book releases, research papers and presentations, and media appearances) visit:

Author's website: **https://chris-h-hardy.com**

Blog at: **http://chris-h-hardy-dna-of-the-gods.blogspot.fr**

BOOKS OF RELATED INTEREST

Wars of the Anunnaki
Nuclear Self-Destruction in Ancient Sumer
by Chris H. Hardy, Ph.D.

DNA of the Gods
The Anunnaki Creation of Eve and the Alien Battle for Humanity
by Chris H. Hardy, Ph.D.

The Sacred Network
Megaliths, Cathedrals, Ley Lines, and the Power of Shared Consciousness
by Chris H. Hardy, Ph.D.

The Immortal Mind
Science and the Continuity of Consciousness beyond the Brain
by Ervin Laszlo with Anthony Peake

7 Reasons to Believe in the Afterlife
A Doctor Reviews the Case for Consciousness after Death
by Jean Jacques Charbonier, M.D.

Seven Secrets of Time Travel
Mystic Voyages of the Energy Body
by Von Braschler
Foreword by Frank Joseph

Curanderismo Soul Retrieval
Ancient Shamanic Wisdom to Restore the Sacred Energy of the Soul
by Erika Buenaflor, M.A., J.D.

Field Guide to the Spirit World
The Science of Angel Power, Discarnate Entities, and Demonic Possession
by Susan B. Martinez, Ph.D.
Foreword by Whitley Strieber

INNER TRADITIONS • BEAR & COMPANY
P.O. Box 388
Rochester, VT 05767
1-800-246-8648
www.InnerTraditions.com

Or contact your local bookseller